INITIATIONS

INITIATIONS

BY

PAUL SÉDIR

TRANSLATED BY MOUNI SADHU

AEON

Published 2007
by Aeon Books
www.aeonbooks.co.uk

The moral right of the author has been asserted

All rights reserved. No part of this book may be reproduced or utilized in any form or by any means, electronic or mechanical, without permission in writing from the publisher.

British Library Cataloguing in Publication Data
A C.I.P. is available for this book from the British Library

ISBN 9781904658306

CONTENTS

Chapter		Page
	Foreword	7
	Verses from St. John XII, 20-26	13
I.	A State of the Soul	15
II.	Andréas	18
III.	Orientalisms	23
IV.	A Rickety Child	25
V.	The Proletariat	26
VI.	A Test of Vedanta	29
VII.	The Brahman	35
VIII.	The Durakapalam	41
IX.	A Brahmanic Evocation	53
X.	Comforts	57
XI.	The Spiritualist	61
XII.	The Magnetizer	67
XIII.	The Unity of the Spiritualists	71
XIV.	Uncertainty	75
XV.	A Mental Vision	78
XVI.	In Plaisance	81
XVII.	A Man Attached to the Earth	85
XVIII.	The Mummy	90
XIX.	The First of May	93
XX.	The Invisible Enemies	97
XXI.	The Vineyard	102
XXII.	An Avalanche in the Himalayas	107

CONTENTS—*continued*

Chapter		Page
XXIII.	Probation	113
XXIV.	The Tiger	118
XXV.	The Prayer	124
XXVI.	The Phap	126
XXVII.	Aviation	129
XXVIII.	At Court	135
XXIX.	Towards Christ's Initiation	139
XXX.	The Spiritualist Tower of Babel	142
XXXI.	Théophane	148
XXXII.	The Comets	152
XXXIII.	The Inundation	158
XXXIV.	The Chinaman	161
XXXV.	The Pyramid	169
XXXVI.	The Ave Maria	173
XXXVII.	The Virgin	187
XXXVIII.	The Louvre	191
XXXIX.	In Compiègne	193
XL.	Christmas	201
XLI.	Antibes	205
XLII.	The Battle	208
XLIII.	Resurrection	213

FOREWORD

" INITIATIONS " by Paul Sédir, as well as his other numerous but not very large works, is unknown to readers in the English language. So far, not one of his books has been translated. Perhaps there are deep reasons for this strange fact, as many far less valuable works on mysticism, occultism and psychology have been translated and made available to the English.

Spiritually, Sédir was too far ahead of his own time and the disasters of the two world wars, together with the uneasy period of false peace between them, were needed to bring the lonely, but ardent mystic closer and make him more understandable for our present generation.

Some of Sédir's books were written before 1914, and in all of them the sensitive reader can discover a warning about the impending catastrophes. In " Initiations ", for example, there is a fascinating chapter (No. XXXIX) entitled " In Compiègne ", where one can find an amazing prophecy about both great wars and the exact position to be occupied in them by France and other nations.

In my younger years, when the spirit of occult investigation still burned in me, I took the trouble to verify, at least geographically, some of the most intriguing statements by the author of " Initiations ". As far back as 1922, I spoke to people, who personally knew a lot about the existence of the mysterious Monsieur Andréas, and even about his home in a Parisian suburb.

In the previously mentioned Chapter XXXIX, the mysterious places in North-Eastern France still testify to the events described in it. So obviously, the author knew of them from his own personal experience, which I could see for myself when I visited those places a few years before 1939. Sédir was by no means just an imaginative fiction writer, who fed his readers on his own literary inventions.

If we are prepared to accept this fact, then his books take on a tremendous personal meaning for us, lifting a small corner of the great veil that covers the mystery of the human drama on this little planet, so lost amid the immense vastness of the manifested universe. But this discovery must be made by the reader himself, he must live through and digest it. And that is the reason why I will not express my own opinion about his works.

Even so, some chapters of " Initiations " have such a power and ability to revive in us the lost faculty of intuition, that I described an account, heard from one of Sédir's contemporaries, about the encounter with the "Master of Masters" (almost identical with the chapter "Resurrection" in "Initiations"), using it as the final item in my own book "Ways to Self-Realization: a Modern Evaluation of Occultism & Spiritual Paths" (published by the "Julian Press" of New York and George Allen & Unwin Ltd., of London).

One of the main difficulties in introducing Sédir's book to the English-speaking world has been the fact that, as some of my literary friends have pointed out, it is "too French". But now, fortunately, English literature is steadily being enriched by a great many translations from other languages and cultures, and it is not necessary to learn other tongues in order to read and become acquainted with valuable foreign works.

However, I must confess, that it has not been an easy task to translate the fine philosophical French of Sédir into English, for one has to use all one's "technical" knowledge of it and adapt the somewhat unusual terminology into an understandable form for contemporary readers.

The gist of this book has been deftly summarized for us in the opening free quotation by Sédir from the Gospel of St. John (XII, 20-36). And Sédir made a definite effort to convey to his readers, the words of Christ, in which the Great Teacher of humanity states that His presence on this planet cannot, and should not be taken merely allegorically, but directly and literally.

One may retreat in awe from this statement, or one may see in it the hidden, tremendous Truth. "Initiations" is intended to show a mysterious path, but a completely real path, upon which one is able to prove for oneself the truth, as conveyed to us about two thousand years ago. The attentive reader will find quite a number of texts in the Gospels of Christ, which speak about the continuing relationship between our Spiritual Teacher and His flock here and now. And that idea is of such enormous importance to a man who is lucky enough to grasp its significance and to see its realization with his own eyes, that he would never dare to divulge that immense mystery.

Judging by the final chapter we can gauge that "Initiations" was started shortly before World War I and completed immediately after it. This means, that for about fifty years it has remained beyond the reach of English-speaking readers. This is a great pity for there is no similar work in our literature which would have such a deep significance for just the present period, so close emotionally and politically to those fateful years before the autumn of 1914.

In an impeccable literary style Sédir tells us about the most intimate and essential problems of man on this earth—the true sense and aim of his life. A deep thinker and occultist of vast experience—for he was not merely a theoretical exponent——, Sédir, in the second half of his life, came into contact with the " Central Light ", about which St. John used the inspired words : " The Light that enlightens every man who comes into the world ". How did Sédir manage to accomplish this formidable and so seldom attempted task ? Through meeting the " bearers " of that Light (Andréas and Stella), who then led him to the living Centre Itself (" Théophane ").

Every occultist and spiritual seeker knows that, when a genuine disciple writes about his true Master (the Light Incarnate), it is the Master who actually directs the pen of the writer. Such accounts are very rare, and can be fully appreciated only by those who have also met a similar Master during their lifetime. Therefore, Sédir's " Initiations " had such an unforgettable charm for me, that I felt an obligation to undertake this translation which will be one of my last works, and so give it to the world at large.

It may be useful to give a brief explanation of the background of " Initiations ". Behind the figure of a Parisian doctor, whose experiences with the mysterious Monsieur Andréas and finally, with the Master of Masters, which form the main theme of the book, is hidden the author himself. At the end of the XIXth and beginning of the XXth centuries, Paul Sédir, who died in 1926, was well-known among the circles of French mystics, occultists, Hermetists, and other "initiatory" organizations throughout Europe. In the original French editions of " Initiations " we find : " Ce roman incrédible fût vecu! " (" This incredible novel has been lived ! ")

In spite of his great erudition and abilities, his search for the Ultimate, Living Truth was not yet completed by the time he reached his forties (he died at 55 years of age). Indeed, he was near to an inner breakdown. Then happened that which has been described in the first chapter of " Initiations ", followed by the further dramatic developments, which reached their peak in the last chapter, entitled : " Resurrection ". In other words, a happy epilogue to a life rich in passionate searching, hard struggles, elation, disappointment and suffering, ending in the ultimate bliss of association with the eternal, immovable Centre, manifested in " Théophane ".

The foremost value of this unusual book, like the very few also written by genuine disciples of true Masters, lies in the author's account of his personal experiences, described so humanly and simply, and his gradual development under the tuition of Andréas, another highly advanced human being whom Sédir met. This is because it is a fact that everyone of us will and must, in due course, pass along a similar path in our evolution through eons of lives.

Details may, of course, differ according to the epoch and planet, when our entering on to the conscious Path will occur. But it is essential that we know as much as possible about the Path, so that the events of our incarnations may not take us by surprise or unprepared. Another important point about "Initiations" is the demonstration of the ineffectualness of self-styled "teachers" and old occult and philosophical methods, invented by men who themselves had not attained the fullness of the necessary wisdom, and who had not yet joined the CENTRE, Which is ALL.

This Centre is by no means unknown to esotericism, but it has different names in the various languages: God—in all the great religions; Ain-Soph of the Kabbalists and Hermetists; Nirvana of Buddha; Supreme, or Real Self of the Maharshi (see my "In Days of Great Peace"); the Father's Kingdom of Christ; the Pleroma of the Platonist philosophers, and so on.

The sole important fact is that the CENTRE has visible manifestations in different epochs, in the persons of Spiritual Giants, who then influence the fate (or Karma) of the inhabitants of the innumerable worlds which belong to the cosmic Creation. All of these great Beings are ONE, as confirmed by the last contemporary Teacher—the Maharshi.

What is "new" and even striking in "Initiations" is the idea that a Representative of the WHOLE (the CENTRE) is always present on the planet, and *can be met* by spiritually ripe sons of man. The thorny Path to that ripeness is shown by the example of Sédir, and told in a simple but unsurpassably charming manner in his books.

Because this work was written about half a century ago, it contains a few small anachronisms, but they are insignificant by comparison with some of the actual prophecies, the fulfilment of which was seen by our own eyes during that time.

Sédir also predicted the rise and decline of that which he terms the "Eastern infatuation". The Yoga movement, which started all right ideologically at the end of the XIXth Century, has gradually degenerated during the last decades into the plague of false "teachers" and "kings of yogis", as they like to style themselves, although true Eastern occultists never accept any bombastic names or titles. These have been followed by corruption, "initiations" for money, and the erroneous conception that every newcomer from the East is a competent " teacher " simply because he has a dark skin, and so on. The recently noted examples of sheer immorality and materialism on the part of such visitors (even in the country where I am writing these lines), and their exploitation of naive and undiscriminating Westerners, only lend support to Sédir's criticism, which he expressed about fifty years ago. And in Chapter XX—" The Invisible Enemies " he also predicts that this " infatuation " will not last for ever.

I hope that the present edition of " Initiations " will fulfil its purpose, and that the deepest truths expressed in it in an amazingly simple and transparent form, will enlighten many of those who have eyes to see and ears to hear. This book has a subtle connection with my own recent work " Theurgy: the Art of Effective Worship ", which can be studied concurrently with it.

Finally, I also hope that the sensible reader will study the initiatory dialogues between M. Andréas and Sédir, reading them many times, until the Light enters his own heart.

Mouni Sadhu.

Melbourne, Australia.

INITIATIONS

THERE were certain Greeks among them who came up to worship the Lord at the feast. Therefore they came to Philip, who was of Bethsaida of Galilee, and said to him: Sir, we would see Jesus.

Philip went and told Andrew, and Andrew and Philip spoke to Jesus. Jesus answered them saying: The hour has come when the SON OF MAN shall be glorified. Verily, verily I say unto you, except a grain of wheat falling into the ground dies, it abideth alone; but if it dies, it will bring forth much fruit.

He that loveth his life shall lose it, and he who hateth his life in this world shall keep it for the life eternal.

If any man wants to serve me, let him follow me; and where I am, there also shall my servant be; if any man serves me, My Father will honour him.

Now is my soul troubled. And what shall I say? Father, save me from this hour; but for this cause I came unto this hour. Father, glorify Thy name!

And then came a voice from heaven saying: I have both glorified him and I will glorify him again!

The people who stood by and heard it, said: It was as thunder. Others said: An angel spoke to him.

Jesus answered again: The voice came not because of me, but for your sakes. For now is the judgment of this world: now shall the prince of this world be cast out. And I, if I be lifted up from the earth, will draw all men unto me.

This he said, indicating what death he should die.

The crowd answered him: We have heard out of the Law that Christ abides for ever; and how sayest thou: The Son of Man must be lifted up? Who is the Son of Man?

Jesus answered them: Yet a little while the light is with you. Walk whilst you have the light, lest darkness comes upon you; for he that walketh in darkness knoweth not where he goes.

Whilst you have the light, believe in that light, so that you may be the children of light, and darkness will not swallow you.

Thus spoke Jesus, who then departed, disappearing before them.

(St. John XII, 20-36.)

Chapter 1

A STATE OF THE SOUL

I WAS just entering my forties. The busy existence of a suburban doctor had not extinguished all the dreams of my youth. It was a beautiful time, in which I was free to abandon everything in order to find a rare book or to converse with a mystic.

My memories were always directed to my old friend Desiderius, dead these twenty years past, and to those unknown persons whom I had met at his funeral. So, every evening, when tiredness did not prevent me, I delayed sleep for some time and turned over the pages of the books, which my departed friend had left to me, especially the small black one. And always my eyes were attracted, without any apparent reason, to the names of *Andréas* and *Théophane*.

A banal accident interrupted the usual monotony of my days. My blundering maid-servant had made a hole in a magnificent embroidered silk wall decoration, which had been bequeathed to me by my late parents.

This splendid panel presented a bouquet of peach branches full of rosy flowers, mixed with snow-white cherry-blossom. The stems, leaves and ethereal petals stood out in relief from the background of the fabric like a multicoloured boss. The half-tints, the transparent shades, the exquisite combinations of colours—all were made with the easy tenderness of a pastel by La Tour.

As a result of the accident, three flowers had been damaged, and I had already spent fifteen long hours searching for a competent embroiderer who would be able to repair the damage.

I was sent from the suburb of Marais to Epinettes and from there to a professional school at Plaisance. Finally, I was told at the school that, close to the Lake of Saint-Fargeau, I might find an antiquary who sold all sorts of weird curiosities. His wife, an artist, would probably be able to restore my treasure to its original beauty.

So, one morning, I left Billancourt where I was then living and headed for the heights of Ménilmontant. I had known that suburb of Paris fairly well for quite a long time as I had previously paid frequent visits there to a cobbler, who was also an alchemist.

Nevertheless, it took me a considerable time to discover the street for which I was seeking, but the walk was pleasant in the fresh April sunlight.

One could believe oneself to be in a suburban subprefecture. The lilacs in the small gardens already had swollen buds; the new leaves of the acacias were growing over the fences of the old-fashioned houses, built in the Paul de Kock style; on the green nature-strips groups of children were playing, while the organ of Barbarie, so dear to the hearts of old Parisians, was sending forth its melodies on the air.

As the street rose to the gate of Pré, bushes replaced the walls, and on my way I often encountered small public houses, booths covered with bituminous board and bowling alleys.

On entering the street where my antiquary was said to live, I saw a lawyer's carriage outside the house in question. It was a large, old and comfortable vehicle, and on momentarily glancing into its interior I was astonished to recognize the travelling equipment of my venerable professor of histology, Dr. B., which he had designed in order not to lose any time when on his visits. Papers, drawings for the Medical Association, electric light bulbs, a small typewriter—everything was there.

I did not wish to explain to the professor the reasons for my visit to the antiquary, which would be unavoidable if he appeared on the way back to his carriage. Therefore I continued my walk. The vehicle was standing exactly outside the house which I had to visit, so I decided to return in a quarter of an hour or so.

The street led to the fortifications of Paris. Just at that moment a flock of sheep passed led by one man and two magnificent dogs, the last remnants of the lost race called in French " old Beaucerons ".

Then a man stopped close to me, evidently also in order to watch the passage of the beautiful animals. He was one of those individuals, who on first sight impress upon you a feeling of confidence and kindness. He was tall, exceptionally dignified in the best meaning of the word and perfectly dressed, which was rather strange for this suburb and hour.

His manner was aloof, but full of graciousness. He said to me : " Do you too love these country dogs ? "

" Yes," I answered, " I also have a passion for them, especially for the shepherd dogs."

" Just as myself ! No doubt we are old shepherds ourselves." And he added smiling, " You do not recognize me, eh ! Doctor? No matter ! We will meet again ! "

He bade me farewell and quickly disappeared in the direction of the fence, before I had an opportunity to stop him.

But that face was not unknown to me, nor the way of holding the head, and particularly—that look. But where had I met him?

And what mysterious words he had used. When he mentioned
'the shepherds' I had felt a slight shock in my breast and at the
same moment, a wave of force had penetrated my while frame.
What had he wanted to say? As if dreaming, I retraced my
steps. The carriage had already departed, but a new surprise
awaited me, for on the name-plate I read these words:

ANDREAS

Antiquary and Restorer

Repairs of all kinds

Andréas, that mysterious signer of '*Letters*', that dandy whom
I had seen at the funeral of Desiderius. Then, I saw him in my
mind as on that morning, long ago, when he was the leader of the
unknown heirs. Yes, his eyes, his posture! It must be he, or
perhaps the name was only a coincidence.

I tried to restore my calm, and began to examine the little brick
building. The whole of the lower storey formed the shop of a
broker. Behind it was a garden, which extended to the street along
which the sheep were passing. There were vegetables, a few flowers,
some exotic shrubs, and in a small courtyard were hens, a recess
and a well.

The roof of the shop served as a terrace for the unique upper
floor, which was built back from the street frontage.

Through the bars of the terrace balustrade, a tall, silvery-grey
dog turned its large, be-whiskered head and watched me carefully.
On the roof of the building there was a structure like a small
observatory.

I went to the entrance. Inside I saw some table vices; the stand
of a jeweller, amply provided with files, punches and pliers; there
was also another stand—that of a joiner. In a corner were the
tools of a snarler, and from a lattice hung all kinds of scissors and
gouges used by a sculptor in wood. On small tables there were
plenty of pots, bottles and basins. A more odd collection even
Balzac himself could not have imagined, or dreamed up in order
to depict a type of old handicraftsman.

Chapter II

ANDREAS

WHILE I was occupied with my observations, a man came through the door clad in a long sleeveless tunic, like those worn by smiths. His appearance, the size of his torso, the thickness of his arms, all indicated extreme strength. His muscles were smooth, like those of Tartars; but in spite of that, his face was one of an honest Frenchman, perhaps a little severe, like an old soldier's.

It was only later that I was able to read goodness, fineness, intelligence and many other qualities from his face.

I was so sure that I was now dealing with a worker that I asked him: " Is Monsieur Andréas at home? "

" I am he," he answered, both surprising and disappointing me at the same time, for he was by no means similar to the elegant young man whom I had seen long ago.

However, I said to him: " It so happens, that I have with me a damaged embroidery for repair. I have been sent to you because it seems that your wife is the only artist, who can do the work and make good the damage."

" Well, Sir, please come in. If you have a little time perhaps you would like to look at these prints, as I have something very urgent to finish. But I will be back in five minutes."

Then the man returned to his blacksmith's workshop, not omitting to send me a long, penetrating look, which astonished me, as it was so unexpected.

I began to think that I was facing a true collector, for in the shop, or rather, studio, I saw some very beautiful engravings and exquisite pottery, which were genuine rarities. I decided to win the confidence of this Andréas. I joined him in his courtyard, telling him that I preferred to be in the lovely sunshine and fresh air. The large dog came up to us and sat between his master and me.

" Be quiet! " the blacksmith told it. " This gentleman is a friend."

" Give him your hand Sir! These dogs like to be treated as persons," he added smilingly.

And the dog actually came closer, sniffed my hand with its large, cold nose and then returned to the terrace.

The workshop in which I joined the master of the house was

arranged for iron working. In its most picturesque corner the powerful repairman moved here and there, setting his beak-irons and making up the fire. A cat spied on us from the top of the fireplace. Sparrows and redbreasts chirped in the branches; on the first floor a contralto voice was quietly singing a noble, old refrain, while the voices of children playing in neighbouring properties came to us from the distance. The whole atmosphere was quiet, happy and yet active.

"I think that all these old things are of interest to you," said the man in a deep voice. "I have plenty of them. Look here! This is a damascene sword. The secret of its tempering has been lost. But look, how beautiful the workmanship!" And he bent the steel blade into a circle. When he released it, the blade resumed its original straight form. "I think that it was tempered in the boiling fat of a he-goat."

"But that sounds like an old woman's prescription," I told Andréas.

"I beg your pardon, Sir, but the fat of a he-goat has a different chemical formula from that of a sheep. And their properties are different."

He continued to speak for a minute or two about rather trifling matters, while still hammering at a small piece of metal. When he had finished he examined my embroidery.

"It is a very beautiful thing," he commented. "It comes from Quang-Si, and there are Japanese influences; but no matter. I have seldom seen anything so lovely. Do you know how it should be placed on a wall, so that the full effect will be obtained? No? Then listen! The shadow of the camelia is grey when full daylight falls on it, and then the rose colour appears brilliant. The shadow of that horizontal twig is also horizontal. So the whole thing has been made to be looked upon with the aid of the setting sun, when hanging on the eastern wall of a room, and with the beholder seated on the floor."

Surprised by these ingenious remarks, I asked Andréas some further questions about the embroidery and ceramics of the Far East. He gave me names which I pretended to be anxious to know.

Andréas smiled and added : "Dear Sir, you have no confidence in me. It is true that you have not known me except for these past few minutes. But we will agree. My wife cannot do this repair for less than two hundred francs and she will need three weeks for it. I will give you a receipt for your panel, stating its value and guaranteeing you against the risk of loss. Anyway, here is the worker herself."

A woman, already in middle age, came slowly down the stairs. She was of medium size stature, well built and simply dressed, but in good taste. Beautiful grey hair framed her radiant, although somewhat tired face; her charming expression was one which immediately wins sympathy. The way of holding her head, her posture and the elegance of her hands surprised me, for she seemed to be a truly grand dame.

"Stella," said the blacksmith, and instantly something very sweet pervaded the air and seemed to catch me by the throat.

Never, even with a pair of young lovers, have I seen such love as flashed between these two elderly people. The vibration in his voice, the smile in his eyes, the wrinkles of the sun-tanned face, which seemed capable of encountering and resisting all the storms and hurricanes of the earth, the whole attitude of his body, all expressed the unspeakable tenderness and immutable gravity of sentiment, which belong to the superhuman ones.

My emotion was sudden. There was no longer any doubt. I saw before me the Andréas and Stella of Desiderius. Was it possible? In the next second my doubt returned; I concealed my inner difficulty for the moment. For, after all, what exact proof did I have about the identity of these two people?

"Stella!" the blacksmith said again. "Here is a work which may concern you : I quoted two hundred francs and three weeks."

And the smiling woman voiced her agreement in a few words. Now I had a better look at her. Taken as a whole her features expressed opposite qualities. The mouth was prudent and good; the nose imperious; the chin resolute; the contour of the cheekbones denoted energy, almost to the point of violence; the curve of the eyelids showed the most noble melancholy; the planes of the forehead and temples were very sweet, and in her eyes I saw the blissful light that shines in the innocent pupils of children. On the whole, they were two enigmatic beings.

Andréas refused to accept a deposit for the work. But I insisted. "You don't know me," I said to him.

"Do you think so?" he answered with a smile. "The deer is calling the tiger," he added, quoting the well-known proverb of Laos.

Then finally I exclaimed : "Who are you?" my mistrust vanishing. "Where did you learn all that I see you know? Did you live for a long time in those oriental countries, for you are so well acquainted with such small details?"

"Actually, I travelled there and I always brought back some souvenirs, as well as errors and truths. For example, on your right palm I see a sign, which, according to the yellow-skinned

soothsayers, tells me that you have been occupied with the occult science, and not without success. But another sign shows me that you possess a very rare advantage over the majority of amateurs."
" What is it? "
" If I told you, you would lose it," he answered in a grave tone. " You have had to seek a lot, so remember, that the True Light comes from God alone."

I realized that this man *knew,* and that I had just touched the aim of my whole life. I had sacrificed everything in my occult search : family, pleasures, a profitable position. But twenty years of that searching had led me only to an impenetrable wall. Among those whom I had considered as masters some had promised me more than they could perform ; some I had to reject because of their racial or religious intolerance. Still others had pitilessly abandoned me, or they had wanted me to leave and go in search of their truth in some far off countries. But isn't the truth everywhere?

And all these failures had discouraged me. Was this man really my Andréas? And this woman? And the whole time spent here? Was I on a good path?

My partner in conversation continued to speak : " No miraculous phenomenon is a proof of the Truth, for how can you discriminate about the force which produced it. Did that force come from evil, or from good? Likewise, science itself is no proof : for where is the brain which could contain all the arcana of immense Nature? How can we judge which amount of science is suitable to the spiritual, intellectual or physical states of the disciple, and which to his past and future environment; to the beings for which he is the leader, and to those which he must follow?

" But don't believe, Sir, that I know something. I do not know anything, not even the depth of my own ignorance."

" Nevertheless, what do I have to do in order to advance? " I asked Andréas, carefully seeking for suitable words because my technical and staid vocabulary seemed to me to be inadequate with this man, who was so simple. I, who had been initiated into a large number of degrees, affiliated with all the European sects which are in touch with Illuminism ; I, who am the soul of many of them ; I, who have written so many savant-like pamphlets, that my foreign correspondents have called me a very learned master, until I finished in believing what they said ; I, who have performed magic rituals and renewed the cures of Paracelsus, who has ' given the Light ' to many men and women who have listened to me with respect; who has believed himself to be impavid and impassive.

But here and now I felt my ivory tower shifting at its base; I was disorientated. And now I was sorry that I had not taken a more sincere attitude towards this unknown man: it was a desire to come at least to a synthesis, to an inner rest.

"I will answer you when you will come and lunch with us," Andréas told me. "Would you like to fix the date?"

I accepted without hesitation, and then took leave.

My professional occupation prevented me from thinking any more about all this conversation with Andréas. So, when I returned to him, I was more doubtful than ever. The habit of analysing evidently obliterated the voice of intuition in me. Therefore I noticed how backward I was in not guessing about the unknown man of the Boulevard de Sérurier.

CHAPTER III

ORIENTALISMS

STELLA had spread the table under an arbour. While waiting for lunch, Andréas invited me to drink a little white whisky diluted with water. He explained that this brand, made from grapes collected at night, was not harmful, because it did not destroy the fatty cells of the body, which might be of importance to a man of my constitution, not too rich in those cells. Smoking quietly, my host questioned me.

"Here are my points to be queried," I told him. "I shall do my best to be as brief as possible. We can begin with the Buddhist philosophy. It claims matter to be indestructible and eternal. But why? From where come the movements which animate the world? Should we follow them or try to escape from them? Who instilled in us the desire to live, which we bear within ourselves? And who inspires the opposite desire in some of us?

"Being as we are, we have to fight against the magic power of our senses through our mind, which, nevertheless, is itself a function of the same forces, which we want to destroy. On the other hand, the arhats impose on the meditators an experimental procedure both positive and analytical. If the extinction of ignorance annihilates the power of the senses, then the disciple should preserve his consciousness after his death, in order to escape Karma and reincarnation. In other words, he must previously discover through his own intuition, the existence of the invisible universes, about which his rational meditations cannot give any proof .

"The Mahayana enumerates eight branches of the Path. I admit that through the *first* one, which is knowledge, one has to recognize the void of physics; and that the *second*, or the five interdictions, and the *third*, abstention from the ten sins are obviously moral. But the practising of the six transcendent virtues, belonging to the *fourth* path, seems to me to be impossible. For, if I become a monk, if I have no possessions any more, how then can I give alms? Being full of egotism, of vanity, of disdain, because I believe myself to be better than others, how can I practise the love of all that exists?

"The different forms of Buddhism, like the Singhalese, Tibetan, Japanese and Tartar, cannot give to a seeker or follower more than a long list of provisional syntheses, or compromises between the state of the disciple and the ideal for which he is seeking. Obviously, suffering is inseparable from existence; but nobody can prove that existence has been created by ignorance. If I am insensible to a certain pleasure, it is no pleasure at all for me, but even so, it does not cease to exist. Therefore, it is always possible that I might again be attracted—in some more or less distant future—by the charm of the same pleasure. If I resist it, I am depriving some cells of their natural opening. And then I, the Buddhist, careful of every form of existence, would kill some energies.

"I am not trying to suggest that I should satisfy all my passions; but I am simply exposing the antinomy of two Buddhist rules. And also, where today can I find *not a master, but a doctrine*?

"How can we choose between a dozen of Japanese sects? Chinese bonzes do not know much today while, in Tibet, how are we to discriminate between those belonging to the cult of Bompa, to the school of Yogacharya, or the tantrics of Kala-chakra? There still remains Siamese Buddhism, but I don't have any documents about it."

"All this seems to me to be reasonably true," said Andréas.

"Now, let us take the mysteries, which come directly from Brahmanism. I admit that Yoga has been created in order to allow the human spirit to receive the seeds of the greatest possible number of forces, and to strive after them. I was never especially interested in the different codes, which permit control of sounds, music, optics, magnetism, muscular force and passions, simply because it seems to me, that if one could reach the CENTRE of all these things, then all these dependencies would be conquered as a natural result. Therefore, I studied only Raja Yoga.

"But please pardon these details: I merely wanted to provide you with the elements of a certain diagnostic."

CHAPTER IV

A RICKETY CHILD

SOMEONE called out from the street. Andréas went to see who it was, and then returned to me with the visitor. It was a simple woman carrying a sickly looking baby in her arms.

"Doctor, please look at the child and see what is wrong with it," Andréas said to me. After examining the child I decided that it was rickety from hereditary alcoholism.

"I do not believe so," said Andréas. "It must simply be a xiphoidan appendix."

And actually the end of the sternum was bent inwards and quite soft. "I have something for bones, but I am not a doctor and have no right to prescribe medicines," said Andréas.

"But I will immediately sign your order, if you wish!"

"Thank you very much Doctor, but I do not wish to involve you. Here we have something much simpler, which mamma can do as often as she wishes."

He then placed the baby on a chair, and asked the mother to pass her forefinger along the little sternum.

"Do you feel anything?" he asked.

"Yes, Sir!" answered the woman. "It is as if cold water was flowing inside my finger."

"That is all right. Do you see this little moving point?" And in fact the cartilage seemed to come forward in little jerks.

"Oh, Sir! I am so thankful to you!" said the poor woman tearfully.

"Ah no! No!" replied Andréas, making faces in order to entertain the baby. "When a mother loves her child the good God helps. It is He who should be thanked, and only to Him should all requests be directed, instead of gossiping with neighbours. Do the same thing every time the little one falls asleep. Well now, good-bye! And if this will not work my doctor friend is here."

But when we were alone Andréas said: "You were right, that sickness was due to alcoholism; but it is better that the woman will not condemn her husband. Shall we go in to the table?"

CHAPTER V

THE PROLETARIAT

BUT during that lunch we were not left quiet for even three minutes. A procession of visitors continuously interrupted us. They were all workers, both men and women, who came running for advice, until the whistles of their mills and factories called them back.

I was compelled to note that, even if Andréas did not count many admirers among the intellectual or social élite, he had plenty of fervent friends among the simple people. Often the whole of his workshop was full.

Some bad rheumatism, a wound, a quarrel with the foreman, a dispute with the boss or union were the usual causes. And Andréas seemed to have knowledge of all these affairs.

He knew the factories and their engineers, the small industrialists, the members of friendly societies and the secretaries of committees. He spoke all the slang and understood a mason, a mechanic or a fitter, as if he was a member of their crews. The ideas of all that environment were an open book to him. He knew how to touch the hearts and the hot heads; he foiled the plans of the ambitious ones, and he spoke with ease about their wives and children, as well as about the village parties. Quite a number of families were indebted to him for the fact that the father of the house came home on Saturday evenings steady on his legs and with his pay almost untouched.

"How do you manage it," I asked Andréas, "so that all those people listen to and obey you? When I worked in hospitals I found it very difficult to satisfy, or rather not to hurt them, and they were my most manageable patients. One could do what one wanted with those little blackguards."

"Ah! It is very simple. I lived with them. You are a bourgeois. A thousand shades of difference separate you from them. You cannot feel as they do, and that is what prevents you from understanding them. Anyway, it is the same obstacle which may close any realm of life to us: the impossibility of going out from our own ego."

"Even so, isn't it the same for us to assimilate metaphysics as to penetrate a state of the soul?"

"Perhaps so; but do you know, I am ignorant of both metaphysics and psychology alike."

I looked at Andréas believing that he was making an epigram, but no, he was not smiling and, speaking seriously, he continued: "To understand, to cognize, is not the same as to perceive or conceive; it is to take something with us, to be born together, to organize and incorporate with the assistance of all the means—intellectual, aesthetic and even physical. If you want to know what a worker is, you must become one yourself, and without any thought of return, otherwise you will merely be declassed. And that is not at all easy. At least, go and watch the workers, try to realize what they are thinking, how they feel, and do it without any preconceived ideas."

"All right, but is it what the Privat-docents term to observe impartially?"

"If you wish so!"

"It seems to me that the actual inventor of such a method was Abailard?"

"No matter who! We have to remember only the fact, that in order to really know anything, we should utterly renounce the personal equation, temperament and individuality. By means of systematic meditation we can attain it in our mind. Brahmans speak about it and Jesuits approach it in their own way. But if we consider that the intellect is being constantly changed through psysiological conditions, and through magnetic, sentimental and spiritual ones, then we may feel ourselves compelled to seek for another organ of cognition, a more central and higher one. This organ is just 'the heart'. No object can be known to us if we do not love it beforehand. And perfect knowledge can be obtained only by him, who is 'poor in spirit', who is simple to the point of unity, stripped to nakedness, and humbled until he considers himself as nought.

"So, the Gospels may contain in them a system of logic?"

"Yes, among thousands of other things. But let us continue with our workers. Parisians as they are, they have plenty of self-love. They do not know that actually they are a very rich ground from which grow powerful trees and charming flowers. They see only the fact that they are close to the earth and that everyone has stamped upon them for many ages. But, all land needs a plough from time to time. Workers know very well that they have only a few abilities and little education. But they do not like it when someone reminds them about the fact, even by just a glance. They do not want to be treated as pariahs. On the first contact with a gentleman they immediately become like a porcupine. They firmly believe that they are despised simply because they have no collars and crude language. That is why they are afraid of hospitals : they imagine that in them they will be subjected to experiments, because they do not pay for treatment. They would prefer to give their money to a first-class doctor, but they will probably not fulfil his prescriptions. The foreman is always unpleasant to them and they cannot bear the sight of him, because officially he is a more important worker than the others. Also, he admires the boss and incites him in his evil tendencies, especially regarding economies where they are concerned."

" How can that be," I interrupted him, " you seem to condemn savings? "

" Hoarding is not inscribed among Heaven's laws. Otherwise, the manager or proprietor also has plenty of troubles. Very often he is too willing to make profits pitilessly, and is apt to consider his employees merely as machines. A small proprietor or boss may easily forget, that he himself was once one of these workers whom he harasses all day long; a well-armoured safe has been established in his heart and he plays the rôle of a small tyrant.

" Apart from that, an insurmountable mistrust often separates these two classes of men. Each is convinced that the other is exploiting him. Cares of leadership make the chiefs anxious; social discord make the proletariat ill-humoured, while trade unionism does not bring all the needed services, because it is like a caricature of true brotherhood. Based as they are on material grounds, unions have the spirit of division and intrigue, while injustices increase. In order for these groups to provide the real social benefits, which are expected from them, it ·would be necessary for their members to be able to unite themselves on the one general idea. But how many centuries will be necessary so that among the masses will spread the individual tendency to forget oneself for the benefit of the community? "

" So what then for the moment? "

" Let everyone do his best, each one in his own small field of action. It is very good to go to people with just friendship instead of many words. Anyway, if we want our superiors to come to see us, we should first go down to our inferiors. You can be sure that if, in a discussion, people will refrain from personal objections, remove preconceived ideas and ask about HIM, then Heaven will inspire us with good just and soothing words."

Chapter VI

A TEST OF VEDANTA

BECAUSE of such a beginning, our meal was finished very late, and as I had some visits to make, I had to leave.

On my next call, Stella directed the conversation to things metaphysical.

"Actually, my proper place is on the first floor," she said smiling, "but I very much like to hear discussions about these things, although I am rather ignorant of them. You were criticizing the Buddhists, Doctor, on your previous visit, but does Brahmanism find more grace in your eyes?"

"I don't think that Buddhism would suffer much because of my criticism, and likewise Brahmanism because of what I will now express. However, I beg you for your attention.

"The Vedas teach that *man* contains within himself a representation of everything that exists in the *Universe*. In both exists a central pivot, on which different speed-multipliers gear the cog-wheels of both machines. This pivot in man is the Atman, the peak of the unconscious Highest. It carries along the mind. It seems that the latter can take into its possession some of the successive cog-wheels of the unconscious.

"Therefore the aim which is recommended by highly developed Yogis is to augment, to deepen and to sublimate the conscious sphere until the Atman is reached."

"All of this is perfectly exact," said Andréas. "You know that Gupta Vidya possesses, among all knowledge, the original property of becoming complicated, because of the complexity of the intellect with which it is assimilated. Its authentic manuals, which I was at least able to read in the crypts are only summaries, the most detailed of which consists of no more than twenty pages, inscribed on palm leaves, rendered indestructible by a special process. They are merely note-books. And the pupil must discover for himself a personal adaptation of each general rule. But I am preventing you from continuing your exposition. I beg your pardon, for I am reaching the age when one likes to have a kind listener."

"I feel that I am getting great profit from the remembrances, which you have so kindly let me hear; but now I will continue my explanations. It seems to me that my mind is less burdened when I am telling you my doubts. Here is what I am not able to understand about Raja Yoga, but please stop me if I begin to err.

"For example, I am holding a stone: the sensation of that contact needed an infinitesimal amount of time in order to be felt. The voluntary return movement by which I open or shut my hand takes approximately an equal length of time, about thirty-three thousandths of a second, or so it seems to me. A yogi tries to become conscious of both these currents and of the cerebral phenomenon which occurs in that short interval of time, which I just mentioned. When he will reach the conscious discernment of the nerves through which runs the current of sensation, its reflection, of the cerebral cells involved and of the phases of the ideas obtained, then he will almost entirely control his mind.

"This means that the mind will not be bound to the brain any more, but can be transported to any point of the body. Such a yogi will see with the ends of his fingers, will hear with his eyes, and so on. He will then begin a similar training of the hyperphysical sensations, of thoughts, of memory, of the thinking principle itself and finally, of the consciousness of the self. Coming by way of an *abstract neutral realm,* in which resides the peak of the conscious element, he will throw himself into indescribable experiences, which will make a '*liberated one*' of him."

"Very exact!" Andréas interrupted me, "at least according to my personal studies."

"Well," I continued, "I did begin such work. I obtained a certain formless state of the mind; I came close to monoideism, or a feeling of being near to attaining it. Then suddenly, every time, I was ejected back into the tumult of everyday life."

"Yes! There is a WALL."

"Well, but is this wall a providential one? Should I leap over it, or destroy it? Did I myself build it before? Is it an enemy or a friend?"

"Doctor, I cannot tell you about it. It is you who should see the thing for yourself. You can destroy this wall, turn towards it, leap over it, or dig under it. But do not try anything yet. Wait! Your exercises apply to only certain of your abilities; you commit the same error as a novice athlete, who develops his pectoral muscles and biceps without first thinking about widening his thorax and strengthening his heart."

"Yes!" I exclaimed, happy at encountering a new idea. "Your point of view differs from that of the Brahmanic one, but do you know of a more *central principle* than the intellect, but which does not belong to the *unconscious?* All Hindu Scriptures place the ' mental moon ' above the ' vital sun '."

"That is true for the world in which they live, but we have something different."

"What is it?"

"You have seen its name thousands of times Doctor, when you were still a child."

"But what book is it in?"

"In the Gospels," murmured Stella in a low voice. "Jesus speaks incessantly about our heart."

"Our heart! Our heart!" I answered. "It is a symbol, a figment of rhetoric imagination."

"Oh no! Oh no!" said Andréas forcefully. "In the Gospels there are symbols only for those who live in the realm of allegories. What meaning has a word against a deed? What value has a system before facts? What is knowledge before power? To know a phenomenon fully, one must first experience it thousands of times."

"But what you say is simply bankruptcy for science! Did you ever so much as exhaust science? Do you have some unsuspected powers with which to act in your hands? If what you say is true, then all my dreams are destroyed; then I have to forget my books, my hieroglyphs, my figures, schemes. Then I have lost my twenty years of study. I am a wreck!"

"Doctor, I had to suffer doubts like you," answered Andréas in an affectionate tone. "I was desperate to the point where I had no tears left. And yet I was supported by pride, a great pride of having climbed a path along which no European had ventured for centuries. Today I know that I did not perform that climb by my own force. But at that time I believed only in myself.

"Disasters fell on my head without forcing me to bend. I never stopped advancing; I surpassed all my fellow disciples. And suddenly, I felt myself *alone*.

"My masters were pitiless. They thought 'if he falls, that will happen only because he is too weak to ascend further and we will merely waste our forces in supporting him'.

"I had learned so much, seen so many things, fought and solved so many contrary enigmas, that in my eyes there was no longer any difference between good and evil, right and left. Was there a God, was there a Devil? Is creation something orderly, or is it simply chaos? And myself—who am I? Slave or free man? What will I become? Will I succumb? Is nothingness awaiting me? Or is there a glorious eternity prepared for me? And so I kept on repeating my work, travels and reflections, passing incessantly from fear to weariness. All those philosophies, dialectics, theologies, practical mysteries which I had experienced, the poisons, terrible and ghastly presences, the desperate sentences of those who had abandoned all illusions, what had I to conclude from all those things?

"In initiatory ecstasies I could perceive the forms of the gods of Nature and science. As a bridge-builder for Kipling, drunk with the occult opium, I could sometimes detect the secret conversations of those powerful beings.

"But of all this, for me there remained only an infinite tiredness. What should I become? Should I not, like those adepts of Benares, ask from Matter, victorious in spite of all, its philtres of oblivion?"

Impressed by the living story and Andréas's confidence, I listened with the utmost attention. At last I had found a man who did not speak merely from hearsay. I had found a true experimenter. I could foresee the end of my long struggles, for I felt hope, a clear hope, like the final dawn. And Andréas continued, always quietly smoking his long Flemish pipe that was brown and smooth like those used for opium.

"At the time of that inner crisis, I had reason to be anxious about my personal safety, in spite of the fact that everything around me seemed to be quiet. I knew that orientals carry grudges, are very patient and learnedly constructed, and that I had already created certain mistrust. And this is how it happened.

"My destiny demanded that I be admitted to almost all of the esoteric associations—Muslim, Hindu, Chinese, Sivaites, Tantrics, Javanese witch doctors, Red-caps of Bhutan, mountaineers of Nan-Chan, all of them initiated me into their magic. I knew the lost idioms and rituals which can only be whispered into one's ears; the horrible objects which can be obtained only for the price of hideous crimes, and stones and herbs so rare that they can be procured only by months of wandering. I lived in hermitages lost in the midst of forests, prepared subtle poisons and irresistible philtres. I accompanied fearless hunters who dared to tear a claw, a tooth or fur from a living tiger, because their ritual rejects these things if they come from a dead beast.

"The monstrous forms of gods from *the other side* appeared to me many times in the smoke of holocausts, and in the steam of recently shed blood. My dreams were often troubled by the evil, ironic looks of these beings, before whom the most powerful and sagacious men are like pygmies. The clever conjurers who, through their adroitly made calculations of correspondences, are able to stay these titans for a second or so and extract a reply from them, are actually only laughing-stocks for them. And often the conjurers serve these gods simply as toys.

"Gradually I convinced myself, that only the theory of magic is an exact science, but its practices offer too many possibilities of error, and too many factors in it are imprecise. Whoever wants to extort some secret forces from Nature, through violence, is throwing himself into the clasp of Destiny. And even if his debates lose their vice for a moment, it makes it only the more inexorable and painful.

"Everything that matures needs a definite period of time, fixed from the beginning. If a man has a desire to have all powers, it is because he already possesses the germs of them. But, because he is too impatient, man tries to raise them by artificial means and therefore receives nothing more than frail plants, destined to die under the first buffetings of the storm.

"But these conclusions condemned all the toil of my youth: I had either to close my eyes against the evidence, or begin everything again from the starting point."

"I am astonished," I said, "seeing how clearly you explain my own position to me. How could I take so much trouble in order to seek so far in darkness for the simple, brilliant Truth, that is so near?"

"Everyone does the same, dear Doctor. So, be comforted because of the fact. It is very difficult to escape the temptation of the mysterious. And I remember that at the beginning of my stay in India, the adepts to whom I turned for instruction anticipated me very well.

"They explained to me, that I was wrong in seeking for far off foreign symbols, when my own religion offered me such wonderful things. They quite firmly told me that, for Europeans, our *eternal Master* will always be Jesus, and that the attitude of those who trust Him can never be frustrated.

"Well, I retained their words in my memory, without actually 'hearing' them! What a pity that I did not try to live, morally and intellectually forgetting my 'ego'. When those Brahmans thus spoke to me, I should have put aside the preconceived ideas, that they tried to discourage in me, and then those two minutes of spiritual clarity would have spared me the lost years, which will never return. Yes, there have been many times when I have been weak enough to regret that irretrievable loss."

"Weak?" I asked him, a little surprised.

"Well, yes, it is weakness to believe that something is useless."

"And now, what do you think about the warning, given to you by those Brahmans?"

"I consider it just!"

"Then one should follow one's religion and go to church?"

"One must follow one's conscience, after having enlightened it as well as one can."

"Actually, man possessed a conscience long before the existence of all the ecclesiastical organizations."

At that point Andréas undoubtedly read my thoughts because he smilingly interrupted me.

"Doctor, don't let us err, neither you nor myself. We are not bishops. Therefore we have no right to judge priests, their theology or their casuistry. If you believe that Christ is always living, then follow His words: they will suffice for everything."

The peculiar tone with which Andréas pronounced these words impressed me. I felt anxious when almost involuntarily I repeated: "Christ, eternally alive?"

And immediately, with some fear I perceived what extraordinary consequences such a hypothesis could have. It was because the words of Andréas impressed me so much by the positiveness of their meaning. He was no conversationalist and his expressions were of the simplest. But behind his discourse which was as simple as usual, and without any gesture of under-lining on his part, I more and more perceived a mysterious gleam, very sweet but very strong, announcing truly a supernatural Presence. This duality perplexed me. I did not dare to put any direct questions to Andréas about his possible relations with Desiderius and even with Théophane. I would only show myself in a naive light if he wished to deceive me, or mistrustful if he was sincere. I awaited the moment when I would be delivered from these uncertainties, for they were painful for me, because the whole meaning of my life was to be decided during these few hours.

After a pause my companion continued, as if speaking to himself: "Yes, when I consider from different aspects the deeds and words of this divine Being, I cannot but feel pity for the indecent imaginings and stupidities, which have been written about Him.

"The Brahmans themselves only shrugged their shoulders when I told them that many Western 'spiritualists' believed that Jesus had been initiated by the Essenes, Egyptians or even Lamas; that some spiritists represent Him as a medium; magnetizers as a Du Potet of the past, and occultists as a magician. I told them that all of these people often pretend that they too have achieved His greatness, to say nothing of those who even place themselves above Him, simply because they are living two thousand years later."

"Oh! Yes!" I interrupted Andréas, "I have heard that such humbugs expressed such ideas about the famous Mr. ——."

"Don't say the name, Doctor. Don't let us judge, merely compare," replied Andréas as he rose. "Better for us to learn that deep indulgence of Christ: 'Father forgive them, for they know not what they do'."

Chapter VII

THE BRAHMAN

ALMOST two months had passed since my initial visit to Andréas, and right from those first weeks he had been sending me patients from his suburb. Although it was quite a long way to travel, I voluntarily occupied myself with his sick acquaintances, as this gave me the pretext to call on him again.

So, one morning, after having made my usual rounds, I again directed my steps towards his home. Turning a street-corner, I stopped opposite a laundry, which I patronized and also attended.

Of course, I knew its whole staff of female workers well, those courageous girls, who were frustrating their youth, risking anemia among the faint vapours of linen and the sickening heat from the iron stoves.

This babbling, arch little world, sincere in its harshness, cordially accepted me and therefore from time to time, I was entitled to chat with and buy the girls a few shillings worth of chestnuts. Last week they had told me that the apprentices' holiday was approaching. So, this morning I walked up to the suburb of *Temple* and bought a magnificent marcasite ring, gold-plated and set with rubies made from glass, which the jeweller sold me for the 'sacrificial' price of only 'a crown instead of a pound or so'.

Then I went to the laundresses and first presented the ring, after which, with the permission of the proprietress, I also gave them a bottle of white wine. They assailed me with requests concerning the cure of their minor ailments. And in the meantime I was able to learn many things about the wife of a policeman, a clerk in the mayor's office, a sweeper, and so on.

"And now, you know, your friend Monsieur Andréas has a Chinese with him. He came yesterday evening and I was even frightened of him when he came in to ask the way, for I had not yet turned on the lights. He doesn't speak French well, but he is a handsome man."

"He is not a Chinese, because he hasn't a pig-tail."

"But his face is yellow," and so on.

I escaped as soon as I could, and in order not to intrude on Andréas, I went to a nearby wine-seller's shop for breakfast. Then later, around two o'clock, I called on Andréas.

His 'Chinese' turned out to be a magnificent bearded Hindu

with a turban, who held himself as straight as a column and v
was evidently a high-caste de Kuhu. After we were duly int
duced he relaxed a little from his triple pride of being an Arya
an aristocrat and a priest. And so we began to speak free
enough, although desultorily. We discussed such themes as Engli
culture, archeology, medicine, astrology, epigraphy, agnosticis
and monism. All of these gave us an opportunity to form mo
excellent opinions about one another. At intervals Andréas inte
posed a remark. Finally the Hindu began to glorify the ' scienc
of sciences', that is, Raja Yoga.

Nevertheless, it was truly a pleasure to listen to him. He wa
rather more fluent than eloquent, but produced such happy con
binations of ideas with such ease, that it seemed impossible for on
to tire while following the development of his conversation.

Facts, theories, pictures, all were bound together, opposed t
each other and yet joined to themselves without end.

It was a brilliant web, a dense composition, just like an entangle
sculpture of warriors, monsters, geniuses, gods, bayaderes, all i
such abundant luxury that the brain of the visitor became as i
numbed into dream-like periods in which everything seemed to b
possible and easy : all mysteries explained and all utopias reason
able.

In this way I listened to the Brahman, when suddenly Andréa
interrupted him saying : " I am taking the liberty at this point c
stopping my guest so as to put some questions to him." And a
the Oriental remained silent Andréas continued : " If my memor
does not fail me, your books recommend that we should neve
begin any practice of Yoga without first having successfull
followed two systems of moral training. Otherwise practica
exercises would become dangerous and perhaps even deadly fc
an imprudent disciple."

" Your words are true," agreed the priest.

" Well then, would you like to oblige and give us the details c
such preparations ? "

" Sir, I will not be teaching either you or your honourabl
friend anything new, if I say that all this concerns the te
observances and ten purifications. Here are the first ones :

AHIMSA—which is the non-causing of any pain, either b
    thought, word, or deed to any living being.
SATYA—always to speak the truth, by intellect, word an
    gesture.
ASTEYA—indifference or lack of desire to possess anything, b
    intellect, thought, word or deed.

BRAHMACHARYA—chastity of the body, words and thoughts.
DAYA—the practising of goodness towards all creatures, even towards demons.
ARDJAVA—inner equality of mind and feelings when performing all the requisite activities, and abstention from all forbidden actions.
KSHAMA—a virtue which permits the supporting with patience of all pleasant and unpleasant things.
DHRITI—the preserving of a firm resolution in disaster as well as in happiness.
MITHAARA—or right feeding, the accepting of meals to only one quarter of the stomach's capacity.
Finally, SANCHA, which is purification of the body through religious rituals, and purification of the heart through discrimination between the Absolute and the relative."

"Now please tell me the ten remaining formulas, belonging to the second series," said Andréas.

"These are they," said the Hindu : "Firstly,

TAPAS—moderate physical penance.
SANTOSHA—to be satisfied with everything and to have recognition of God for the same.
ASTIKEYA—practice of the Vedantic Doctrine concerning things due and undue.
DHANA—charity given to worthy persons.
ISWARA-PUJA—the cult of the Lord according to ritual.
SIDDHANTA-SRAVANA—knowledge of religious philosophy.
KRITI—shame for errors committed in religious or worldly affairs.
MATHI—the following of the prescriptions of the sacred books with faith and love.
JAPA—repetition of daily prayers.
Finally, VRATA—the abstention from deeds prohibited by religious rules."

"So," interrupted Andréas, "it is only then, when the disciple becomes incapable of omitting any of these precepts, that he would be able to practise Yoga?"

"Yes, Sir!" replied Nagendra-Nath (which was his oriental name). "Such is the pure doctrine of the Rishis of the past, although modern followers often forget, or distort it."

"I know, my dear Brahman," said Andréas. "Forgive me for asking you to recite all these details to us. However, it will be useful for our doctor friend to know them." He accented the word *our*. " I had to decipher those venerable texts in my youth, just before I reached my sixteenth year, and I was entirely absorbed in that reading for twenty-one days and nights."

The priest's gaze glowed for a second under his long weary looking eyelids, but with a simple expression of worldly politeness he asked: " So you have been in my native land Monsieur? Which states did you visit? "

" Many of them," softly replied Andréas. " All because I was seeking for the stone, which can be found in the stag's head."

I must mention here, that, in India, people attribute a special virtue to that hypothetical stone as being the supreme protection against snake-bite, and a certain occult fraternity of great importance makes this symbolic belief its pass-word, just as the sentence pronounced by Andréas.

" Quite true ! " said the Brahman, with the same mood of indifferent politeness. " I have with me just such a stone, and even a flute with seven holes to charm the cobras."

" Your country really is rich in curious things," said Andréas. And rising, in order to take his pipe, he remained standing with his right leg crossed over his left adding: " Also one of your countrymen, an old man who walked with the aid of a bamboo stick, gave me a vina (Hindu musical instrument), whose sounds can charm even the grey serpents. As far as I can remember, it was in the Kingdom of Oudh, close to Rudrapura."

At this Nagendra seemed to lose his impassiveness, for the sentence pronounced by Andréas was just the same as the one used by wandering members of the Agartta to permit themselves to be recognized by their subordinates in a lower degree of initiation. However, because of my presence the priest limited himself to merely rising and bowing before Andréas.

" Please be seated," Andréas told him, resuming his own seat. " We may return to our training. I will allow myself a few remarks, which you will immediately understand, providing that, for some minutes, you will forget who you are and who your teachers were. Now listen !

" To begin with, where could you find a man who would be able to live here, on this low plane, without causing pain to any creature ? This match will suffer when I light it and also when I extinguish it. In one breath I sacrifice millions of little beings. To express the truth means that one knows that truth. But if I know the truth, then what purpose has Yoga ? To be indifferent to everything is lack of politeness towards God : all that He gives us is precious, because it is only through the best use of His gifts to us, that we let Him (if I dare say so), make new and more generous munificences. To be chaste? But if my parents had been so, my spirit would still be knocking in vain at the gates of this earth and such enforced inactivity would be a hellish torture for it. To be good to all creatures? In point of fact only the ONE is really good. Further, if I am good, that means that I have reached the goal. And then there is no need for any Yogas. The impassive moods? For that purpose one should necessarily pass through all experiences, and then all initiations would become useless. For no one can be impassive in the face of pain if he has not already passed through it sometime 'before'. And this is another 'petition of principle'. To be grateful towards God for everything He sends us, even the worst of sufferings is something that only a FREE man is able to accept in this way, but not any student of Yoga. As regards ritualistic observances, I leave them to you, since because of the simple fact that you were born in the blessed land of Bharat, the Vedas for you contain all the truth."

The Hindu bowed again and said: "For me you are opening horizons such as are seen from the top of Mount Meru!"

Andréas continued: "Yes! My venerable Brahman, you have your own way; yellow men have theirs, Muslims also, and so do the Christians. We are walking upon the artifices of the goddess called 'Illusion', so let us guard our ways. You have come from America via London, where you were showered with honours, decorations, tea-parties and discourses. But you have to return to your hermitage, make sacrifices and pay extraordinary fines to the temple because you, a priest, left your sacred soil and lived among the Mlecchas, those stinking eaters of cow-flesh!

"And then you may see how the lowest ranking chief of police, in his khaki uniform and mounted on his Australian horse, might take a fancy to make you run from one end of the country to another, calling you a negro, an idiot idolater!

"The Anglo-Saxons speak about fraternity, but don't always practise it. Didn't you notice how civilized Americans behave themselves with coloured gentlemen?*

"You allowed yourself to be bewildered, yes just bewildered —although nobody could have any doubt about the fact for even a minute—by the beautiful female listeners of New York, Boston, Philadelphia, and the beautiful ladies dining in the Carlton. And did you for a moment believe that they understood anything of your metaphysics? But you are separated from Westerners by a

* Sédir wrote this before World War I, when conditions in India and all over the world were, of course, quite different from today.—M.S.

wall! Please pardon me for telling you all these things so bluntly, but it is necessary that you be well informed as to how things actually are."

The Hindu, a little offended, looked towards me.

"My friend!" said Andréas. "It is of no importance, for he himself leans on a beggar's stick when he walks."

"Oh!" said Nagendra visibly relieved of his previous uneasiness, I know very well that all your actions are guided by the greatest wisdom, so I have not the slightest doubt about this gentleman." And he made a deep bow to me and another to Andréas. Then he started a long discourse in Hindi of which I did not understand much.

On the following evening, at the express invitation of our host, I returned to hear new themes discussed. Andréas and Nagendra spoke in French and English, as well as in several vernaculars. Sometimes I heard the name of a mullah, or Russian general, or a Muslim leader mentioned. And in that way, from the two men, I learnt plenty of things that are not usually known about the Asian world. A journey by the Czar, an ethnographical mission of the Japanese, Lazarists apostleship, the construction of a railway, a stock-exchange crisis, and other apparently not too important events were discussed. They showed me the springs that work behind it all, so that once more I could recognize the old Hermetic axiom—'*everything is contained in everything*'.

Esoterism occurs in truly unpredictable circumstances, and how wise these men were! What a depth of view! What cleverness! Quite definitely, Andréas must be just that hero of my small black note-book. Of course, since that time he had advanced very far, briefly, he had achieved Attainment, and seemed to have reached the last, the highest degrees of initiation.

But my subsequent visits again immersed me in my usual perplexity.

CHAPTER VIII

THE DURAKAPALAM

It was not any new, questionable points which gave me trouble, but always the old enigmas, always the old antinomies. I repeated them to Andréas with a sickening persistence. He listened to me patiently, and as a kind of answer he told me some stories from his own eventful life. In general his conversation always included one or two words, which when said seemingly by accident, illuminated some problem from a different angle, which then broke my short-sighted logic.

Here is one of the most marvellous of those stories as Andréas conveyed it to me during the course of several visits.

"Before leaving Paris, I contacted and came to an understanding with some men, who corresponded with certain Hindus, so that everything was anticipated and provided for. Hence, on my arrival in India, I was immediately able to turn to the right people there.

"On disembarking in a small port of Malabar, I had to walk slowly through the township, clad as a priest of Siva, with a certain amulet around my wrist. Hardly had I passed through the Indian quarter, when a man belonging to a low caste came to me and let me recognize him. He then led me to the countryside from where a light cart transported us to the Ghats. From there we began climbing upwards until evening. The difficult route did not allow me to enjoy the freshness of the night, nor the serenity of the surroundings.

"Bushes and stones absorbed all of my attention, to say nothing of a fear of wild animals and poisonous creatures. Shortly before dawn we came to a kind of granite plateau, covered with coarse grass burned by the sun. Far ahead the plateau outline was made irregular by some heaps of stones which formed a circle. My guide directed his steps to a rocky mass, which was very similar to the cliffs of Cornwall. I only had time to glance briefly at the magnificent sunrise over the sea on my right, before I had to crawl into a vault formed by these rocks. At its end I found a kind of hole and I entered into it after my guide. A sloping passage led us to a dungeon where reptiles lived in considerable numbers among bleached bones. The Hindu produced a whistle in order to remove the serpents and after a few more steps we entered a narrow ravine. I must confess that I found the view of the blue sky very pleasant.

"We then entered a new tunnel, a short one this time, and at last we were in the fresh air, to find before us the moving scene of a town in ruins. The pandits confirmed for me that the Deccan has many dead cities, destroyed by catastrophes or wars. Later, I learned that this one had been completely isolated by an earthquake, which in disturbing the rocks had formed a circle of cliffs, whose smooth walls defied every attempt at descent. The position of the city set below the level of the plateau through which we had passed, as well as the chalky nature of the soil easily collected and held rain-water. And that was why the ruins were covered with luxuriant vegetation in which birds and monkeys crowded. It was a really fantastic picture. Broad streets that had been damaged by the passage of the centuries were bordered by crumbling palaces. Here and there I saw some columns of rosy marble, small ponds and sometimes baths, encircled with balustrades, slowly being destroyed by the pressure of the plants, while monumental flights of stairs with their long sweep of steps were gradually disintegrating. All had been invaded by the green vegetation and its flowers, reverberating with the concertos of birds and chattering monkeys.

"It was an extraordinary orchestra, with deafening passages and majestic silences full of secrets. Everywhere there were large trees, whose magnificent foliage would prevent the curious—who might venture here from the surrounding cliffs—from seeing anything beyond. My guide was hurrying between the loose columns and over cross-roads, which became glades. The enormous sculptured façade of a pagoda suddenly reared itself before us. We had reached our goal. A Brahmin appeared and greeted me in English. He took me to the balcony of a shadowy gallery, ordered fruit and refreshing drinks to be served, and invited me to take a few hours rest on a camp-bed. But the as yet unknown vistas that surprised beyond expectation, prevented me from falling asleep.

"I examined the temple. The beauty of its mass as a whole, the richness of detail, measurements and proportion— all made it equal to the most famous monuments of Benares and Ellora. As far as my memories of the Tantric lectures allowed me to conjecture, I judged this building to have been erected in honour of Ganesha, the elephant-headed god. It was composed of an enormous band of circular galleries, containing five other precincts with several floors, concentrically arranged and filled with doorways.

"The central gallery, which was also the highest, was filled with the temple buildings proper. Later I saw that there were three altars, under a canopy, supported by richly decorated, massive columns.

"Each altar was composed of a solid block of stone having a base of about ten feet square, serving as a support for a truncated five-sided pyramid, one of which was higher than the others.

"The roof was an elliptical terrace on two fulcrums, from which rose the fourth and fifth altars. Between these two altars, the centre of the terrace opened out towards a lower nave to give access to a colossal statue of a god, whose aureole surpassed the whole of its surroundings.

"The bas-reliefs and friezes, in their entirety, represented the legend of Mahadeva, more or less as it is described by the Skanda-Puranas. No wood or metal had been employed, only stone.

"Parama-Siva and his twenty-four *murtis* were visible on the first altar. On the second one Daksha among the Prajapatis, made her penitence before Siva, then gave birth to her sons: the first thousand being the Haryasuas, and the second the Sabalasuas, who govern the subtle essences of the universe, or *Tattvas*. Next came the sixty daughters, resplendent among whom was *Uma*, the wife of Siva. So was depicted the long legend of all these figures, each one representing a symbol of a definite cosmic force. All this was shown on the four faces of the altar, the five sides of the supporting columns and on the five faces of the last pyramid.

"The third altar told of the downfall of Daksha, and the transformation of her daughter *Uma* into *Parvati*, on the Mount of Himavan; when Siva himself, under the aspect of Dakshina-murti, tried in vain to initiate the *Mounis* in the shadow of the banyan tree, again repeating the attempt on the top of Mount Kailasha. During that initiation the Asuras were dispersed over the earth and there committed thousands of atrocities. Then the Mahadeva (Great Spirit) emanated Humara, or Subramanya, which means a spiritual fighter.

"On the upper terrace, the fourth altar showed the incidents in the births of another son of Siva, Ganesha the Peaceful. Finally, the fifth altar, according to the myth of Linga-Purana presented the fivefold Siva and his twenty children. These fivefold aspects are: *Sadhodjyata*, through whom the whole of life is reabsorbed; *Vamadeva*, who accomplishes the law and ritual; *Tatpurusha*, who fixes creatures in the supreme science; *Aghora*, the terrible, who teaches Yoga, and finally, *Isana*, who is the form of all forms, synthetizing the Union, Reason, Penitence, Knowledge and Religious Observance, as well as twenty-seven other qualities of the soul, which has conquered deliverance.

"Along the outer peristyle crept the *serpents of eternity,* with their seven heads; at regular intervals stood the symbolical guardians of the mysteries, and the holy elephants, the bearers of the occult science and the bearers of the temple, lowered their trunks to the visitor and gave shelter, all of them being fashioned in granite. The ceiling disappeared in a chaos of sculpted demonic forms confined, according to the Scriptures, to the inferior, invisible worlds. Behind the cactus plants, euphorbias and thorny figs one could see, in the shadows, the thick-lipped, beastly and canine faces of vampires, Pisachas, Kataputanas and Ulkamukhas Pretas. Columns supported long bas-reliefs where rhythmical Gandharvas danced. To the north there were images of Soma and Indra; to the east, Yakshas guardians of treasures, presided over by Kubera and Yakshini his wife; to the west a terrible army of Rakshas, commanded by Khadha-Ravana, the dispenser of victories, and the south formed the main entrance.

"At the end of the day the Brahman returned, the same one who had met me. He had the long face of his race and the beautiful eyes of a circumspect Roman prelate. He explained to me, that all of this old temple, which had actually been transformed into a laboratory, was at my complete disposal, and its hosts considered themselves to be my servants, because of the high personage who had introduced me to them. I thanked him according to the exaggerated form of Eastern custom and good breeding, and then we began a tour of the building."

"'There is a mental attitude in which, firstly, I beg you to establish yourself,' my new guide told me. 'It is not to hurry, to consider that you have plenty of time before you, and then you will be set face to face with entirely new things. Impatience or even haste will be only obstacles for you rather than assistance.' I promised to do my best in order to realize that calm, which I knew was a distinctive sign of the sages, of whom I had become a disciple. I therefore asked that some allowance be made for me and I prepared to take my first lesson.

"The temple housed several kinds of laboratories and workshops. However, I did not find any rare minerals, or precious oils, or apparatus belonging to psychological magic in them. The savants who worked there studied only what Europeans call *physical forces,* but with very sensitive instruments. These had to be insulated against the magnetic currents of the earth and atmosphere. This result was achieved by manual processes of manufacture and no machinery was used. Metal parts, wires, everything was hammered, forged, laminated and prepared by hand, with a patience hard to imagine. I saw one of the workers hammering a piece of copper with a watchmaker's hammer from sunrise to sunset, while another took over from him at night, and I was told that this work went on for months.

"I will spare you a description of all the apparatus and mechanisms which my guide showed to me. However, there was one item, which was used for such an unimaginable purpose, that it transcends all the most extraordinary fantasies of science-fiction novels.

"As we walked through that museum of machines, Sankhyananda (which was the name of my guide) drew my attention to a large cube-shaped chest, made from a yellow substance, like gold, but as transparent as glass.

"'This is a *Durakapalam*,' he said to me, 'which you may translate into your language as a telemobile. We use it for our travels to other planets in this material universe.'

"I opened my eyes wide in amazement, but my companion continued: 'You see here, an application of the Tattvas system, which your monist philosophers partially re-discovered in their theory of the fourth dimension. Here is the chain of reasoning which we ourselves use.'

"I will recount to you only a part of the detailed exposition of the Sankhya physics which I heard and so give you merely a resumé of it.

"There is a universal substance which is unique and all existing objects are only different forms of it. We perceive these forms only through the medium of our five senses. Therefore, they can be classified under the name of the sense which is able to register these forms. Each sense is sensitive to certain kinds of atomic movements: hearing, seeing, touching, tasting and smelling belonging respectively to the vibrations of ether, light, air, water and earth which, at the same time, are movements of atoms. So, ether is movement in *all directions*; light movement along straight lines; air movement of vortexes; water balanced movement, and earth cessation of movement.

"Apart from this, each of these elements possesses as secondary things, the qualities of the other four. Ether apart from sound, also has colour, form, taste and smell. You can see for yourself all the other applications of this law.

"Finally, each of these kinetic forms is represented in the human mentality. Therefore, all things can correspond one to another, under certain conditions.

"But we were primarily concerned with the acoustic fluid, the properties of which were described to me by Sankhyananda.

"'Sound,' he told me, 'possesses, apart from other qualities, those of mobility, fluidity and softness. We call it *Sneha*. Long before your physicists discovered it, we knew that sound emits calories. Also, that it incites movement through the impulse of the power, which we call *Pranamitva*. Stringed musical instruments, rhythmical melodies, the noise of thunder, all these show us the existence of these different properties. In short, that form of the universal substance which we call *Akasha* possesses a specific quality like sound, and as generic qualities form, movement and heat.

" ' Numerous long experiments have taught us that some classes of sound contain the most perfect forms, while others are richer in calories, and yet others emit more movement. We know how to distinguish between these different kinds, how to produce them and even augment their intensity by means of different psycho-physiological formulas.

" ' Similarly, a fakir can raise himself into the air and remain suspended for some time by the use of particular sounds under a certain nervous tension. In other words, nervous force can influence and act upon matter through sound. That is what we have achieved!

" ' Here is another point: a conception of SPACE is one of the most difficult to achieve. You Europeans do not recognize anything but physical space. You call it ' the REAL SPACE ', but for us it is quite illusory. Our *real space* is that which some of your geometricians and mathematicians call ' hyperspace '. Physical space is finite because, if it were otherwise, that is, infinite, only an infinite number could measure it. But there cannot be any concrete infinite number. On this point Tradition agrees with our reasoning, and I hope that you will be able to experience it.

" ' Now, if space is finite, it must have a form, which is a *spherical* one, because there is no reason why space should extend itself more in one direction than in another.

" ' *Space* is the place for all creatures, and your memory will certainly tell you about some cosmogonical personages, who symbolize it. Such dwellers are subjected to the inevitable law of transformation. Such are the elementary truths, which will suffice in order for you to clearly grasp the principle of the telemobile.

" ' This machine must be able to transport itself into all the planes of space and to exist in them. Therefore it is necessary for its materials of construction to be unalterable, and its motive power must be independent of all the physico-chemical and fluidic forces, which means the superior essence. It is the accepted thing that we do not quit our visible universe.

" ' These conditions seem impossible to achieve, but nevertheless they have been achieved and here is the way in which it has been done. Our chemists in the crypts can produce metals which are indifferent to all physical agencies; but in order to obtain metals unaffected by forces belonging to other planets, one should first know that world, which has to be explored.

"'How can we get free from that vicious circle? Our observations of the firmament have been preserved for about two hundred centuries. They contain investigations from the point of view of mechanics, mathematics and biology, and can also be referred to astronomy and astrology. Even now, every night, new slips are being made out and calculated. They are centralized, classified and synthetized. And for every celestial body we establish a hypothetical table concerning all its physical, chemical and natural properties. Of course, all this is only a calculation of probability, which we try to develop in that way, but exact calculations show us that the chances of error are infinitesimal.

"'So, if our investigator and observer would transport himself in the telemobile closer to the planet nearest to our earth, he would then be in a position to rectify the tables we had prepared for that planet. Subsequently, our engineers and chemists could invent another machine, to investigate the next planet, and so on.

"'The old and venerable magic, which in each age manifests itself according to circumstances, in relation to its outer form, is not a matter of guesswork. Quite the opposite! It is a positive and exact science!

"'And true magicians are not any emotional demi-savants, but engineers, physicists and chemists of the INVISIBLE.

"'Naive people who hypnotize themselves by pentacles or mantrams in order to obtain superior forces do not know that these drawings, and so on, are, for them, just unknown cinematic schemes, whose realms are mysterious spaces of four, five, six and seven dimensions. Even to imagine such things would be madness for your philosophers. Even so, there exist active beings in these spaces, thinking intelligences, working bodies and organisms, creating machines and art objects. The pentacles are just the lines of force of these machines, frames for those invisible statues, for those inaudible symphonies, for all those unknowable creations, which nevertheless fecundate some noble hearts and deeply human minds.

"'You may consider, along with Descartes, that all matter is like space and all space like matter, that is, that space is full; or you may imagine matter as being impenetrable space with emptiness inserted in it; or as a system of pre-established harmony; or you can ascribe to the world's properties of mutual attraction and repulsion. All of these opinions would not be irreconcilable with ours. The more you will advance in Wisdom, the better you will see that traditional doctrines are quite sufficient to settle all the differences that endlessly arise in the confined field of exoteric philosophy.

"'Yes! Space is substantial. The simple forces which fecundate it exist independently. To take possession of both is the dual problem which our telemobile pretends to resolve. We already possess the special acoustic energy, about which I spoke to you at the beginning of this interview. Therefore, let us seek after the *point of support*, a centre of fixation and finally, a directing apparatus. Elements of matter like atoms cannot act on one another because they do not mutually touch. If it were otherwise, then they would have to touch each other on ALL their surfaces, because of their infinite smallness. Then matter, becoming a full solid, would remain immobilized. Hence we have to imagine atoms swimming in a more fluid environment, constituted by other atoms, much smaller and endowed with tremendous speeds, incessantly hitting atoms of the ether and so involving it in vibratory movement. This hypothesis is supported by differential calculus. We have to verify it through numerous experiments made with the aid of optical apparatus much more powerful than your microscopes, of which the legendary 'magic mirrors' are merely sketches.

"'How is matter itself organized? The answer to that question would perhaps give us the data which we still lack. The atomic volumes of the so-called *simple* elements have been established, and despite the uncertainty of these calculations, it has been found that the atomic volumes of the elements belonging to the same family are in simple relation to one another. There is no need to remind you about Dumas and Wurtz.

"'If a lucky chance would put into the hands of a chemist, a factor capable of changing the position of atoms in an element, it would be possible to transmute say, chlorine into iodine, or carbon into rubidium.

"'And this active factor does exist. Our sages know about it; our books mention it. It is the *Vyoma-Panchaka-Akasa*. Among other matters the *Mandala-Brahmana* describes its five forms. The fourth, the *Surya-Akasa* has the property of special condensation. And we have found the substance which is capable of receiving a considerable charge of these spiritous molecules, which can permeate all the material forms of the third dimension. Our accumulator or battery has the form of a block '*in quarto*', composed of five or six hundred thin sheets of crystal. You know that in the language of alchemists, crystal is the sky of Saturn. These sheets are cut according to a form which reminds us of catacoustic surfaces.

"'When it is necessary to charge the apparatus, one of our Sannyasins begins to train himself in order to obtain a certain nervous tension. He then shuts himself in a room to repeat a particular mantra over the block of crystal, about a hundred thousand times on the average. This is required for the harmonious vibration of the crystal blades, in the crypt situated about sixty feet deep, to be heard, in the laboratories, which are built on the surface of the earth. Such in essence is the motor of our telemobile.

"'But this machine needs a housing, a protection against the changes of temperature, of electric storms, of attacks from unexpected visitors, and all the accidents possible in the course of interplanetary travel, any of the smallest of these accidents being deadly for the operator of the apparatus.

"'Let us remember, thinking along Western lines, about the theory of *pangeometry*. Whether one accepts the system of Euclid, or that of Bolyai, spherical geometry remains the same, whereas, in hyperbolic geometry the circumference, if its radius grows, tends not to be a straight line, but a curve, different from the straight line, but always remaining tangent to it. It is the *horicycle*. This fantastic curve, being parallel to the straight line, creates surfaces and volumes which develop themselves naturally INSIDE the Euclidian space and volume. That is what we have achieved inside of a material physical body.

"'Matter in such a form, invulnerable to all mechanical factors and all known physical reactions, is a precious metal, which we transmute by means of special prolonged hammering and tempering. In the state of gold, this metal condenses the luminous ether, the Taijas, whereas this cube-shaped chest is filled with Surya-Akasa, if we can but use such an expression, when speaking about that imponderable substance.

"'Don't touch it!' the Brahman warned me as I went closer to the resplendent chest. 'You might be in great trouble if you come in contact with it. One needs to submit oneself to a special training to make one's organism able to stand enormous electrical tensions, if one wants to use this apparatus without any danger. For this there is a particular kind of Yoga. At the moment, we have no one prepared in our temple. Otherwise, in this season, the fluidic state of this country is unfavourable. But, if you will remain here for some time, you might see the actual experiment.'

"Such was the first lesson given to me by my guide," said

Andréas after a short pause. "The following recollections are ones which I gathered and retained in my memory to a certain degree.

"The whole problem actually consisted of finding an accumulator able to absorb the force of sounds, that is, acoustic fluid, if you like this expression, as well as the nervous fluid, with which a human being perceives sensations and conceives ideas. The raw materials for such an apparatus was a metal, extracted with infinite care from certain alumina. The transparent chest, or case, about which I have spoken, had in its centre a small device, which was similar to a book of crystal. In order to charge it, seven priests first submitted themselves to a severe training for forty days. They had only one meal daily, consisting of oats, the brains of certain animals and very 'electric' fish. They lived in a cell, the walls of which were painted a mauve colour and decorated with diagrams of the force to be captured. They had four hours of rest in every twenty-four, and the remaining twenty hours were divided into four periods of five hours each, so arranged that the middle of each period coincided with sunrise, midday, sunset and midnight. These priests had to become able to see, to touch, to hear, to taste and to feel that sonic force. It was done through the repetition of the mantrams of that force, and through mental concentration on its properties.

"This training was performed only in the periods indicated by the astrologers with the help of a minute study of the magnetotelluric variations. The very position of the cell was chosen from the map of these currents.

"The training occupied forty days, and finally three days of continuous sleep were imposed on the operators. Then, for seven days, six of these priests charged the machine through the imposition of their hands, without taking any rest, sleep or food. I was allowed into their presence on the evening of the seventh day.

"They looked fantastic. After having necessarily lived in darkness for seven weeks, because solar light contains some rays unsuitable for the project in which they were involved, the skin of these men had taken on the colour of old ivory; their deep-sunken eyes were brilliant with a concentrated light which shone from under their dark eyelids, and they were sparing in all of their movements so as to economize their forces. They had been put into the crypt in which the telemobile was located, about sixty feet under the earth's surface and ordered to sit at fixed points on the skins of lynxes.

"Imagine the absolute silence of that place, its strange

atmosphere, and ghostly manners of its occupants! I recall it all even now, dear Doctor, just as it was the first time I saw such a scene." And Andréas began to explain the whole thing in pantomime, walking forward and returning again, in order to show me the position of the actors.

"Then there was the seventh operator," said Andréas as he continued with his narration. "He entered into the transparent case, and its twelve edges were soldered with a special paste. He sat diagonally across the inside of the case, his legs folded and hands joined together, according to a certain asana. The accumulator was behind him and at the height of his eyes there was a disc of polished gold. Under his elbows were placed two handles of crystal connected to the accumulator by two silver rods. The operator sat on a hollow seat filled with powdered carbon made from a certain kind of laurel. For a while he remained immobilized, breath suspended, eyeballs already reversed as in Dhyana. All of this was performed in silence, by the light of a wick immersed in the oil of camellias. I observed all of this while squatting in a small recess and looking through a narrow pane of violet glass. This was because the powerful currents which were passing through the interior of the crypt made it dangerous for those who had not subjected themselves to the special training, to be in the cell.

"Finally, the operator pressed his elbows against the handles two or three times. A piercing whistle hit my ears followed by a tremendous noise as of raging seas. And suddenly the case disappeared from sight. I was so surprised, that at first I believed that I had been hypnotized. But nevertheless, all the time I saw the six immobilized helpers, I heard my guide speaking, and I had no fever. So, I had witnessed disintegration, and a most extraordinary one at that. My guide explained to me, that the apparatus was so strongly saturated with the sonic fluid, as also was the body of the operator inside it, that their astral counterparts remained in the cell, visible to a clairvoyant and expressed by a geometrical figure painted on the floor: just what Western occultists and magicians term a *pentacle*.

"A week later, Sankhyananda invited me to descend again into the crypt for further observation. The six operators were already there, like silent statues. I waited for about an hour. Then a fluorescence passed the penumbra and the operators extended their hands towards the pentacle.

"A steam-like cloud floated in the air. Then suddenly and silently, the transparent case with the operator inside was back, in the same position as at its departure. He was lifted from it, rigid as a mummy, and was quickly transported into the next room where a hot bath had been prepared for him, together with massage, friction and ointment, all administered to him with the greatest care. Later they carried him into the fresh air at ground level and fed him. He then began to give an account to the head of the community, walking very quietly around as if he was not the hero of an almost incredible Odyssey.

Chapter IX

A BRAHMANIC EVOCATION

"You see, dear Doctor," said Andréas to me, when I paid him a further visit. "We Europeans have not yet finished spelling the alphabet of Wisdom. Nor have the Easterners," he added with a smile. "Even so, they seem to know much more than we do, but that is only because they spell a different alphabet."

"A different alphabet you say?" I interrupted Andréas, being somewhat scandalized, because so far I had believed in the esoteric dogma which says that there is ONE science, ONE religion, ONE Power. "Then are there several kinds of Knowledge?"

"Certainly, Doctor! Take for example myself, who am not a great scholar at all, yet I know a dozen systems of chemistry, and still more of physics, as well as of psychology!" And Andréas continued to smile. At last, evidently trying to comfort me, he added: "Here you have another story.

"The Brahmans teach that cosmic forces are organized, each one forming a kingdom, analogous to the classes studied by natural history. They believe that magnetism is a world in itself, while electricity is another world, and so on. How can we verify this hypothesis? How to perceive, analyse, and use these unknown universes? Perhaps by inventing very sensitive apparatus, or educating our nervous system. Materialists would like to choose the first method, while mystics would prefer to use the second. My masters used both, because they always try to resolve the antinomies.

"Let us take one of the earthly magnetisms, which we may designate with the letter 'C'. The Brahmans have defined some of its properties, and then they have found that some cells of the human psychic forces represent the same characteristics. And, as they say, because everything has its corresponding elements, they presume that, by setting the first ones in motion, the others will automatically manifest themselves. It would seem that some variations of magnetism 'C' are related to certain solar spots, and in the human organism its point of emergence is, according to their words, the navel.

"You know that certain somnambulists pretend to see through the solar plexus or through the forehead. In the East they know the art of transporting the physical senses to any desired point of the body; that is Yoga. And so they have established a method of training, which allows them to feel and think through the solar plexus.

"Anyway, it is nothing more than to prepare a person to choose the hour and place where strong 'C' currents are passing. The experimenter, when carried into this fluidic wave, fully conscious, makes his observations and with the help of a fixed 'support' again returns to the physical plane in the foreseen moment of the ebb of the currents. That is what a diver would do if he were not limited by the necessity of taking a fresh breath.

"These are very brief summaries of the explanations which were given to me. I at once asked to be allowed to participate in such an experiment. But I received rather an evasive reply: 'You will have to wait as, so far, nothing has been decided. Moreover, the whole enterprise is of a very delicate nature: one risks one's health and mental balance.'

"I answered diplomatically, that my masters ought to be much better able to judge me than I myself and it then seemed that both parties forgot the project.

"Some weeks later Sankhyananda spoke about imminent earthquakes, 'C' currents and the difficulties attendant on their passage through the temple. I immediately understood the meaning and so renewed my request, with the result that I was accepted for participation along with the five other operators.

"Water flowing through a channel dug for the purpose of conducting it would be an exact description of the processes which had to be used. This 'C' magnetism always hurls itself down towards points of lesser tension: it seeks equilibrium. But, I thought, it undoubtedly does so with crashing and uproar, for it was also referred to there as the 'Storm of the Subterranean Regions'.

"There were weeks of severe training as concerns food, sleep, attitude, breathing and incantations, everything being done with a minuteness that was almost tyrannical.

"I do not know how much eternal value these works bring to a human being, but, for some time, they provide a man with a delightful feeling, both physical and mental. One again becomes young, with active senses, lucid thought, and an understanding as clear as a tranquil lake. The serenity of Nature penetrates you. You are then free of all apprehensions and cares and days pass in peaceful joy.

"Our experiment took place just before sunset. A circle of rocks in the neighbourhood had been selected, the earth inside them swept clear and on it figures and characters signifying the properties of the Subterranean Storm were traced with coloured powders. The position of articles, perfumes, clothes and their orientation were fixed according to recognized relationships between the power to be studied and different minerals, plants, odours, spaces, forms and sounds. Most certainly you know a good deal about the theory of signatures.

"I was ordered not to move from my appointed place under any circumstances, even if the earth were to open under my feet. Then when everything was ready and all were in the desired attitude, we were told to adopt a certain psycho-physical state of Dhyana, in which the consciousness remains vigilant. I saw my companions including their chief, who was standing naked before us murmuring his mantrams and holding perfumed sticks in his hand, while sea-weed burned along with nauseous gums.

"Suddenly, I had the sensation of descending into a very old palace, situated at the bottom of a large mine shaft. The architecture of this building and the beings which populated it formed marks on the landscape, just as in spiritist photographs phantoms are seen toning down the contours of material objects. Gradually, the air became drier and, in spite of that the insupportable smell of the asafoetida did not reach me any more because, in the peculiar state in which I was, respiration occurred only once every half hour. But even so, another odour filled my nostrils and throat. Heavy, fatty and bitter, with a sour taste, this terrible smell was accompanied by a sudden tremendous noise of thunder, in the very centre of which we were placed. My bones trembled under these deep vibrations and I suffered the nightmare of a seemingly endless fall. My muscles contracted against my will; my body was terrified and wanted to fly, but I knew that it would be death for me and my companions. One cannot expose oneself with impunity to the naked rays of the secret powers.

"Added to all of this was the anguish of not knowing what to do, a fear of not perceiving a possible sign from the master, and the anxiety of being able to hold on to the end. I had a very unpleasant time and it appeared to me to last for a long while.

"Then, in the midst of my efforts at control, I suddenly saw, in the centre of our circle and a little above our heads, two eyes which looked down upon us with curiosity, cunning and power. Gradually a face traced itself framed by hair hanging in curls; then a body was formed standing on one leg, while the other was folded back. All of it was adorned with sumptuous fabrics and sparkling jewels. Several arms were attached to the shoulders, perhaps about twenty of them, all gesticulating. The hands with their agile fingers seemed to say things, just as those of the deaf and dumb do. Two of them, on the breast, incessantly performed a gesture which kindles the magic fires of hell. At intervals, lightning flashed everywhere.

"This fantastic form, gigantic, modelled in black against a black background, radiated terror. It gave the impression of being an enormous machine, living, intelligent, no doubt so far obedient; but like an antedeluvian monster, only partially domesticated.

"Intense cold seemed to annihilate us, while continuous and penetrating growling reached into our marrow. I blinked and saw that sweat was streaming from the body of our master. The leaves on which we were sitting became yellow and shrivelled. We knew that it was a sign that the Presence had finished speaking. Soon all the phantoms disappeared under the radiance of the moon, which already stood high in the sky.

"We raised ourselves painfully: we had been 'there' for six hours, exposed to the most terrible panic that the hostile, invisible forces can devise.

"I slept all the next day and the succeeding night, as our European nervous systems do not possess the flexibility of the Hindus. On awakening, at the usual time of my morning meditation, I became aware of having made a great step ahead. I understood that the powers unveil themselves progressively, to the measure of the eye that contemplates them. At first they appear to be blind and random, but later, one discovers a certain logic in them and then, as a consequence, one finds that they can be given names like—fluids, currents, vibrations and laws. Finally, you come to see that these forces are the work of those beings which polytheism calls the 'Immortals'.

"But always, always I started to doubt, that I did not know anything. If only I could one day feel the Life! Ah! I wanted that with all my soul. But I was completely ignorant at the time that, the most effective help for realization of that vow would be given to me by a woman."

And as he said these words, Andréas fixed on Stella a grave look, full of ineffable tenderness.

Chapter X

COMFORTS

ANDREAS was absent on one Sunday when I went to see him and I had to wait for several hours. So, in order to make me more patient, Stella showed me the whole of the inside and backyard of the shop. There were cartons filled with engravings, furniture with drawers full of knick-knacks and glass-cases packed with rare objects. She displayed her embroidered laces from France, Geneva and Honiton for me. Then she showed me turquoises which became green after being macerated with pieces of roots from ash-trees; rough opals in wooden bowls; tarnished pearls awaiting attention; the frame of an Irish crowth* drying in the sun, which was being restored according to old miniatures, and still thousands of other curiosities.

"You cannot imagine how patient, careful and even punctilious Andréas is," said Stella. "Here is a violin case. He cut it from a log, taken from an old pear-tree, which, for several months beforehand he had subjected to the action of the sun, using a system of lenses for that purpose. For varnish, he first prepared a special resin from the maritime pine tree, and, as far as I can remember, covered the case with at least twenty layers of it. Here is a cauldron, bought in a suburb: from it he will make a Tibetan vase. These pieces of ivory have been soaking in these bottles for months, so that they will get the right colour."

Besides the repair workshop, there were, in all that stock, the elements of a true museum: Flemish wainscots of the XVIth Century, old theorbos, calumets of the Redskins, locks with secrets, compote dishes from Persia made of delicate porcelain with Zoroastrian cypress design; a priceless Japanese tea-pot fashioned from greyish-yellow clay and encrusted with micá; porcelains from China, some of them belonging to the green variety with inscriptions of blessings in the Ta-Tchouang dialect; sonorous stones, chased gongs, rare coins, rings of iron styled à la Marat and Rocambole, some with a stone from the Bastille; official advertisements, engravings, portraits, rolled upholstery, Tibetan daggers for the expelling of spirits, masks of Siberian Tungouses, and many other things.

* Ancient Irish musical instrument.

"All of these things have their stories," said Stella. "I will tell you about some of them one day in the future. But look! Here he is!"

And in fact, Andréas had entered, looking kind and friendly as usual. He asked my permission to work during our chat and immediately started his task of finishing the repair of a pewter ewer.

I was only too eager to tell him about my misfortunes of the past week: fatigue, errors, rancour, impatience, loathing, laziness, and so on. "You will still have a lot of other similar things," Andréas told me as if giving me a kind of consolation.

Stella offered us tea made from bricks, which came direct from China. "In Tibet it is called 'Kiapa ka kig'," said Andréas. Anyway it was delicious. My host listened to my complaints, all the time filing away with good-humoured patience. And once again I found myself wondering about this person, so simple, so vital, so correct in his manners. He was affectionate, but without comradeship; patriarchal without posing, briefly—he was so human.

He was just like a very wise old man, who loved me along with all his other children. But I also knew that if anybody approached him with an open heart, he too would feel the same certainty of being a Benjamin of Andréas's heart. Does it exist, an unknown state of love? I wondered. For my impressions at that moment surpassed in freshness, pure enjoyment and vividness the purest sentiments I had ever before felt. I could feel myself calm, certain, resting in the shadow of a serene and stable affection.

Then Andréas started to address me as 'thou' instead of the usual and more formal 'you'. But I was not at all astonished, for beside him that day everything seemed to me to be natural and clear.

"Resume your self-possession again, get your breath, find your peace once more. He, whom you love, that Ideal Being, although still outside you, nevertheless becomes your host at times, He is the hero of eternity. It is true that enemies encircle Him and fog hides Him from you, but His victory is sure and His influence on you will remain wholesome. Do you believe that He did not foresee the quagmires on the path when He invited you to follow Him? Nothing comes to a man except by his own will. If there is something you can do, it would be useless and harmful if some other man were to undertake it instead of you.

"Take a bad pupil: he did not learn his lesson of yesterday. He then offers marbles to his more studious neighbour. And when he has copied the lesson will he really know it? He has only lost his time and lied, but during the examinations at the end of the year his ignorance and laziness will be exposed. Therefore, do not avoid the toil which you encounter, do not imitate a dunce: otherwise you will retreat instead of advance. This haste, besides alternating with some discouragement, reflects in you the trouble of our own epoch. Life boils, desires irritate and forces themselves shrink and then decay. If you could but see the spirits of contemporary people, you would find perhaps not five, not even two men in a thousand who are seeking the True Light with pure motives.

"You know that the treatises of magic promise power over the invisible and over men. This promise is of itself understood in the lessons of magnetizers. Can't we find in the midst of our positivistic and utilitarian civilization, societies which propagate these absurd doctrines concerning the influence of will-power over all the 'important' things of life: riches, success and other nonsense? You may well feel that such 'apostles' are either silly dupes or cynical foxes. But even so, they have certain success.

"These savants proclaim that the material universe is perfectly organized, that everything happens according to justice because, as they say, everything is submitted to the laws of causality and the preservation of energy. Well! We agree! But the same persons would like to have the universe of morals drowned in anarchy, and the invisible universe in chaos. What inconsistency is this?

"They cannot deny that justice acts on all planes, so why do they incite men to revolt against their destiny, instead of teaching them to make use of that destiny? Why do they consider that the spiritual debtor should not pay his debts? Why do they teach attack and robbery in the darkness?

"Take, for example, a naive man whom these people try to persuade that, by performing certain training, he may be in a position to hypnotize an enemy, charm a buyer, or tempt an indifferent person. What right have they to teach this double crime: to injure by dark means and to compel the forces, created for spiritual purposes, to serve materialistic egos? How is it that those people do not see that they only foment envy, discord and hatred? Moreover, they create hellish fire in human hearts and in the world, and they act through the inspiration of the Invisible forces, which have been captured illegally. Are they not the blind leading the blind into the abyss?

"Almost always, in the same way, the earth corrupts the clarity which it receives. I remember that in Russia, under Czar Alexander I, a friend was sent into a certain district and there established the basis of a small association called the Children of Heaven. Some of the peasants started to work and soon they created brotherhood among themselves. But it wasn't long before persecution started and a good man tried to defend them before the government. Only after innumerable applications was he able to arrange for those poor people to live in peace, without being bothered by the administration. His name was Lopuchin. But what the Czarist state could not do, the Spirit of darkness did.

For the children of those spiritual workers began to listen to the false 'sages'. And as a result, the Doukhobors—for it is they of whom I am speaking—were perverted through the books of a writer of wide-spread reputation, finished up in revolt, mental alienation, hatred of work, and in the worst kind of madness.

"Similarly, when man, generally speaking, is able to realize that he bears in himself the germs of occult powers, he tries as quickly as possible to develop these powers by any means, perverting them into hypnotism, suggestion, volition and magic.

"But for those who have realized God's teachings, let them voluntarily accept poverty, of body, spirit and even of mind. And I can assure you dear Doctor, curiosities which you will now sacrifice will some day be repaid a hundredfold."

So said Andréas. And this serious teaching revived my courage. I saw the horizons very clearly and a power was awakened in me. Through it I became conscious of the vanity of my titles and diplomas, and the uncertainty of my knowledge.

I felt deep gratitude towards this elderly man, who was so hospitable and towards the woman, who was so good.

After all, why should I investigate whether or not they were friends of Desiderius in my younger years?

Would it not be much wiser to accept and to use what they offered to me so graciously?

Chapter XI

THE SPIRITUALIST

Just as I was about to communicate a part of my reflections to my companion, who was putting his workshop in order, Stella announced that dinner was ready. During the meal I heard quite a number of people come into the shop. When Andréas and I joined them, I was quite surprised to recognize among the fifteen or so visitors, some faces already familiar to me from the schools and societies of neo-spiritualists. And so I found myself greeting an old doctor, a magnetizer; another, a younger man an astrologer and homoeopath; a cabinet-maker of Picpus, famous in his suburb for the healing of fractures and sprains; a typographer, a liberal and mystic; a craftsman saddler, a disciple of Boehme; a captain in retirement, who was a president of a group of spiritists; an electrician, a follower of Kardec; a bookseller; agnostic bishop; a pharmacist who was a Hermetist; a pastor still a young man with blond hair and a clean look, and an old republican, a Fourierist of 1848. In the eyes of all of them I could see sincerity, ardour and conviction.

I always had great sympathy for the idealistic innovators, for they perpetuate the beautiful tradition of the Celtic race. Those men of the people, who had raised themselves beyond their proper class through the power of their work, who had remedied the gaps in their education through their own intelligence, often original, rich in noble elation, candid in spite of disillusionment, joyous in spite of shocks, disentangling themselves from among the thick brushwood of old utopias; all of them showed to me with great vividness the best aspects of the French soul.

Nothing could stop them from the attainment of their aims. whether the hardships were large or small for they simply accepted such things. I knew some of them who, on leaving their workshops or offices about seven-thirty in the evening; ate a small piece of bread in a dark street, in order to be present at eight o'clock for the opening of a conference; and then about eleven they walked back to their suburbs to save the cost of a bus ticket, so as to put it towards the purchase of an important book. Such simple sacrifices, without any glory, yet how moving they are! What ardour were they unable to offer us in their work, or what confidence in the future of our race? Its noble old blood still does not seem to be exhausted, and the light of its Spirit is not yet completely extinguished!

Later I began to see that the people invited by Andréas did not know him properly. Some of them believed him to be a healer; others considered him to be a survivor from the early groups of Kardecists; or an extraordinary doctor. Two or three of them presumed that he was an initiate of some Eastern sects. All of these people smoked and drank, except for a member of the Blue Star. The main theme of the conversation concerned the forthcoming Metaphysical Congress announced for the Spring.

Andréas did not take much part in the talk. He answered his questioners rather evasively saying that he 'did not know', he 'was not qualified enough to give advice', he 'wanted to remain quiet', that 'there are enough savants to scrutinize things abstract', and so on. I could see that all of these brave men seemed to be a little disappointed. Then, as I knew many of them, I thought it might be good to intervene. So, on my own responsibility, I said that they should not ask Andréas to take any part in the Congress, and that they should not even mention his name there, but, if he had some advice to give, they should try to follow it.

Andréas seemed to accept this. Then the programme was explained to him, the names of the organizers given, as well as those of the speakers, and the aims put before him. He was silent for a long while and finally, he turned to me: " Don't you think Doctor, that, unless its members are almost saints, such a congress will remain sterile? Especially if its participants merely hope to shine before the audience, to boast of their work, to blacken others, to collect press-cuttings, and so on. And his words starting with irony, ended with a benign smile.

" That is why," interrupted the typographer, a dark, thin man with a passionate face, " the Egyptians held their congresses secretly and only among initiates! "

" Yes! " answered Andréas, " and they were not the only ones to do so. But today, it is useful to have everything open: so it is written in Heaven; must it be otherwise written in the Gospels? "

" Yes! " said the pastor, and he immediately quoted the book, chapter and verse.

" On the other hand," continued Andréas, " perfection does not belong to this world; one cannot expect that all those seekers will remain anonymous. How should we act? Seek a label, a flag, a title, which could unite all of you; range yourselves under a rule of tolerance, so that no person or school intrudes on it; let every group have its secretary, but no president, and let all the participants be equal. Individual action would bend itself better to the influence of the Spirit. But, alas! You want a congress, so have your congress; at least do not found it on a money-making basis, or on a single man, but bolster it up with an ideal."

"We can arrange it quite well," said the cabinet-maker with his strong, coarse voice. "We are all brothers aren't we? We have different opinions, but there is nothing wrong in that. Let us discuss in order to explain. You know that myself I do not like to read since it puts me to sleep, but to listen to talks, yes, I understand that."

"Quite so!" agreed Andréas. "Let us learn to listen to others and let nobody try to put himself before the rest."

"Did you see the programme," asked a young probationer. They intend to study magnetism from its physical and therapeutic aspects, which means fluids, od, etheric double, spiritist phenomena and transcendental photography : for you know, they have photographed the phantom of a living man. They are seeking how to get experimental proofs and confirmation in support of esoterism."

"Well, my dear master," answered Andréas, "have you a suitable person?"

"No," said the lawyer, "but I am working on sociology."

"So! Who has a good medium, a healthy, strong and courageous woman?"

"I do!" said a magnetizer from the country, a jovial, kindly giant of a man.

"Then give me your hand, so there! We will ask Heaven to deign that we will see another side of magnetism, beyond the three well-known poles. Do all of you want that?"

"Yes! Yes!" We answered together.

"Put your attention on the fact that I am making no suggestion," said Andréas; "I am not using any will-power; I am only asking. Well! What do you feel now?"

"My forefinger is pulled away, but it is painful, you know!"

"It doesn't matter, let us continue!"

"Now it is the middle finger; its flesh is becoming taught and frozen. Here is the third finger, which feels hot as if I had it close to a candle; the little finger is trembling, as if it is being electrified; the same with the thumb and in the bones, where I feel a fresh current. I do not feel anything else."

"Will you remember those five effects? Here is what really happened. The spirits of your fingers have, for a moment, been set free from all ties with the general magnetism of your body. And every time that you ask for this, but, having your hands clean you understand, this freedom will be rendered to one or another of your fingers for a minute space of time. And then you will be able to use them for the sick. The forefinger for ailments of the liver, the middle one for bones; the third for the heart; the little one for the nervous system and the thumb for psychic diseases. But your hands must be clean. I mean that your conscience must be pure. Has this never been mentioned before?"

"No, Sir!" some of them answered.

"Mind you, I cannot magnetize myself," said Andréas.

"It should be possible to take photographs of those invisible effluvia, and even try to obtain coloured prints of them."

"Would you permit me to investigate the matter?" asked the pharmacist, who was also a spagyrist.

"Certainly," said Andréas, "who am I to allow or forbid anything? What I am showing to you is nothing new. I spoke some time ago about similar things to the Baron du Potet, but I don't think he made any use of them."

"How is it that you know du Potet?" someone cried; but at that same moment the officer, who was a spiritist asked:

"And what about the dead, Sir?"

Andréas seemed to hear only the second question.

"Well, as regards the dead, it would be best if you left them alone," he answered softly. "However, I know very well that you will not take my advice. But at least, pray before your sessions, and seek the means to avoid overburdening your mediums."

"Yes, but if we extinguish the lights, sceptically minded people will certainly accuse us of fraud."

"Why don't you try to use lamps fitted with mauve or violet glasses, and use oil scented with cinnamon or cloves in them."

"And what about the use of animals or blood with perfumes?" suggested a disciple of Eliphas Lévi.

"No, for an animal would suffer too much, and after all you do not know what a scent actually is. Better to try the following: take a solid, square-shaped table. On the opposite corners, under the top, attach two small pieces of copper and zinc sheets, and connect them with a wire, thereby creating a kind of solenoid. Let your medium sit on a chair on the same woollen carpet as that under the table, and you close the current over him. It is possible that, under such conditions, you may obtain the movement of objects without touching them, and that with a minimum of fatigue. Keep the assistants in equal numbers and the leader of the session must be a cold-blooded person, especially when you may take the fancy of putting an electric current in the wires."

An old disciple of Hoené-Wronski, who sat hidden in a dark corner retorted: "All of that is good and interesting; but the phenomenon itself doesn't convince, unless one already possesses the Eleutherian conviction within oneself. A doctrine, a synthesis would be necessary."

"A doctrine? But you have it, my dear Professor," replied Andréas. "The tables of Messianism are as true as it is possible to get. Moreover, there are so many theories and so many systems!" Here Andréas directed his words to a medical officer. "And you, Doctor, you are a well-known person, you should form a foundation where the mediums could be accepted, their health cared for, their minds readjusted a little, and where they would be set free from any material anxiety during two or three months each year. For a start, it would be sufficient to find, with an independent person, a house with two or three rooms, set in the midst of a forest. In this way you will obtain far more interesting phenomena and less fraud. Many famous investigators have been duped; but the poor mediums have a lot of justification, since they are engaged then dismissed, annoyed, unsettled and poorly paid."

"But," shyly asked a tall, pale young man, an amateur, contemplative catholic, "isn't it all rediscovery, rejuvenation?"

"Well, yes!" Andréas told him with a smile. "All of these things are new yet old. For some time from now you will see something new, but beware, for the fruit will be poisonous. Even so, for a few years now our atmosphere has been receiving some new forces, but at the present time, I can think of only two or three human beings who could operate them."

Many of the visitors wanted further information, but Andréas anticipated them by saying: "No! No! I don't wish to add anything more, for such people prefer to remain unknown. However, you are free to seek them. What they have discovered is already within the reach of all of you."

"How can that be? What should we do?" asked several voices.

Andréas started to laugh mischievously. "But you know very well and from a long time ago, what we should do in order that Heaven will surrender a secret to us. Don't you remember? And you, it is already over twenty years since your mother was so sick? And you, in the year of your big strike, when I encountered you one night on the bridge of Tolbiac? And you, Doctor, when you were assisting in Nice? You were still an intern and you allowed yourself to mistake a tube!

"Yes! But since that time I put all my attention on what I am doing you know," replied the doctor in a very low voice.

"Well now, returning to what was said by our friend 'Alexander the Great' (Andréas often called the saddler that because the latter usually held his head leaning to the left), it would be good if someone in your congress rendered homage in public as a recognition of your predecessors. Let them be remembered and let the names, which were suppressed because of human intolerance, be mentioned. They had to endure misery and sarcasm all their lives. They were the ones who opened the way for you, so do not forget it! Theirs are the tears which watered the field from which you start to reap the harvest."

Then the old gentleman from 1848 said: "Gentlemen! May I be allowed to say how imprudent I find all of you, since you ignore the discipline of secrecy, which the old initiatory brotherhoods and their inheritor—Freemasonry, so strongly did and still do recommend. And what? You already teach the crowds how to put people asleep, to act from a distance, to catch fluids, to hypnotize? What more have I to say? And not one of you is able to foresee that such instructions can be read by criminals, or simply by utilitarians. Don't you believe that Mesmer is responsible and suffers for all those low abuses allowed by hypnotism? Don't you believe that your reports about exteriorizations make you guilty of a certain numbers of invultuations? Otherwise, are all your theories of reincarnation and your preaching about Karma only empty phrases, mere lip service?"

At this point the old enthusiast looked at us with indignation.

"He is right," said Andréas. "But he speaks as if in a desert. All of you are courageous men, very nice ones. But you are only too pleased to see your prose published and your names adorned with eulogistic adjectives. Nevertheless, think about the measures to be taken during your congress, against any possible misuse of your discoveries.

"But it is late now; you all live a good way off from here, and you must rise early tomorrow morning. Depart quickly, and when you come back again to see the old tell-tale, he will have other things to say to you."

CHAPTER XII

THE MAGNETIZER

Some days later, when I went back to see Andréas, I found him talking to a magnetizer, who had come from the country. His cures did not please the group of doctors in his town and he had even been called before the police-court. This pleasant man was very angry and did not cease to hold forth against those ignorant in methods of treatment, who take so much from poor, sick people and who heal so little. He insisted on quoting stories to support this and to show their keenness for profit, their lack of devotion, intolerance, and so on.

Andréas tried to calm him and said: " At this moment you are acting just like those speakers in the Masonic Lodges, who, because some priests don't appear to be too worthy, include the whole body of clergymen in their condemnation. I am not a church-goer and I don't have unlimited confidence in official science; but I do know that there are good people everywhere. I know some priests who are worthy of admiration, as well as some doctors. Similarly, every organization, speaking generally, has a fair number of misers, egoists and ambitious people. You say that doctors make people pay them too much. But that isn't correct in relation to doctors in the country or in quarters : their six or seven years of study have cost them dearly; they have had to pay for their diplomas. They also have to pay licences, maintain a certain standard, as well as support wives and children. What right have you to demand a kind of self-denial from them, which even one man in a thousand doesn't possess? "

" But why do they try to prevent me from curing? Perhaps because I can do it better than they themselves? "

" Well! But you are a competitor, so they fight. Such is life! I agree, that it is far from being idealistic, but find me one who has realized the ideal? The fines which they will make you pay will substitute for the licence which you escaped paying."

" Well, I suppose," conceded the magnetizer, " that it really is pretty much just as you have said. I wasn't thinking about such things. It is true that they have to pay for the right to practise."

" At the same time you cure by a natural process, without having studied, or, at least, after very summary studies by comparison with those of the medical faculty. And also, we can be frank with each other, isn't that so? You can cure, that is agreed, but the patients still pay you, although much less than to a high-ranking doctor. And finally, are you sure to cure in every case?"

"It is true," said the magnetizer, "that I have also had a few failures, but very seldom."

"Yes, I know! But that is not what I would like to talk to you about. I am thinking of the sick who leave your quarters looking as if they are cured. Are you absolutely certain that they are?"

"Certainly! I am convinced of it," answered the magnetizer. "But what are you trying to say?"

"Simply this: often you only apparently cure and then for only a certain time. Later the disease returns in a different form. Or perhaps, you make your patients immortal?"

"Of course not!"

"Therefore you only partially cure them. I like to talk in paradoxes, but bear with me for a while. You are a believer in the theory of fluids, and as sickness is a bad fluid, you expel it and replace it by a good one. Very well! A colleague of yours would prescribe herbs, another would act through his will-power, while yet a third may use spirits, and finally all would arrive at almost the same end. But where do those bad fluids that you expel go? When you have cockroaches in your kitchen you close all the holes and the insects go to your neighbour. Did you ever ask yourself where the morbid forces go, which your curative power causes to withdraw? They go in another direction, seeking another organism, which is ready to accept them."

"But then, Sir," said the man in embarrassment, "I should not magnetize any more? What do you want me to do?"

"Oh yes! Continue, you do good! You have a duty to help through the means which Nature has given to you, and you act very well. I only wanted to make you realize that you are not all powerful, and that you are only a little stronger than doctors, only a little, and it so happens because you believe in Life."

"I can see that you are destroying the confidence I had in myself. So please put something else in its place: tell me something!"

"Well, I am not going to tell you that if someone falls ill it has happened because he deserved it, and that he should be left to suffer in order to atone for it.

"Oh, no!" interrupted the magnetizer. "If you told me such a thing I wouldn't listen to you any more. I see little in such theories of the savants, I am from the people and am as I am. My father was not in a position to give me any wider education, I know only one thing : when someone suffers and I am able to remove his sickness, I would be a bad person if I didn't help."

"I know," said Andréas, "you have a brave heart. You never spare yourself and you are right. On the contrary, I advise you to continue your magnetism. But how to prevent the bad fluids from going further afield and causing harm? Through magic? Certainly, it is possible to conjure and attach the evil to any place ; but later, a terrible storm will burst over your head. Through your own means? But you can't see those fluids. By helping yourself through the use of a somnambulist? Yes, if your medium is perfectly lucid and if you are able to protect him, for in sleep a person is much more vulnerable than when awake. Then, there is not such a medium who can see everything, just as there is no savant who knows everything. Therefore, the only resort that remains for us is to turn to a Master of Life and Death."

"To say the Lord's prayer?" asked the magnetizer with a pout. "But what about those 'good women', who spend their lives in churches. Can they ever cure? On the contrary, they are mostly scandal-mongers of the worst type."

"Leave the devotees alone. God merely ordered us to be charitable. When you were a little boy, and you brought home good reports from your school on Saturday evening, your father used to give you a few pennies on Sunday. Continue to be like that. Help the poor a little more than you do now, never become angry, and when you find yourself facing a sick person address yourself to God saying : ' I don't know how to manage this : help me ! I am going to pass on to this sick person the vital force Thou hast given to me. Cure him with it and deign to arrange things afterwards.' Then you may operate as usual."

"In that way the good Lord would have a lot to do, if . . ."

"Don't worry about it," interrupted Andréas. "You know that in a castle the steward is more of a bully than the master himself. Ah well ! With the good Lord, the more one is simple, the better He will listen to you. And never forget that the sick are cured only because He wants it so. Even so He cannot wish that someone will suffer. Just the opposite, He would like everyone to be happy. That is why we always get a little less suffering then we should according to strict justice."

"But why is it necessary for people to suffer? God could well let us avoid it."

"Yes! If we didn't have stubborn heads. We are obstinate about not doing what He has told us to do. When we sit for too long in a hotel we have a headache the next day. It is not God Who sends us the migraine ; it is Nature which is reacting. Diseases have no other causes. When a man behaves himself badly, this fact naturally embarrasses other beings, visible as well as invisible. There is no reason why they should let themselves be trampled on, so they protest. And then, this creates diseases, disaster or ill luck. That is why we should say to God: 'Cure this ailment if such be Thy will.' This is because it may be that, while the person in question is enduring the disease, he may not endure the grief of a monetary loss so well, if it replaces the malady which you, as a healer, want to remove from him."

"Well, I understand that. So to resume, I must do the best I can, but not be obstinate even in healing."

"That's right! You see, there may be twenty different ways of breaking a leg, but they all mean a broken leg. Similarly, there may be twenty ways in which to cure: therefore the man who heals may not necessarily be a good one. Even a tough and avaricious doctor will cure providing he is learned. In the same way, certain invisible beings can send a healing force to someone because, in that way, they obtain a hold over the sick person."

"But then, all of it is quite a dangerous business," cried the magnetizer.

"Oh, yes! It is dangerous! But you have nothing to be frightened of from that side, provided that you are well aware of being only an instrument in God's hands. For God never allows those who have confidence in Him to be led astray."

Chapter XIII

THE UNITY OF THE SPIRITUALISTS

When I returned to Andréas, there was a young tradesman, a saddler, enquiring after the proper means to use so as to achieve unity among the different spiritualist schools, during the famous Congress, about which we spoke previously. Andréas tried to inject some reality into the noble utopias of the enthusiastic mystic.

"Firstly," he said, "modern spiritualism is still in a sketchy state: even its vocabulary has not yet been established. In every school a technical term can take on a different meaning. The same idea has been given various names, and so earnest prior study is necessary in order to know where one is."

"Perhaps a dictionary could be published?"

"Yes, if you could find a spiritualist with sufficient authority for everyone to accept his definitions. Otherwise, your dictionary will represent only one school."

"But what if a doctrine could first be fixed?"

"Go from your room and visit some of the groups of spiritists, magnetizers, astrologers, occultists and theosophists, and bring me back the elements of the body of your doctrine! Nevertheless, all of them claim that they are tolerant. But in every one of those schools, their 'tolerance' consists in showing that all the others do not possess more than a part of the truth, while the school in question alone embraces the whole. Even so, this multiplicity of theories is only natural, necessary and useful. Truth has innumerable faces, and one has to know all of them. Further, unity in Nature can flash forth only from multiplicity. Finally, a conflict of ideas and feelings alone can create true tolerance."

"Then, my project is not a viable one?" asked the young man.

"That may be so, but in your place I would still launch it. You will see a general skirmish among the great priests and that is an instructive sight. Then later, when making your intervention at a suitable moment, you may be able to deduce important knowledge from the battle, and to understand that the only possible point of unity is the one, which, in all systems, does not belong to intelligence, but to the heart; not to knowledge, but to power; not to theory, but to practice. It is morality."

"Yes!" objected the craftsman, "But if spiritualists agree on nothing more than morality, then it would not be worth unifying them, because the highest spiritualistic morality is equal to the highest materialistic one. To do good for the sake of good, not because of fear of the visible, or invisible police and not because of the hope of reward: Epictetus and the great Catholic saints also teach the same."

"You are right; but still try to unite those people. You see, one has to dream, for dreams are useful, but one should not get drunk on dreams. Where are we? All on the earth. Where do we want to go? All together to the Absolute. But the distance is enormous, so immense that only astronomical numbers could give us the right idea. And we cannot all take the same path, because we are not identical. Look at how travellers depart in different directions: they will see different landscapes, cities, people, monuments, museums, and so on. Thus it is with different religions and initiations. But all of those travellers accomplish identical actions: they walk, for example, otherwise they would not be travellers. Such is the role of morality. Without it—even though accumulating knowledge of mysteries, rites and sciences—one cannot advance. With it—even though lacking everything else—one advances faster since one does not stop because of curiosities along the path."

"In other words," concluded the young man, "spiritualists need common sense, so that they do not undertake work which will not lead to anything good."

"Exactly, my dear friend, do try to preserve a sense of reality. When the day comes when two spiritualists will be incapable of saying anything bad about one another, they will do more for the purpose of uniting different schools than if they make twenty congresses and sign twenty volumes of exhortations. What do you say, Doctor?" added Andréas turning to me.

"I agree with you completely," I answered. "I believe that all of us are guided without even knowing the fact. But our guides, good or evil, don't tell us about their plans just as a general doesn't entrust his to a private. Also, the chief of Darkness, being clever and shrewd, knows how to generate the fatal curiosity in simple human hearts, under praiseworthy pretexts. Therefore, let us be prudent."

"But God will not allow a sincere man to be misguided!" cried the follower of Boehme.

"However," replied Andréas, "it is still necessary for such a man to first recognize that he can err, and that he does not rely absolutely on his own knowledge and intelligence: he must have modesty."

"Yes!" observed the young man, "we have only to remain

sincere, to become humble and to give proof of courage. God will do the rest, because the cult of the Spirit is beyond all religions and all adepts. And it is only by uniting ourselves with the Father, through the Son, that we will be entitled to bear the name of spiritualists."

During these last remarks our friend the pastor came in familiarly and joined in the conversation. He exposed the attempts by some of his colleagues in viewing the reconciliation between catholicism and protestantism. For my part, I thought that this was a day of noble utopias.

"It seems to me," continued the minister, "that we, as supporters of free thought, represent the universal principle of individualism and emancipation; we are involved in religion somewhat like scouts. Whereas the Catholics, being conservatives, followers of tradition and things systematic, represent the past. To wish to fuse together both of these tendencies seems to be very risky. Priests and pastors, being the ministers of the same God and His solicitude, must know that the divine activity, which occupies itself with man is Providence. Through its care our highest aspirations find fulfilment and without compelling us, Providence offers us the means to get out from the quagmires in which we are swamped again and again by the fatidical burden of the past and the uncurbed emotional transports of the future."

"I see, Sir, among your co-religionists an indefinite division into sects. Also, a bond of rationalism, either in philosophical or historical studies, which leads to obliteration of the divine sense of the Gospels. Isn't it true that the most knowledgeable section of the clergy recognizes only a man in the Saviour, and only symbols, or scientific work in His miracles? Isn't it the very teaching of the anti-christian Eastern initiation?"

"No one deplores such a state of the mind more than myself, my dear Doctor," replied the minister. "That is just the error that catholicism doesn't commit. But you theologians—please pardon the liberty—hypnotize yourselves too much over the past, and exaggerate the value of ritual. The letter kills the spirit, and the government of your Church seems to be too political. Therefore, the only grounds for agreement would be, not the divinity of Christ—because, unfortunately, too many of my colleagues don't believe in it——, but just moral action, charity."

"Actually, controversies are quite useless, since the disputants are not realizers," said Andréas. "Find me one unique pastor and one priest who are saints. I mean men of common sense and strong will-power, who have realized the practical ideal of their religion. They will soon be reconciled to each other. Such men, whose whole existence is a continuous evocation of Providence, have the power to offer unity in all their efforts, physical as well as moral. The Oneness will descend into them, they will learn to incarnate it and become capable of building it into an organic body in the social collective."

" Ah, yes! " cried the young worker. " Such men could perhaps convince the Consistory and the Holy College, the politicians and the indifferent people! But I have read certain apologetic books, which want to experiment in the phenomena of mysticism and to catalogue millions of factors, which contribute to the organization of a collective religious, or political soul. And yet they cannot even arrive at listing the forces which produce a microbe! "

" Your example is a little too simple," remarked Andréas with a slight smile. " But taken briefly it is true. In order to conquer matter we have to study it with material means; but Spirit does not permit itself to be captured. It escapes when It likes. That is the eternal Spirit through which our own immortal spirit becomes perfect. Religion is the only one on the top : to juxtapose religious forms means to make a mosaic. What is necessary is for the faithful of different religions to raise themselves to God : there they will be one. The Eternal is the living God, and this must be experienced.

Wishing to get our host to unveil for us some obscure points on the history of mystical brotherhoods, I said : " These attempts at unification are not at all new." And I quoted names, mentioning the Rosicrucian order, the Philalèthes, the Inner Church of Eckartshausen, and so on. But Andréas cut off my manoeuvre by remarking that we could miss the last bus. Usually he detained me till well after midnight, but I realized that I would not be able to make him say anything further this evening, and so I left together with the Boehmist and the pastor.

Chapter XIV

UNCERTAINTY

CIRCUMSTANCES were such that I was able to return to Ménilmontant only after long weeks of delay. This interval was alive with difficulties: business, friendships, relatives, all become sources of disappointment for me. I accidentally heard some malevolent stories about Andréas, and some apparently respectable people complained about him. My doubts returned again. Because I never dared to ask him about Desiderius, my confidence in him was weakened, so much so, that I decided some day to go and take back my embroidery, in order to sever relations with him.

However, I did not judge Andréas, as some obscure premonition warned me not to do so. I knew how worldly handling can misinterpret everything, but still I wanted to erase any thought of him from my memory. The illogicality of these impulses threw me off balance: at that time I still had not had much experience about the purgatory of the human soul.

Yet, when I arrived there, the very sight of that small house was sufficient to restore serenity in me. Stella received me with her usual charming cheerfulness and showed me her work.

I had, she told me, to prepare some pasteboard from Chinese paper, which Andréas would cover with a non-transparent varnish of his own invention. Then I could cut out petals for the missing flowers, so that my new embroidery would be as translucent as the original one.

" Wouldn't buckram be sufficient? " I asked, astonished at so much work.

" No! It would be opaque. Anyway judge for yourself."

And really, the panel was in admirable order, it being impossible to distinguish the darning. I was delighted, and warmly thanked Stella. But, when I wanted to pay, she bluntly refused to accept anything telling me that her husband would scold her if she did.

In spite of that, I thought, some people had described both of them to me as being close and not too scrupulous.

Andréas, who, at that moment, had come in unexpectedly, approved of his wife's attitude. " Anyway," he said, as if compelling me to accept this present, " some day you will have ample opportunity to repay us for it."

We sat under the arbour and Stella let us taste some special liquors, which she had prepared herself from some old recipes. And so, helped by the desultory conversation, I was able to tell my host and hostess about my tergiversations and, by means of hints, something of the idle talk circulating about them. These confidences made no impression on them.

"Many other stories about me are also being related and I am delighted," said Andréas. "I much prefer to be attacked than to be incensed. As was said in the Bible, everything has its weight, number and measure. Isn't that so? There are quite a number of slanders circulating throughout the world, and I would rather they fell on me, who doesn't care about them, than on others who might be affected and harmed by them. It is Goodness which feeds Evil, for only Goodness possesses Life. It is much better to be the food for evil, than to nourish oneself by Goodness. Better to be attacked than to attack, provided, however, that one remains humble."

"You are answering the question that I already had on my lips," I said. "Nevertheless, I know an old naval doctor, whom you most certainly have heard of, who teaches that not defending oneself against slander or calumny is like suicide."

"I don't deny that slander can wound; but, if you repel it, it will go to a neighbour. Moreover, the sole fact that a thing is directed to you means that it was destined personally for you."

"Is that a doctrine of abandoning oneself to God's will?" I asked.

"Yes! But don't let us fall into quietism: we should undergo suffering and do it well."

"To reunite the passive with the active?"

"That is the thing! Examine the last period of your life. Don't you see from where your present doubts are coming?"

"No!" I had to confess. I was unable to rise from the effect to the cause. "Perhaps it is my occult studies and attempts at Yoga? Should we not, as St. Paul says, try first and judge afterwards?"

"Of course! But," added Andréas with a smile, "you are a European, always pressed to act. To act is an excellent thing; but first of all do deliberate for a few minutes and ask for Light. This is a precaution which never harms any work."

And, because I remained silent, he added again: "Look Doctor, you have done a little training, yes? Fixation of the gaze, formation of mental images, establishment of volition, development of will-power, a great operation according to the ritual of Eliphas Levi?"

As my smile admitted to all of this, Andréas continued: "It

can be seen from your face that you are overworked : the liver is not too good and also the lungs. Suppose that a genius did appear to you, but what more? Imagine that you have a power of, say, ten units, do you believe that you would be able to direct a force expressed in a thousand?"

"Yes, but a driver, with a single action, can start a locomotive!"

"No, these forces are not of the same order. A magician is acting, say, through his astral power upon beings of an equally astral nature. Likewise the driver knows certain laws which direct matter. Just when a magician is evoking those mysterious forces in order to know them, he makes the so-called 'petition of principle'."

"Of course you are right," I said.

"Your magic could only put you in contact with a being a little stronger than you are. Mind you, I am speaking only about the power, not about the Light. A chemist who discovers a new compound is taking a risk of poisoning or blowing up himself, together with his laboratory."

"I believe," I said, "that I will not make any more attempts at magic operations."

"In such a case," concluded Andréas, "straighten your shoulders! Assume your responsibilities! Consider only one aspect of your training and recapitulate it. Think of all the cells of your food, all the molecules of the tinctures, drugs, furniture, plants and animals which you used, all the fibres of your body which you set in movement for that purpose, all the invisible beings, which your will has enslaved. Now you must repair this disorder and ruin."

"That is only just," I said.

"So be in peace : Heaven will do something for you," finished Andréas with paternal stress.

And once again I departed with my serenity restored. In the mouth of this man, so simple as he was, the most abstract metaphysics became clear, common sense.

His straightforward look inoculated me with force; his smile dissipated my pessimism.

I left full of confidence, almost ashamed of my recent restlessness.

CHAPTER XV

A MENTAL VISION

On my next visit to Andréas I found him ready to leave. He invited me to accompany him, rather asking as if I would be useful to him. His courtesy, exquisite as it was in all its forms, seemed to flow spontaneously from him like a fresh spring. And a special charm appeared in his attention towards his guests.

St. Francis of Assisi must have had similarly attractive manners. Andréas really loved his visitors, and those of them, to whom he rendered the greatest services, observed with confusion that he behaved himself towards them as if it was he who was indebted to them. It was in this way that I recognized what is meant by a truly humble man.

" I am going to Plaisance to see a sick person," Andréas told me. " Aren't you afraid of this trip? "

" Oh, no! " I answered. " I like to walk; but wouldn't it be better, in order to save your time, to take a cab or use the circular railway? But he said that he would prefer to walk, in fact, through the years, I never saw him using any of the city's conveyances. Perhaps he imposed this fatigue on himself as a kind of penitence. And perhaps, thanks to his power of attention, he used those hours of walking for mental work. Anyway, I often noticed that he seldom chose the shortest route.

This was the first time that I went with him. Walking endlessly through the noisy streets I didn't even notice the length of the journey. Andréas had a quiet gait, like runners who are able to do fifteen leagues at the one time. He smoked a lot, but spoke little. And I must mention, that every time I went with him, I found myself in a very special nervous state.

The views along the route did not distract me from a certain inner tension, through which the subjects of our dialogues were elucidated almost before they were formed. It seemed to me as if I were on a platform from which I saw the inner side of things, in truth from their right aspect. I was no longer aware of my body and never felt any fatigue; on the way back there was a feeling of having learned a lot of things other than those which he talked to me about.

I used the opportunity to speak to Andréas about another of my studies, about my attempts to practise contemplation, and all my trials and efforts to reach a tangible result.

At that moment Andréas said to me : " And the most evident of your gains is now the beginning of consumption."

Then to my great surprise he enumerated to me, different pathological symptoms about which I never spoke to anyone. I did not dare to ask him how he could know these details. He continued to give me a long technical exposition of Yoga. As if frightened of being pedantic, he avoided the use of the Sanscrit terms, taking care to translate them in a very exact and ingenious way.

" In general," he concluded, " breathing exercises, if practised with moderation, are useful. But, if you add a voluntary tension, either magnetic or mental to them, you break the Law. The amount of oxygen, carbonic acid and quantity of food have all been fixed in advance for everyone. In going beyond these limitations, even with the apparently noble intention of intensive psychic practice, you will only provoke reaction. No matter how subtly we try to reason, we will never prove that we are doing good, when using a bad procedure ; it will be only an apparent good, of a temporary nature, which will quite soon bring evil."

I remained silent, seeking some objections, but being unable to find them. In the face of my silence, Andréas continued : " I will tell you what I saw during one night, when travelling to Tibet for the second time. During my sleep I was shown a battalion of soldiers working to establish trenches for access in order to attack a fortress, which I could not see. The estafettes arrived and set out again at the gallop. The moon lit up the whole scene ; then I realized that this dream was of an intellectual kind. It was a curious thing, that the soil, rocky and greyish, seemed to move like a throbbing heart. Suddenly there appeared a group of beings, whose enormous heads were out of all proportion and who immediately reminded me of those pictures of the Chinese sages, which you know well, Doctor. This phalanx directed itself to the General's tent. It was led by an extraordinary macrocephalus, whose body was quite transparent. He spoke to the General in hard tones, and little violet flashes flew from his mouth. Immediately the movements of the scouts and pioneers were changed. Many of them, clad in red, were expelled from the camp : I saw them running here and there, through the fields, then falling one after another on to the soil. Their comrades, who remained in the camp, gradually became similar to the beings with the large heads. The siege was abandoned and they directed their steps across the moving plateau to a fairy town, which I saw on the top of a mountain range. I knew that this enchanted picture was only a mirage. The ascent continued for many years. From time to time the climbers encountered the fantastic forms of antediluvian animals, monsters known only to clairvoyants. Suddenly the battalion was surrounded by the Reds, whom I believed to be dead. An officer with long hair was in command of them. They advanced quietly against the crystalline beings, which at the moment they were captured, fell on the earth as if reduced to ashes. The rocks took on the appearance of mould, and in a short while luxurious vegetation arose from them. Then all disappeared and I was awakened. Daylight was coming and I climbed the neighbouring knoll to enjoy the dawn, as was my usual habit."

"How beautiful it must have been," I said, forgetting the vision, "if one can judge from what I saw in the massive Belledonne!

"It is unimaginable. The lowest valleys are about 9,000 feet below. The clarity of the atmosphere, the purity of the air, the unspeakable silence, the moving drama of colours which unfolds on the horizon, before the sun suddenly arises, all these immensities enter your soul like waves, and renew it. So that morning, standing amid the icy breath of the eternal snows, murmuring the formulas of the Path, which I followed at that time, I realized the meaning of my vision. I was upset. I don't think you need the whole decor, which helped me to understand it."

"It seems to me," I answered, "that the arid soil, was the mental plane, which is not fertile in itself, and on which only illusions can be built. The red soldiers and scouts represent feelings, while the crystalline beings are what Boehme called "own will". That vision teaches us that a man has no right to cut the throat of any vital manifestations that Nature puts into him. To wish to rule the movements of the thinking principle would be a dangerous illusion for, in order to recognize which of our mental images have to be obliterated and which reinforced from the point of view of omniscience, one should first possess that omniscience."

"And, moreover, our unique instrument, the brain, is not capable of reflecting more than a very small corner of the university," added Andréas. After a short silence he continued with a sort of half smile.

"Well, my dear Doctor, you have caught one of the meanings of my vision very well, but I will spare you my conjectures. Solitary people are apt to be talkative when they find an obliging listener, especially when they are growing old."

Chapter XVI

IN PLAISANCE

I WAS prevented from answering Andréas, as we started to cross the boulevard of St. Michel; but on reaching the Luxembourg, I immediately renewed our conversation. "I realize everything you teach me," I said. "However, I cannot yet be convinced."

"You are right, Doctor," exclaimed Andréas, "we are being given a judgment, an analysis and we have to use it."

"Let me state precisely. Here is what I cannot explain to myself. Providence is just and good, isn't that so? Why therefore does it allow men to invent methods injurious to evolution?"

"Certainly, what you now put forward is a hard problem," answered my companion with a grave nod. "You should be decentralized mentally," he added after a moment of deliberation.

"I don't understand," I replied, "what is meant by to become decentralized."

"Yes! That is true! I have a bad habit of using absurd comparisons. You know, understanding works like an algebraic system, or an epure of descriptive geometry, but then there are also differential calculus and superspace."

"I continue not to understand," I confessed after reflecting for some time.

Andréas made a gesture expressing doubt and asked me: "If you come to understand, would you promise me, that you will continue to behave yourself, just as if you didn't know about it?"

I wanted to assure him in the affirmative, but, under the wise gaze of my questioner I felt the vainness of my answer, and I had to be content with saying, that I would do my best.

I remember, that at that time, we were in front of the beautiful park of Couesnon, which was later removed to make room for a tram-depot. Then as evening started to descend, Andréas stopped, raised his head, which he often held bent downwards, and looked into my eyes for a few seconds before saying: "Blessed are the poor in spirit! That is what can be read in the *Book of the Lamb*. Otherwise, man's spirit is known only to those who can live in the atmosphere of the Consoler. But we ourselves, we cannot breathe this rare atmosphere. Nevertheless, every test tones up our lungs and shows precisely the sketch in us—which everyone of us carries

—a statue of the Logos. But we could never animate that statue by our own forces. The Logos alone can infuse the Life, His Life into it. But many blinded men think that this statue is alive. They attach themselves to it; they make it their work; their thing, and so they aggrandize the Shadow, and believing that they are going to *Being*, they lead themselves astray to Nothingness.

But some have doubts in their erring, and it is they who are not completely overrun by pride. They can hear the warnings of the guardian-angel; they start to feel the inconsistencies of this world, and they learn to forget it. And for every step that they take to the centre of the world, Heaven approaches them with a hundred more. Everything you have read, everything you have heard of the exotic and mysterious, only repeat to you the axiom— 'every action creates reaction'. Your hand cannot raise itself to the firmament unless your arm and body press on the soil with an equal effort. You would call this the law of the binary, isn't that so? During the long years of your studies, the grey cells of your brain stored things away and the white cells became more refined. You discovered many unknown organisms and called them by Greek, Hebrew, Sanscrit, Egyptian or Chinese names, according to your momentary attitude. You took force from every place that you could; you made of yourself a kind of decorative and useless athlete, occasionally able to perform an extraordinary effort, but condemned for all of your remaining time to a punctilious regime. People admired you, and you became proud.

All bodies are born, grow, and then decay. Could invisible bodies escape this law? No! All these organs, all these premature powers have to be restored by you. And this will now lead you on to the descending path."

Andréas became silent. We had reached our destination and penetrated into the worker's town, full of single-storied houses of dirty bricks, with wells full of noisy brats. A fat, old woman recognized Andréas and invited us into a sad looking room where, from the middle of a reasonably clean bed, a man turned his anxious gaze on the visitors. He was one of those pariahs, which great cities create by the thousands, worn out since their childhood by working too early, and for whom alcohol alone gives the power to live, in spite of bad food, bad hygiene and carelessness.

Together with his wife, he poured out a string of lamentations.

Andréas, standing with his hat held in his hands, listened attentively, nodding his head with compassion and seeming to be merged in thought. Finally, the old man finished his complaints crying with all the voice that still remained for him to use : " In

any case, the good God is not a just one! And after all, those are only stories created by exploiters, there is no good God at all!"
"What! The good God is not just?" grumbled Andréas. "And you are a just one? Must I tell everything before the missis?" he added in a low voice, as the man's wife went out to fetch small glasses for liquor. Then, leaning towards the man, he whispered a few words into his ear.
"How do you know about that?" exclaimed the frightened man.
"Hold your tongue! Hold your tongue!" replied Andréas in a delighted mood, as it now came his turn to play with the old fellow. "Be generous, give and take! Don't complain any more, and I will not disclose anything. But," and he threatened him with his forefinger, "you must follow a right way!"
The woman came back. We touched glasses and drank, and then came her turn to complain. "Will he recover, my good, Sir?" she asked. "What will happen to me?"
"Ah!" answered Andréas. "I don't know, mother. Here is my friend, a doctor, who will tell you about it. It is a grave case, isn't it, Doctor?" I was already embarrassed enough by my patient. From the point of view of medical science the man was finished. But Andréas was there, so I decided to confess the truth.
"Yes! It is a very grave case and it will be a real miracle if he recovers."
"So, mother," asked Andréas, "you really desire to preserve this old rascal—your husband?"
Instead of replying the old woman started to weep.
But Andréas took her affectionately by an arm, clasping it in his own. "Be comforted, things will be arranged. But do not quarrel again, either of you; then there will be no more pain. And remember that there are people more unhappy than you are. Did you hear that, did you?" he asked the husband. "Then goodbye, see you later. Are you coming with me, Doctor?"
I was a little disappointed, for I had expected to see a miracle.
"Why didn't you cure him immediately?" I asked Andréas.
"Well! But firstly, it is not I who will cure him. And also, he does not need to be on his feet immediately, he still has some money and can wait for a week or so. Apropos, Doctor, what would you, an occultist, do in order to cure this man?"
"He is very sick," I replied, "and I will not say too much. Anyway, I could try to transplant the disease into a tree, or an animal."
"Well, and so direct it there where it has no right to go. Also, I would very much like to see your reaction if someone burdened

you with a disease belonging to the gods. Certainly you would groan a lot from such a blow."

" Of course you are right, and I never even dreamed about it. Well, what if I throw another spirit against the spirit of the disease? "

" If your spirit is weaker, your patient will deteriorate. There must be a simile in that matter in the Gospels. Now, if your spirit expels the sickness or even kills it, you will be responsible for everything which will arise as a result. What if the genius of consumption will seek his comrades in order to take revenge on you; what will you do then? And if, on becoming furious, these entities will start to attack innocent people? "

" Then I cannot see any solution whatever. Perhaps to limit oneself just to ordinary medicine? "

" Not at all, Doctor! Just when something impossible appears before us, it becomes interesting. We must be persistent. Or Heaven may remit the debt of the sick person, or may change the way of repayment."

" I would very much like to believe you, but I am not convinced," I retorted.

" I know! " replied Andréas with a smile. " Good-bye, Doctor, I wish you well. Come to visit me next week, perhaps on Wednesday, will you? "

" Yes, certainly! " I said, being a little distracted by my own thoughts. I had expected a nice, slow walk on the way back, filled with conversation, convenient rest and new things. For I had so many things to explain, so many projects to submit. But Andréas had already disappeared into the darkness of the approaching night, which was occasionally interrupted by the glow of far off street lamps. And so I returned to my home in a pretty melancholy mood.

Chapter XVII

A MAN ATTACHED TO THE EARTH

Two months earlier I had received an order for a large work dealing with a certain point of pathology from a society of scientific publishers, and I had sent off my manuscript some days ago. Now, on returning from a walk along the Rue du Château, I found in my mail a letter from the editor announcing the return of my manuscript under some unimportant pretext. This was the first disappointment. Fortunately, my days were too filled with work to allow me to be disturbed by the fact. Two weeks later, while passing the School of Medicine, I saw a new book, treating of the same subject as had my own. I turned over its leaves and found that it was a copy of my own work, except for some insignificant changes in it. My former disillusionment now became true and simple indignation.

I was due to lunch with Andréas that morning. I had then not decided whether to speak first to my publisher, or file a law suit. I caught a bus and arrived at the lake Saint-Fargeau rather late.

It was the beginning of July. Everything in the suburbs caught my attention and interest, renewing my sympathy for the people, and my admiration for all the inexhaustible and gushing force which they spend without counting. It was that little agitated world of midday, the drinkers on the terraces, the costermongers oppressed by the police, the glitter of gay clothes, the tents, the white walls, the varied shop-windows, the cries, the smells, the gestures, the funny as well as tragic words, and so on.

Hardly had I shaken hands with Andréas and Stella, than, being as I was preoccupied with my own affairs, I started to tell them about my disappointments. My host and hostess laughed and filled my plate, while Andréas said to me, as a kind of consolation: " Let us forget the whole thing. Your publisher certainly honoured you by not taking you for a naive person. Therefore he had to act with caution. Read your contract again; you have not yet gone through it, and I am sure you could not repeat its stipulations."

" It is true," I confessed. " I read it wrongly! "

" Well, Stella! Because he has confessed to his ingenuousness, give him and us a little Tokay."

And so my friends pampered me to the best of their ability, as if I were their son. I rebuked myself. Why was I being so stupid with my rancour, only augmenting still more, the damage which the deceit of a shrewd business man had been able to inflict on me? And I expelled all my feelings of grudge, being reluctant to notice anything apart from the charm of this hour. During our coffee we sat under the arbour. Suddenly the front-doorbell rang, and the servant introduced a man in his prime, who was seemingly a business man. But, in spite of the beautiful weather, he was wrapped in a top-coat, supported himself with two crutches, and walked with difficulty, his face contorted by suffering. Andréas asked him to take a seat and explain the aim of his visit.

About a month ago, without any visible cause, pain had overtaken him, violent, irreducible and often unbearable, which occurred principally in his back. The pains started in the morning and ceased at night, with relief from midday to two o'clock in the afternoon, and sometimes for short intervals. He had consulted all possible doctors and healers; he did not have any rheumatism, nor was he suffering from syphilis, arthritis, or nervous afflictions, and his parents were perfectly healthy. That was what the doctors had told him, adding that they could not understand anything about his sickness, and did not know how to help him.

And this man, whose face expressed a strong will, even stubbornness, confessed his despair and inability to endure such a torture any longer.

"My suffering is terrible," he told us. "It seems to me that while I am speaking to you, just now, it is as if someone was slashing at my back, tearing apart my muscles with iron combs. I am receiving violent shocks, stinging pains, and my vertebrae are being quartered.

Actually, the poor man could hardly articulate as he twisted on his chair, seeking to escape from his lancinating torture.

"If I only knew of an enemy, if I believed in things from the other side, I would imagine that I am being invultuated," he concluded. "Sir, if you cannot help then, I firmly believe that only a bullet will deliver me from this hell."

"One should never despair," said Andréas, "even if one is bound to the mouth of a loaded cannon. Yes!" he added, as he smoked. "Your case is a peculiar one. Are you free this afternoon?"

"Oh yes! I am free!" said the ailing man. "But do you believe I would be able to work with this torture that I have to endure?"

"Well, if you agree, we will make a trip into the country. This changes our ideas, doesn't it Doctor?" said Andréas, turning to me.

"Certainly," I answered, not understanding anything, but presuming that I would be a witness to something extraordinary.

"Go to the country!" said the sick man. "But why? I didn't think that you would like to mock me. Anyway, what does it matter after all."

"Yes!" replied Andréas, as if answering the thought of his questioner. "Perhaps we will find a certain herb."

We departed in a cab for the Vincennes Railway Station. There Andréas bought three return tickets to a small distant station, which we reached after an hour and a half of travelling. At the local inn, Andréas was soon able to hire an old victoria. The son of the innkeeper sat on the front seat, and Andréas gave him the name of a neighbouring farmer. Again we travelled a good league before we saw a beautiful farm with three buildings on it. Andréas and I went into the courtyard, but the sick man remained in the coach.

Andréas asked a servant if he could see the proprietor of the farm. While waiting, we strolled for a hundred feet or so among the poultry and pig-sheds, under the vigilant eyes of two hairy dogs. "Ah!" cried Andréas. "I thought as much!" And he pointed to a well, which workers were digging in a corner of the yard. He went to the well, took a handful of the soil and examined it, letting it drop through his fingers, weighing it and seeming to think about it.

In a few minutes the farmer appeared. "Ah, good day, Mister Martineau, you do not remember me," said Andréas, always eager to speak to everyone in his own language.

"I'm afraid not," answered the farmer. "But I am trying to remember. . . ."

"Well! Don't you recall when you were still a child, about ten years old; you were on holiday with your Uncle from Bagnolet, and you broke your leg in three places?"

"Yes!" cried the man. "Yes! It was you, the man who fixed it! You managed it very nicely too. Yes! Yes! It was you. I was very little at the time, but I still remember your eyes and your pipe."

"Well, yes! I am always the same," said Andréas smiling. "But this is not the same pipe."

"Good, I am so glad to see you again. Come in for refreshment, my wife will be here presently. She is filling the racks."

I followed both of them. We sat, drank and talked; but all the time I was thinking about the sick man, who shivered in the coach outside. Then Andréas said rapidly. "You are making a well, as I can see."

"Yes, the old one dried up. Also, I would like to explain something to you." And the farmer launched into long details about his plans for domestic administration.

"Well," said Andréas after having listened to the farmer, "I will speak frankly to you: it inconveniences me because you are digging this pit."

"How can it be that it causes you inconvenience?" cried the farmer. "Why? How? I know that I am in debt to you, but really, it is a very peculiar thing that you are telling me now."

"Yes, it troubles me, that the well is just where it is," insisted Andréas, looking directly into the good man's eyes. "I came here expressly to ask you to dig elsewhere."

"But," said the farmer, as if hit by a sudden stupor, how did you come here? How did you find my farm? It is quite a long time ago since my Uncle and Aunt died, and my parents are not from this place. And how did you know that I was making a well?"

"By taking a walk," said Andréas softly.

"Oh well! After all, I am heavily indebted to you, I recognize it, and it is your right when you don't wish to tell me about your affairs."

"Listen," said Andréas using the familiarity of 'thou' which did not astonish his interlocutor, "how much have you spent so far on this well? I will repay it to you and I will show you a free place, where the water is better. Here you are only on a side-stream, but I will put you on to the main body of water. And you know that such water is good for health."

"Ah, do you use the divining rod? I don't have any doubts about that," said the farmer.

"Except that I have no such rod. But let us proceed, for we still have to catch a train. Listen, I will pay your expenses immediately. You will stop the workers, making them dig in the spot where I shall direct you. And after tomorrow, if the sounding-line doesn't provide you with a stream of exquisite water, you hear, exquisite water, you can retain my money and continue your former pit."

"Good! That has been agreed," exclaimed the peasant. "We will put it down on paper, isn't that so?"

"Very well. But let us start the filling in of the pit immediately."

As we were returning to the farm-house, the sick man, whom I had forgotten called to us from the distance. "Tell me, have you still something to do that will take a long time? I am afraid of the coolness."

We went to pacify him and then suddenly, as the diggers threw their first spadeful of dirt into the hole, the face of the man changed. He became pale, and opened his mouth, but it all passed in about two seconds until with fear in his eyes he said: " My pains have disappeared."

" Just as I told you," replied Andréas, " the country is good."

The business was quickly concluded. Andréas paid about fifteen gold twenty franc pieces to the farmer, who was somewhat mistrustful, and gave him his address in order to get news about the water from the new well. Then we departed for the station at a fast trot. Our return was a little confused. I did not understand anything, neither did the patient himself. He repeated time and again : " I have no pain any more, I have no pain ! "

When we had to separate on the Place de Bastille, Andréas took him aside for a moment and I heard the man answering in an energetic tone : " I promise you, Sir, it shall be done ! "

When we were again alone, I ventured to question Andréas.

" What connection was there between those pains and the well? Was there any? "

" Most certainly, Doctor," Andréas answered with an indifferent expression. " The soil and the man's back are of the same family."

I realized that he did not want to say anything further.

" But how could you know about it? "

" While strolling ! "

" But how did you find that peasant and everything else? "

" Only by walking around, as I already told you."

Most definitely Andréas was not in the mood to teach me that evening. Anyway he excused himself before he left me, with his usual kind and gracious charm. He told me, that he had some complicated business occupying him at the moment, but I did not learn anything more.

He seemed to be very anxious to be alone.

CHAPTER XVIII

THE MUMMY

On a beautiful autumn morning, Andréas and I were walking along the admirable Voltaire's embankment, whose noble charm and good taste are only apt to be appreciated by fervent Parisians. At that season, old aspens along the bank cover it with their leaves, reddened by the first frosts; the long grey silhouette of the Louvre, the dome of the Institute, the lordly mansions, the outline of the Place Dauphine all located themselves gracefully in the perspective of the delicate light. And the sun, on the right, left in far off shadow the spire of Sainte-Chapelle and the towers of Notre-Dame Cathedral. A right intellectual landscape, beautiful with aristocratic elegance, and vibrating with everything that the ages and generations have impressed upon it by their ardours, sorrows and thoughts.

Andréas smoked in silence, his eyes fixed on the pavement. Then he suddenly turned around before the window of an antiquary, facing the old house of the gentleman-painter the Marquis Desboutins.

In the shop window of the dealer his attention was drawn to the reddish figure of a small Egyptian statuette of the god with the head of a sparrow-hawk. Worn, corroded, coated with verdigris and formless, the bronze did not appear to be anything remarkable.

"Look for a moment, Doctor," he told me. "Then I considered the object with a little more attention, and a feeling of uneasiness enveloped me without any reason for it. Andréas looked at me and added with a smile: "You see, better for us to take that bird; another person might be considerably harmed by it. Come, follow me!" And, calling the antiquary, he bought the statuette from him without even bargaining about it. At the same moment my cane caught in my legs and I would have fallen heavily if Andréas had not supported me. In the beginning, I did not see anything in it, apart from awkwardness, and not until later did I establish a relation between the incident and the bronze statue.

Andréas turned towards the Pont-Neuf and descended the steps placed at the feet of the monument to Henry IV. He did not enter the small garden, but passing behind some fishermen standing there, he stopped on the extreme end of the bank and, with his back to me, began to look silently on the statuette for well over five minutes. Being, by now, acquainted with his strange customs, I stood behind him saying nothing.

It seemed to me that a bluish flame went out of his hands to disappear almost immediately into thin air. Andréas took a newspaper from his pocket, carefully wrapped it round the statuette, tied it up, and waited until a boat going up-stream passed him.

Then he threw the packet into the water as far from him as he could. On our way back we went up to the bridge.

"Well?" I said to him.

Andréas offered me some tobacco, and after smoking for a while said: "Do you recall the story of a mummy in the British Museum, which, for the last eight years, has caused so much annoyance to its visitors?"

"Yes," I answered, "all the newspapers have mentioned it, and I have been told that an English couple have established an enormous file about the whole affair."

He continued further: "When one dies, shouldn't the body be allowed to rot, so that its cells can rest? And isn't it so that, at that time, many spirits attend the man? If his body is prevented from rotting, a certain natural law is violated, cells are made to suffer, some beings are prevented from evolving, and one or more wheels of time are halted, yes?"

"Of course you are right, but I never even dreamt of this."

"When the Egyptian priests embalmed thousands and thousands of corpses, don't you think that they immobilized those wheels with an enormous force? That they chained souls to the native country of their bodies? That they collected a formidable battery of a special kind of electricity?"

"Yes," I said, "that seems to be so. But what was their aim?"

"That is their secret, and it is useless to unveil it. Think a little and you will quickly find out why. For, if in a closed circuit, contact is established with an outside body, would it not produce a short circuit?"

"Ah!" I cried. "The Egyptologists are doing just that, and their plunder must then naturally produce disorders in the midst of the unmanageable realm where it is exposed. Even so, it seems that the sarcophagus in question doesn't contain a mummy any more."

"What is the difference? You well know that, according to the rites, the figures, signs and colours decorating the casket, expressed the vital character of the departed one, and were bound to him by means of special spells. Anyway, they have been translated!"

"Yes, in effect I saw that in the annals of the Guimet Museum."

"Well, now do you understand?"

"Yes, I think so. But could nothing be done in order to attenuate the evil?"

"Oh, if you could find a man capable of seeing things which happened about four thousand years ago, and who would be able to speak to those Atlantean souls, to unravel the secret bonds tightened by the time honoured schools, and to set in movement the thousands of orbs populated by the spirits, immobilized since that time, such a man could perhaps do something in that direction."

In saying this, Andréas cast an air of mystery by which he often conveyed to his listeners, a feeling of an unknown power. Consequently, I did not ask him anything further.

It was he who broke the silence. "I remember, dear Doctor, some fifteen years ago, I was passing exactly this spot with one of my friends, a certain M. d'Annovilliers."

"He who has left the souvenirs about Jean Lorrain?"

"Exactly! Well, he told me that he had dined the day before with M. Sadi Carnot, who was then only the president of the Senate. And that evening, at his request, he gave him a little statue of Buddha in basalt, which he himself had received from an explorer. The latter found it in the country of Song, in High Burma. I too passed there in my youth. This statuette had belonged successively to five or six village chiefs, all of whom had died violent deaths. And the bonze, from whom the explorer had bought it, being a Buddhist, was also honest enough to warn him about these details. The explorer also died by an accident. And, as M. d'Annovilliers narrated this story at the table, M. Carnot, who completely disbelieved in such superstitions, insisted on having the idol for himself. Well, you know how he died."*

"In this way, my Master, if I understood rightly, one should not disturb the order of things, nor violate the course of natural laws, and not even cause beings, which are attached to their countries, to abandon them."

"Yes, Doctor! It is always the advice of the Friend to: 'let the dead bury their dead'. And if some day you go to an old country, leave alone the statuettes which seem to remain forgotten in shadowy corners. Later I promise to teach you how it is possible to touch them."

"And what about the blue diamond of Tavernier?"

"That is another story, we will speak about it some day."

And, having again lighted our pipes, we continued to smoke among the friendly secondhand booksellers and the familiar plane-trees.

---

* Monsieur Sadi Carnot, who subsequently became President of France, was assasinated on the street by a fanatic. (Translator's note.)

Chapter XIX

THE FIRST OF MAY

Some impressive public demonstrations were predicted for the first of May that year, and I had a word with Andréas, expressing my desire to know to what could correspond, in the invisible worlds, political agitations and social movements.

He arranged for us to meet on the eve of the day, and I found him in the company of an elderly woman, whom he presented to me as a clairvoyant.

"We cannot go," he said to me, "together on the other side of the Curtain, as a much greater self-possession would be needed than we have. The aspect of certain beings and the violence of certain vortexes would be disconcerting for us. This woman will go instead and tell us what she will see."

"But would she not court the same risks as us?"

"No! She will not be as uncovered as we would be forced to be. She will be in a kind of observatory."

"Well, couldn't you give that defence to me?"

"Yes, that would be possible if you were very wise; but you aren't obedient enough and you would do imprudent things."

"In that case," I acquiesced, "I have no other choice but to bow to your decision. I was expecting to see something like a magic ceremony, with recitations and mystagogy. But it was nothing like that. Andréas simply said to his medium: "Please be seated and we will start."

The medium settled herself comfortably and immediately went to sleep. "Now, what do you want?" Andréas asked me.

"Firstly, I would like to know what kind of state she is in."

"But, Doctor, she will be in the state in which you want her to be. It is not an odic fluid which I am using. You know very well that there are different kinds of magnetism; that which will be used here is a little known one. I am not using any passes or suggestion, and this woman hears you as well as myself. I will never allow myself to bind anything to something else; moreover, she can see equally well in your wallet as in your thoughts, or in Peking."

I made a dozen experiments in order to verify Andréas's assertions. I found them to be exact. I saw that the medium, even during her visions, still preserved her awareness of the physical plane, but movement was painful for her.

Finally, I asked Andréas to send her into the Invisible society, which study always interested me. The seer turned herself to Andréas with a questioning gaze.

" Yes, your escort is coming," he said to her with a smile.

" What sort of escort? " I asked him.

" Would you go alone into a country completely unknown to you? " he answered. " And, if you can go there by rail within a few days, you would surely not prefer to take several months to walk there. The beings whom she will encounter are neither terrestrial nor even human ; therefore she must avoid their inquiries and curiosity. Everywhere there are customs just the same as here on the earth ! "

" Are they perhaps the same as the beings called ' guardians ', which are mentioned in the *Pistis Sophia*, as well as in the passwords in the symbolic chambers of the F . ·. M . ·. ? "

" Of course ! " And turning to the medium he said : " Now you can go ! "

" In which way is she directed? " I asked. " There are different kinds of spaces? Which senses guide her? "

" Oh, but you want to know everything," answered the smiling Andréas. Wait, we will study all of these later."

" Here come a bear, unicorn, leopard, reindeer, dragon, eagle, camel, cow, beaver, cock . . ." pronounced the medium.

" Well, don't tell us about the whole menagerie," said Andréas. " Just see, for example, what the cock is doing since it is France which mainly interests us."

" So," I said, " on the *Other Side,* there does exist a place, a space, where nations are represented under their animal forms. How can it be? I was under the impression that Egregors are fluidic fields. What then is the animal ? "

" But," replied Andréas with a smile, " everything is in every thing. A stone here on earth can have a human form elsewhere ; an archangel of the Invisible Plane can be a gem in the depths of a rock, or rather can reside there. The enigma of the universe is so simple ! That is why it is not solved. And animal? But everything is animal : myself, the Earth, the Milky Way, an automobile, geometry, Jonah and his whale, it is all a scene lived in a corner of the *Invisible.* What, biologically speaking, does characterize an animal? It is an individual, wilful, responsible, mobile, which maintains an abstract principle under temporary domination, fluidic energies, minerals, vegetative organisms, viscera similar to the stars. We see only the physical and earthly animal species, but there also exist equally earthly ones, hyperphysical, social, religious, human, political, cosmic, industrial, intellectual, and so on.

"Modern theories about radiant matter, ions, electrons, showing that the atoms of cells both organic and inorganic are small suns, can help us to understand the ancient vision of the holy animals, Devas, demiurges, and fiery dragons. If an instrument were invented allowing the ions from which our body is built to be visible, this body would appear like a small nebula as compact and brilliant as that which is resplendent over our heads.

"But you make me chatter like a one-eyed magpie. Look well at the cock," continued Andréas addressing the seer, after a second or so of examination.

"It was so beautiful," she said, "but it seemed to disappear in smoke, and other animals come from out of the fog into which the cock was turned. It could now be described as a fenced field; here is a herd of completely confused sheep, which are stamping and bleating; they are very dirty; around them are sheep-dogs; they defend the distracted animals, but they also sometimes kill and then devour them. Approaching the first group are a horde of small animals, similar to dogs of all colours and shapes. A kind of unmoving monster is close to them, with arms like those of an octopus. It is inciting the animals and urges them to attack the sheep. In their midst is a fox to which they are incessantly turning and which commands the sheep-dogs.

In a corner behind brushwood, a crocodile seems to be sleeping; but crows, magpies and jays go from him to the fox and octopus; they poise themselves here and there over the two groups and augment their confusion by cries and blows of their beaks, while the fox and octopus consult between themselves at intervals and seem to help in increasing the fear of the sheep and the attacks of the dogs. From time to time they devour the wounded ones, which are brought to them. But they do not see that in reality it is the crocodile which directs them. Here comes a man. He bears a fisherman's net and casts it between the two groups. The dogs gradually stop and the sheep start to browse again. The man looks at the three chief animals and compels them to come into a corner, and speaks to them several times.

"That is good," said Andréas, "please rest a little."

"And what is the meaning of it all," I demanded.

"If this woman has invented her little story, or if I suggested it, all of this has no value. But perhaps it is the true picture she saw unroll before her."

"What in that case?"

"That is for you to find out! It can be from alchemy, astrology, or a social phenomenon, who knows? The medium merely saw it. She could speak to those beings, but it would be too tiring for her."

"Then what purpose does this somnambulistic session serve?"

"Nothing very great, dear Doctor. Realize that it is very good to have enthusiasm, but one should not undertake work beyond one's powers. If you or I were pure, if we could recognize ourselves as God's children, nothing of the Creation would be hidden from us. Then we would understand everything, and everyone would understand us. Then, because we would be humble, it would be possible for us, for example, to have relations with the Spirits of the Nations, or political and religious sects, directing them according to the plans of Providence. While waiting for that, we can only work in silence, devote ourselves to and have confidence in our Friend."

Chapter XX

THE INVISIBLE ENEMIES

ANDREAS was on his way to Brittany, on one of the sudden, short journeys, which he occasionally used to make. I joined him as he passed Nantes station. That evening we were due to see a sick farmer together, who lived about two leagues from Vannes, in a grey house, with a large roof, only the top of which was visible through the hedges that bordered the lonely road. The parish priest believed this peasant to be possessed, while the doctor, knowing him to be an alcoholic, would have liked to hospitalize him as soon as possible.

With the taciturn Bretons, Andréas too was sparing of words. In the dark lounge room, where a small lamp animated the shadows, the mother and daughter were busy among pots and pans. The man sat with us, his stick in his hand, hat on head and pipe between his teeth.

Andréas also smoked and we all three of us drank from a pot of cider. A thin cat begged for food and two mud-covered dogs, with bright eyes, warmed themselves on the hearth.

Outside the wind started. It began softly at first, singing in the chimney, but soon it became a furious orchestra, which made the whole of the solid old house tremble. As September storms are rare in those parts, the wife of the old man, being somewhat astonished, half-opened the door to look outside. I saw her take a few steps on to the roadway. Then she came running back. Her face was the colour of chalk and she whispered: " There is not even the slightest breeze on the road." She put the sign of the cross on herself.

Her husband raised his head, as if awakened from a doze. He sprang to his feet and raised his stick with wild energy; but Andréas was already standing and had caught the man's eyes in the light of his own immovable pupils.

The farmer fell on his knees and arms, started to nibble here and there at the furniture, and howled like a wolf wandering in a rage of hunger. The trembling women crouched together under the stairs, and the animals hid behind them. Meanwhile as the storm raged stronger, the peasant howled more loudly. The black demon of fear was casting forth his most obnoxious poisons. I was becoming impatient because Andréas did not move at all. But he had to do something, it was imperative that he did. And yet, minutes were slipping away while the same evil concerto of the wind and the possessed continued.

But now, a dark thing was silently pushing past the door, looking like a large old wolf, mute, supple, with stiff hair, slavering muzzle and brilliant, red eyes. It went forward and sat facing the man, who continued to howl all the time, becoming convulsive under the poisonous breath of the Beast.

Andréas went and stood between them, and the Beast raised its large eyes to his, eyes that were clear, cruel and crafty. But Andréas gently took that big, savage head in his hands and plunged them into the thick fur. Then I noticed that the body of the wolf was as if translucent for a moment. This made me lose my cold-blooded mood. An unspeakable stench came puffing out from the foaming muzzle. Suddenly, the Beast prepared to leap, but Andréas stopped it by holding its shoulders. And so they remained, eye to eye, until finally the reddish gleam that danced in the centre of the savage pupils became extinguished like a blown out candle.

" Get everyone outside! Make the man sit, but quickly! " Andréas ordered me.

I pushed the women out along with the dogs, and wearily raised the man, who was unconscious, on to a seat. At the same moment the storm subsided; the Beast fell on its paws, receded to the fireplace and there disappeared into a vapour. The farmer stretched himself, rubbed his eyes and grumbled. He saw the froth on the sleeve of Andréas's coat and was startled.

" Listen Jean-Marie! " said Andréas, " in an hour's time you will not remember anything, and you will never speak about it to anybody! Depart immediately! You will meet old mother Le Dallo, whom you will reach early tomorrow morning, and you will walk back here. You will repay her those hundred francs you know of, dating back about twenty years, and you will also add a hundred francs for interest. When she dies, you will arrange a funeral mass to be said for her every Saturday. Do you promise me to do all of this? "

" Yes! " replied the man, going to the small plaster statue of the Virgin on the mantelpiece, where he crossed himself and recited the Lord's Prayer and Ave Maria, saying: " I swear to repay the twenty gold coins, to order the masses and never to speak about it."

" That is good," said Andréas, " now go, so that I can see it done. Have no fear, for nothing will happen to you this night on the way."

Three minutes later we were on the roadway and Jean-Marie was heading to the north, while we returned to Vannes.

Naturally, I assaulted Andréas with questions.

"It was all due to vengeance," he told me.

"But the wolf, although it was translucent, it still had weight, and was material because it spoiled your jacket."

"Well," he said, "haven't you studied magic? Certainly you know very well what lycanthropy is. We are here in the country of the were-wolves. In the land where the life of Nature is strong, and man himself is of little intellect and therefore offers many means of action to the spirits of stones, forests, ponds, clouds, winds and uncultivated soil. Then physical creatures become intuitional seers, mediums and invisible creatures are closer to the realm of matter."

"That is one more proof that Nature always goes through the insensible gradations and that men, everywhere, have an innate, intuition of the Invisible."

"Yes! Everywhere man inwardly receives what he needs. Today there is a tendency to say, that the mysterious sciences all come to us from the Orient. But that is not exact. Not only in Western books, but even in folk-lore, one can find all the theories which are taught in the esoterism of India, China and Tibet. We are simply under the spell of a mental fascination, put over us by certain powerful individuals. But it will not endure forever."

"It is true that the book of Zohar contains all the ideas, which I had previously seen in the Puranas. The Brahmanic theory about the chronological periods of time is also present in the book of Sepher and Trithemius, as well as Arbatel. If one would like to compare the writings of Agrippa with certain Fathers of the Church, one could build a pneumatology just as complete and complicated as that of the Vedas. Paracelsus gives the same teachings on medicine, natural history, physics and chemistry as do the Hindu *Samhitas*. But can we still say that the East is the source on which all those European initiates drew?"

"That is true! It is too idle to discuss priorities. You know very well that nobody knows anything, and that there is usually only apparently realization. A cabbalist, a Pythagorean, a yogi, an arhat, a wali, a saint—all of them did not approach closer than others to the zenith of knowledge and power. They possess only approximations, more or less close, and everyone of them is on the top of a mountain. All of them see stones, trees, animals, villages, clouds: that is their concordance. But not one of them sees the same forests, nor the same hamlets: these are the divergences of the traditions."

"You want to say that the subjects with which esoterism is occupied are too far from us, so that we can discern little more than very large conglomerations?"

"Yes! And when a seeker finds something clear and precise, this meeting point belongs to so many different forces, that it is then impossible for him to enumerate all of them, and therefore, to account for the true nature of his work. The scene which we witnessed just now, is the last hour of a drama which began four centuries ago. This farmer and the witch, who took the form of a wolf are old enemies; now, of course, they will be reconciled. But who can count the millions of spirits of every kind, set in motion during their age-old hatred?"

"And who will put all of them in order?"

"God, through certain beings. Every thing is a living thing, everything has its spirit, its intelligence; every physical form is only a form of a spirit-soul. So, supposing that I was able to perform it, if I reconciled those millions of sparks of life, I would still need much more time to do it, than this man and woman used in order to set them fighting. If I turned to the different chiefs of those spirits, I would first have to seek and find them, and they most certainly have already departed very far from this earth. The simplest thing would be for me to turn to God, Who knows everything, and Who, in the twinkling of an eye would then cause all of them to appear and be judged, which means to be reorganized."

"Then the books of esoterism, magic, pneumatology, or angelology, although containing exact data, only incite the seeker to turn to the secondary causes, and not to the Primary Cause?"

"Quite so! And although they always advise us to turn to God, to undertake nothing without obtaining His aid through a pure life, people invariably pass over this preamble. This is because people believe it to be good enough for the crowd, but not necessary for an initiate, as they believe themselves to be. They court knowledge of secrets and curious things and, as an end result, they become misled."

"To sum up, there are many spirits, chiefs, princes, satraps and invisible kings, gods of planets, races, nations, thatched cottages, guides for professions and individual positions, as well as saviours who help us. The Kabbalah, religions, Sufism, Buddhism, Brahmanism, are all unanimous on the ultimate. But it is more prudent and urgent not to seek after them, but to inquire about God alone!"

"Yes! For man should act with the Light which made him man, that is, with the divine spark which was put into him in the beginning. If he acts with one of the bodies of that spark, that is, with his intelligence, his magnetism or will-power, he acts in the appearance and on the appearance, but not in the Centre and on the central plan of the world. Remain in the Centre, in

Unity, in Harmony, and everything you will do will radiate unity, harmony and peace. I repeat to you, that all that has been taught by the greatest of men, all that has been revealed to the most pure of them, does not form even a millionth part of the Wholeness of Science. Everyone has his own path. There are no polemics, no critics, nor battles in this plan of Unity, where we have to dwell. Say what you believe to be true and always realize it. Others do what they have to do. There is the FRIEND to arrange everything, to put everyone in his place, according to the Law which He alone knows. Work in this way and be in peace."

CHAPTER XXI

THE VINEYARD

INSTEAD of returning directly to Paris, Andréas took the train at Chinon and alighted at Ile-Bouchard. From there we took a small country train, together with a whole crowd of farmers and their wives, who were returning from the market. The small locomotive advanced, panting among the hills warmed by the high, summer sun. Divided by walls of rough stone, the series of vineyards presented their vines in rows of dead plants; endlessly followed by the replacement ones, with leaves blued by the use of sulphates. The forecast for the season was bad. The peasants were moaning as the crops promised to be barely half that of a normal year; the vines could probably not be saved. Neither powders, liquids, fertilizers nor cross-breeding helped to halt the renewal of the diseases. The ruin ahead could be seen. Several good years would be necessary to give even a slight recovery.

"But you have had good years," Andréas said to the peasants. "What use did you make of them? You collected your gold coins and you didn't even allow yourselves to have one more pleasure. Did you arrange for roads with your municipal council, or give something to the destitute? No! Well, why do you expect the soil to be better than you are?"

"You don't count," answered the peasants, "all that we have had to spend on new plants from America, for manures, fertilizers and watering."

"A lot of good it did you this year," replied Andréas. In fact, nothing has stopped the disease, and the science of agronomy has to confess its helplessness. So now, you have to return to the empiric practices which the old ones recall as they sit under the walnut trees, canes under their chins and pipes in their mouths.

"Yes!" continued Andréas, "in the old days people went into the fields with the good Lord, but today you are becoming too mischievous. For now your good God is copper sulphate and his angels are the phosphates. Get something from them, now, when you have exhausted the soil. You were too lazy even to plant the seed and that is not natural. You know very well that if a man takes only marc without eating, he will soon die. You should not enforce: you know quite well how to manage your horses and bulls, then do likewise in the vineyards."

And the peasants listened to him, saying nothing, in order not to give the impression of being weathercocks; but in their hearts, some of them recognized that this gentleman could possibly be telling the truth.

"Nevertheless," I said to Andréas, "you would not like to send these people back to the church and the parish priest."

"Why not?" he answered. "They don't need to have the general views of the government. They are born as peasants, which means that they only have to obey their religion. Know well, that catholicism is the best religion."

"Yes! But what relation has it to the vineyard diseases?"

"Very close ones, Doctor, just the same as with the diseases of cattle, with grain, wind and many other things."

"How can that be?"

"In a very natural way. You know that the purpose of Jesus' religion is to unite the whole of creation with God, because it is the religion of the Logos. Do you understand?"

"Yes, nearly! But it seems to me that I would have a lot of difficulties in trying to explain it to philosophers."

"Oh! We are not trying to. Firstly, one would have to make them catch the objective reality of religion. They do not see anything except the whole of the subjective formulas. They see only the intellectual in dogmas, and only moral symbols in the rites. A dogma is something in itself, and ritual contains virtue in itself. Moreover, if a priest is a saint, this virtue is augmented. But, returning to our sheep, we have to take into account—so as to explain the influence which a liturgical prayer can exercise on a physical phenomenon——, that the collective circle of a church embraces more than only the people who are part of that church. For example, the Catholic Church does not include only the priests and the faithful, living or dead, for it also includes many other beings, visible as well as invisible. In the first place they are the spirits of the nations which recognize the Church and then the subordinate spirits which obey it. The church has a certain number of infernal spirits and those belonging to Heaven; spirits of the sciences and arts proper to a particular nation; spirits of cities, villages, rivers, mountains, forests and fields, which depend upon the spirits national or ethnical; spirits of the public, political and intellectual institutions; of machines, houses and palaces; briefly, the spirits of all the varieties of beings and material forms, constructed by Nature's power, or by the will of the human beings, who have offered their faith to the Master of that religion."

"Then it would be possible to invent a spiritual physiology of a religion, state, industry, in short, of everything constituting civilization?"

"Yes," answered Andréas. "Always remember that Nature works only according to a unique plan, and that the same law which rules the development of a star, also rules a grain of wheat, science, virtue, and so on. Now do you see how the kingdom of Heaven is similar to a grain of mustard? Do you see in which inner attitude one has to study the Gospels?"

"Yes," I answered, "I am catching a glimpse of very vast horizons. But," I added, "let us return to our unfortunate vineyards." For I knew how cleverly Andréas was able to elude a question.

"Well," he replied, "let us return. Which is the highest act that a man can perform? It is the one by which he sets in motion his most profound and purest energies, which, consequently, awake the most echoes in all the spheres of his individuality. It is, clearly, the religious act. Now, because everything is interconnected in the universe, and because we cannot do anything which will not have any repercussion on our surroundings, it is the most powerful reason for prayer to stir our most secret centres, and so, through reaction move all the centres of the environment to which we are attached."

"Yet isn't that all?" I asked.

"If in a social community a cell charged with representing the function of prayer, that is, the priest, asks for something according to the forms indicated to him by the tradition, which is formed by the chain of priests right back to the founder of that religion, such a request finds, first of all, an echo in other members of the same community, just as when your heart prays, the other parts of your body feel the effects of the same. The rest of the community, visible as well as invisible, listens to such a prayer, and because God's Name is invoked in it, the parts of the community which are not in accordance with the law, have willingly or unwillingly to comply with it."

"Yes," I answered, "I would like to believe you, but I don't understand it too clearly."

"I'm sure you don't" Andréas said softly with a smile. "I do not tell you these things for immediate use. You will need them much later, as you will forget them for a long time. But, you know, sometimes an earthquake happens within us and sometimes the deep layers of our spirit rise to the sun of the Consciousness, while what was on the surface is buried in the dark subsoil. It must be mentioned in the Gospels."

"Perhaps where it is said that: 'He humbled the strong, and so on.'"

"No doubt!" answered Andréas. "Well, when the parish

priest in a village, along with the teacher, children, a few peasants and some good women went with the Holy Sacrament across the fields of wheat chanting the Psalms in his rough voice, he had invisible assistants at that simple ceremony. They listened to the Latin words, or rather the faith which made those words dynamic, appearing to them like rays of light, barriers and points of fire. Then the little beings, which make the hail and rain or wind, were more obedient than they are to those blunderbusses, which you can see used here and there amidst the vineyards."

" Is it as simple as you say? "

" Yes, it is, for rustic Nature is very sensitive to psychic forces; that is why the witches, or bone-setters get better results in the country than in towns. Religion is so natural a thing, the heart is so much the receptacle of life, that both find their most normal expansion beyond the artificial creations of the human mind."

" Could some reason be sought here regarding the failure of the chemical treatment in the vineyards during this year? "

" Yes, it is possible. The earth, which, in the first place, is a living thing, develops a habit for nearly everything, like simple King Mithridates. Also the chemical product is dead most of the time, and consequently it cannot give something it doesn't possess. It is only a stimulant for the soil, in the same way as alcohol or coffee is for the human body. Apart from that, just as with our bodies, the soil has only a limited capacity for absorption: once saturated it reaches the limit of its output and cannot go beyond it. Then the agriculturist has to seek for something different until, finally, we arrive at the position that we have at this moment, in this part of the country. And sometimes the immanent Justice issues decrees which are executed in spite of all the artifices of human ingeniousness. When for a long time men show themselves to be obstinately avaricious or slanderous despite, for example, the clemency of the climate and goodness of the soil, certain beings—who are lovers of justice—open a particular door on the *other side* Then human avarice and slander enter a place where they obtain life, a certain ability for organic procreation. And this then forms itself on the surface of the soil as mould, a little everywhere. At first the micro-organisms are single cells, which evolve fast enough and become animalcules. The Phylloxera is not of any other origin, and what I have told you is so true, that in this country, through which we are passing just now, there is only one healthy vineyard, and that belongs to a man who prayed."

" Then there is a continuous relation between that which the occultists call the 'astral' and the physical world? "

" Of course there is! All the parts of the universe are in

perpetual relationship; they bathe in one another, except when a wall has been built for local and temporary isolation. It is because of this universal infusion that religions so insistently recommend that we dedicate to God, every action and every thought."

"But what about these poor people, wouldn't Heaven again do something this time in order to save them from ruin? Perhaps, being so close to ruin, they will mend their ways."

"Heaven has already been patient with them for years," said Andréas. "It did not work. However, the good God has plenty of time. If among them was someone who realized what he was asking, much suffering would be spared them. But, alas!"

"Then, why not try to warn this man, about whom you spoke just now?"

"Well, he will be warned," replied Andréas in a tone one uses when trying to get rid of the importunate questions of a child. If only men could realize that they are the objects of incessant cares! We are vulnerable from all sides, from our bodies to the finest points of our spirit. We brush with Death, no, with deaths, several times daily. No, man does not cultivate gratitude enough. Hence we, who have travelled since this morning without any accident, find it all so natural! Ah, how ungrateful we are!"

And then with his eyes half closed Andréas merged into a long and taciturn meditation.

Chapter XXII

AN AVALANCHE IN THE HIMALAYAS

ONE evening, on visiting Andréas, I found him assisting his wife to prepare for a journey. An intimate friend, who was sick, needed her and she had immediately to take the Southern Express. We accompanied her to the Austerlitz Station. I noted how much Andréas tried to secure every imaginable comfort for her, as well as the exquisite politeness of his manners, a gracious attitude which I know of in only two or three old noblemen. I also noted that Andréas knew many of the railway personnel, from the chief to the more humble members of the staff.

The express train departed, and Andréas suggested that we make a night trip into the country, which I accepted with enthusiasm. A night of conversation with such a companion was a rare treasure. I suggested that we take a suburban train so as to reach the silence and fresh air of the fields faster. And so, the inhabitants of Villaine, who had not yet fallen asleep by 1 a m. could see, in the full moonlight, two shadowy figures walking through the fields to the forest-covered hills, dominating the valley of Bièvre.

"There are countries like the vast Tartary, India and China, which I have always wanted to know," I told Andréas.

"Yes, but how many travellers have left their skins there! There are some countries with a definite reputation, and consequently one is cautious about them. But the climates of Turkestan and Mongolia are no less torturing. I remember suffering a lot there myself."

"How was that?" I asked.

"Simply, it was my first journey to Lhassa. At that time, I was passing through a period of strong attacks of moral origin, just the kind you have talked about to me before; but as troubles never come singly, I also had other anxieties and so found myself in the following position."

And Andréas continued, climbing all the while up a short, but steep path. "In the whole of Asia, as you most certainly know, politics and the occult sciences are closely connected and assist one another. So far the Brahmans have remained relatively quiet, but the Muslims are more active and bring a lot of trouble to the Queen of England and the Russian Czar. As regards China, today everyone knows about the slow and silent work of the secret societies against the Manchu Dynasty. The Annamites are always dreaming of regaining their self-rule. And the Tibetans, from their snowy observation posts, watch the movements of nations, agitated as they are throughout the immense Asian continent.

"Things such as the migration of the Buddhist nomads of Tartary, Iranian Muslims, Afghans and Hindus, Taoists, members of the Triad and White Water-Lilly, are all faithfully reported to them by fast emissaries, as well as by a sort of wireless telegraph, which they have known of for several hundred years. The Lamas take much interest in the descent of the Russians to the South, and ascent of the British to the North. Anyway, their sympathies are always with the former.

"I do not wish to bother you with the tedious history of Tibetan policy, nor the vicissitudes of the central priesthood. It will suffice for you to know that the Dalai Lama and the great Lamas of Tartary, are more in agreement between themselves, than the mass of their faithful people know. Their Supreme Council—which includes, apart from the *living Buddhas,* the chiefs of every Indian, Chinese, Japanese, Annamite and Malayan initiation—, one day proposed to try an approach to the head of a great empire in Europe. Anyway, this happened several years ago. They were in need of an emissary, who was well acquainted with things Western, and they looked towards me.

"But messengers, caravans and ceremonies did not allow them to keep these negotiations absolutely secret. The mass of the people, the novices, lamas and even khampos or cardinals, were informed about the course of things by the inevitable comings and goings, which occur during such diplomatic activities. It was therefore necessary for them to find the right pretext which, in the eyes of these people, would justify the importance conferred on my person."

Here Andréas stopped, again lit his pipe and looked down on the valley sleeping in the moonlight, and then said :
"Nature is mild here."

Then walking back a few steps, he remained immobilized in silent contemplation. The sky in the east was already becoming a little brighter; rabbits were running over the roadway, and swallows started to warble around a farm in the valley. Suddenly the sun surged up before us, over the forest of Hay and at the same time a lark shot out from a furrow like a bullet, and started its morning prayer. Andréas returned to me and continued his story.

"At that time, the Transcaspian railway was not yet finished, so therefore my retinue and myself travelled on horseback across the plains of Turkestan. I again saw the ruins of ancient Samarkand and Merv, those centres of the once brilliant Arab civilization. That is where I would like to see you. Fried by day, blinded by dust in the evenings, frozen at night; suffering from thirst all the time, without any possibility of quenching it because of the danger of intestinal diseases, and a prey to the sand-sickness, which makes even the most patient people cross. But I will tell you about all of that some other day.

"After having performed my mission, we set out for Tibet. The journey was peaceful enough, until we reached the high plains of the Hindu Kush. But terrible things awaited me on the 'roof of the world'.

"It was the third time that my destiny had led me to that snowy solitude of the Himalayas. But, although the cold, fatigue and discomforts were discouraging, nothing really affected me when I faced the joys of mountaineering: neither tiresome climbing, dangerous descents, storms, nor terrifying optical illusions. The peace I experienced was even beyond that which I always felt in the midst of a desert. The joys were numerous: the filling of my lungs with the icy air of the peaks; the being intoxicated in the evenings by the magnificent view of the firmament; the enjoyment of the magic of the rising sun, and the dramatic orchestration of colours as it set, and the being drowned in the calm beauty of those nights, when the moon poured its light into the formidable silence, sometimes broken by the distant cry of an animal hunting down in the bottom of a valley.

"In that immense peace, immovable but full of life, the majesty of visible Nature exalts man's heart unto the Invisible, for then it rests closer to the bosom of the Great Mother.

"Everything which is artificial and unnecessary falls away, just like dry bark. The enormity of the material earthly forms, pressing on us from all sides, causes to shoot, from the depths of our hearts, that little and so weak plant, which alone can ascend to Heaven and make LOVE descend from it. It is not without reason that the most remarkable feats in religious history have been performed on the summits: Mount Meru, Nebo, Horeb, Thabor, Calvary— are the mysterious springboards from which flashes forth, with a supernatural effort, the Prayer of the Initiators. They are the harbours of Grace, into which empty the eternal rivers, the nave which brings to the sacrificed one the necessary assistance during the consummation of the Holocaust.

"The sanies of the electro-telluric currents fall to the bottom of the valleys; the mountain air is the purest and the earth is richer in it. Under the snows the rocks are brooding, silently forming the virgin alumina, and the water of the springs flows there, invigorating, saturated with the flavours of the maternal soil. The fragrance of those forests develops the chest; the vast horizons sharpen the sight, the escalade of the abrupt slopes forges the muscles as if of steel; the unforeseen cataclysms of avalanches, and the treachery of the crevasses, enslaves the nerves to prompt obedience to will-power, and the quasi solitude exalts the soul and makes it eager to aspire to the unspoiled heights of the mystical peaks.

" In the intimacy of Nature, the culture of a civilized man dries up and dies. The intimate sense takes its normal place and the instinct of what is true, devoid of prejudices and social conventions, can then freely open its green foliage, in the perpetual spring of the soul, becoming innocent once more. Ah! If only men did not wish to believe themselves to be more of savants than Nature itself, then how quickly they would see that their various systems are sterile and give nothing but insipid fruit; how they would then, without any anxiety about tomorrow, allow the living forces of their inner depths to frolic here and there, offering themselves to the rays of the true Sun, to spread joy in and around them, just like a circle of children dancing before the doors of a thatched cottage. But we don't wish to realize how simple Truth is.

" One night we were camped on the southern slope of a mountain in order to save ourselves from the biting wind, which had made us suffer terribly during the whole day. The sky was clear and nothing forecasted a storm. However, I noticed some small hawks with white heads, in the valleys beneath us, travelling to the north against the wind. I advised my companions of my fears, and ordered them to put my tent, in which I had to sleep alone, being a candidate for the Nomekhanat, between two rocks in the direction from south to north. That night I was awakened by the dull noise of something falling on to my roof of felt. But, as we were surrounded by crevasses and precipices, I preferred to wait until morning to see what had happened, and spent several hours listening to the snow storm, which I had foreseen, battering on the sides of my Tartar's tent.

" When the noise finally ceased, I tried to get out, but first had to clear a path through the snow. The brilliant sun caused the whole of the immaculate plateau and diamond peaks to shine brightly. But my companions, their tents, horses and camels had all disappeared. A block of ice had formed between the two rocks which protected my tent and had thus created a kind of hut with walls of snow. On searching, I saw a strip of felt some hundreds of feet down. The whole caravan had been carried away by the avalanche like a leaf, and I remained alone, with a bag of tea, no water or fire, and about fifteen thousand feet up in 35 degrees centigrade of frost.

"However, I was not over anxious. If my servants really were the victims of an accident, I could, by use of what you call 'telepathy' ask for assistance from the nearest monastery and wait for several days, merging myself into one of the lethargic states of Hatha Yoga. But, if my abandonment had been premeditated, then I could count only on myself; for, in such a case, no lama would answer my requests. Therefore the wisest thing to do was to preserve myself against hunger.

"Certainly, you have heard of the adepts who can, for example, materialize a bag of rice if they have even one grain of it to serve them as a basis, a fulcrum for the operation. But I had nothing apart from tea, which was not nourishing, and snow covered all the places where I might hope to find a plant overlooked by a camel. Hence I could not use that procedure. However, it was relatively easy for me, with a little patience, to collect and absorb certain nutritious particles, which came from the decomposition of the rocks exposed to the rain. The minerals, which you doctors have studied for a century contain everything that man can need. In that way a raw material was not lacking for my purpose.

"So I collected a handful of the reddish powder, prepared an area under my tent, wrote out the formulas and directed the operation. Then, without any apparent reason, these words, read before and then forgotten, reappeared in my memory: '*Make it that these stones become bread*'. And I rose, deeply confused. What right had I to interfere with Nature's plan? What would become of all those microscopic lives, which my will-power might throw into a spiritual environment which is not their own, thereby destroying their evolutionary curve, tyrannizing and enforcing them to accomplish a task for which they are not prepared? But my life was more precious to me than all those powders, on the other hand, if I continued my operation, it would be the law of the stronger, which I would be using. If I did one unjust thing today, what abuse of my powers would I commit tomorrow?

"Time was passing. Soon I would have to defer the projected transmutation till tomorrow. Ideas buzzed in my head. If I resisted those suggestions it would mean death. I had no fear of dying, but I did not want to die, and the pride in me was being wounded more than the desire to live. So I started all the preparations for my operation again, and soon everything was ready. I was about to pronounce the ritual words but, my lips remained silent. Something like a bitter and astringent liquor was descending into me; I felt myself to be so small, both with my intelligence and my body. And so I remained there, like an insect, sticking to the rocky walls, expecting something unknown and happy to wait for it during that night full of sparkling stars.

"At dawn, I came out of the dangerous torpor. The mystic scruples disappeared; I forgot the dignities, the mysteries, the worldly politics, and the lamaic church. I was merely a hungry mountaineer, but still alert and willing to play my best with the snow, cold and precipices.

"I folded the felt of my tent to form a kind of sledge, and bound myself to it as best I could. Then, holding a stick in each hand for steering, and trusting to my guiding star and experience in the snow-fields, I started to glide along an almost even path, at the end of which, after a few hours travelling, I hoped to find some living being.

"I suffered quite a bit of bruising and risked breaking my neck several times, but, by about midday, after having descended almost six thousand feet, I saw a strip of grass and a little further on some trees. I was saved.

"I mustered my forces sufficiently to yell loudly at the edge of the forest, hoping that the echos would reach the ears of a shepherd. I was happy to hear a far off reply resounding in the air, and half an hour later, along the path came running a peasant, happy to serve a holy lama, who sat under a pine tree, with an expression of great nobleness and detachment."

Chapter XXIII

PROBATION

ANDREAS continued his story: "Some days later, after being conducted there by some peasants, I returned to my cell to await, with the greatest of possible calm, further events which I presumed would be of a decisive nature. Soon the ambassador of the Great Lama of Ourga came under the pretext of the celebration of an anniversary. Next day they came to find me with great ceremony, amid an uproar of bells, fireworks and acclamations of the people. The Council of twelve Nomekhans was reunited. I was placed in the centre. A long parchment was presented to me in silence and from it, to my great surprise, I read that I would be elected to a high position, yet had I not given notorious proof of my inability during my European mission. I allowed my gaze to wander indifferently over the assembly, because I felt that they were watching me with all their power of attention. Any other person in my position would defend himself, and death was the usual edict at such secret trials; but my former experience of oriental ruses was useful to me at that time. If they had decided my doom nothing could save me except a miracle. I couldn't escape them by my own powers. But I first had to guess what they expected of me. I knew myself to be superior to them in certain rituals, which the Brahmanic sanctuaries never communicated to the Buddhists. The obvious aim of their clever manoeuvres was to compel me to unveil those mysteries to them. But I did not at all wish to betray the oaths I had taken.

So, in the silence of that hall, in the midst of the humming monastery and merry city, I waited, under the fire of those twelve wills, eager to tear out my secrets from me. As yet no desert had been so terrible for me as this. My dispassion must have surprised my judges. I was led back to my cell, and they placed a superb ring of chased jade on my thumb, as a sign of honour. That meant that the Nomekhans would not attack me in my physical form. But, I had yet to fear tortures of a different kind, the use of which was common to them, and I had never seen one person, among those few luckless people, whom the politicians of the secret councils wished to destroy, who had been able to resist them. Scientists don't speak about this art; but people believe that certain lamas can unleash a horde of demons over you. You will understand that I cannot say anything more about it. And that was what actually happened. Ideas of escape germinated in my brain. But how to realize them? I could never go out alone, and I had no clothes other than a large woollen robe and a large hat. I had no money. I was in despair. Then I wanted to exercise my power of hypnotic suggestion in order to ensure assistance from one of my servants. But my plans had been foreseen: everyone was, so to speak, bewitched by the Grand Council. And I had to use the greatest of efforts so as to ensure that my attempts would remain secret.

"I was caught like a fly in a spider's web. For a week I struggled to perform public rites, with a rosary of beechnuts in my hands as I preached, because they had bestowed on me the decorations and functions of a dignitary, which again meant more chains. Then my enervation increased and consumption started to undermine my energy. This was just what my tempters expected. When they knew that I was weak enough and apt to become impressed and desperate, they came to me and proposed that I take charge of one of the Lhassa monasteries and let me visit it, inspecting it from the cellars to the top story. It is unimaginable just how many riches were accumulated there. Whole rooms were full of crude, precious stones, others were filled with jewels, coins, weapons, art objects, manuscripts, drawings, furniture, collections of plants, minerals, extinct animals, magic instruments and dresses. I was dazzled. In spite of myself, my hands stretched out towards these treasures. But, before the fever of possiveness completely engulfed me, I was able to say to those who accompanied me: 'What is the good of all this? Gold scatters, science is vain and beauty doesn't exist on this earth.'

"Then, changing their tactics, they greeted me as the One whom they expected for the fulfilment of their plans. They unveiled their intentions to me. They wanted to throw one half of the ancient continent against the other, in order to enslave the whole earth and bring it under their domination. I saw myself as a hero, a half-god adored by millions of humans. All beauty, all power and riches were to belong to me, as well as the whole of intelligence and love of which the human heart is capable. A fire began to kindle in my exhausted organism. I hid my hands in my sleeves so that their trembling would not be seen. At my feet were all the treasures of men; before my eyes I saw splendid horizons, the peaks, the ether, and the forests in all their spring glory, while on the lower terraces the novices and monks, bent double before me when I appeared and poured for me the wine of ambition.

"'You will establish the glory of our Lord Buddha over the whole earth,' the lamaic cardinals told me. 'Perhaps you will change the destiny of this world, his satellite that is in revolt. Perhaps you will be able, aided by the enthusiasm of the multitudes, to lead it into submission. You will always live on these mountains, or anywhere else you may desire; unknown if you wish, or the sole object of human attention, if you so prefer.'

"And during the long hours, those intentionally mute, solitary people told me the beads of the sublime concupiscences. The invisible kingdom of Buddha was opened before my mind, and his aureola instantly surrounded me. But, among the fluidic wheels with their diamond-like spokes, through the golden flames that glowed in my brain, on the bottom of the ruby-coloured streams flowing in my breast, far above the canopies of sapphires leaning over my head, there appeared a small flash, fresh like a dew-drop, sweet like a breath of wind in an orchard full of flowers.

"And then I was able to give them my answer.

"Lord Buddha said: 'Everything is illusion, and you cannot destroy illusion by creating other illusions, Allow me, O very wise men, that in a desert as well as in a city, I alone may first completely destroy the basic illusion in myself. For only then will Truth descend and I will be able to answer you. And then together we will serve all the Buddhas and their Father, the Inconceivable.'

"Against these words the defeated Nomekhans retreated.

"My suffering was over. A few days later, a man arrived with a caravan of Chinese merchants. Anyway, it seems to me that you have already met that 'person', added Andréas in parenthesis.

"It was discovered that my health needed a better climate, and I was offered the chance to descend with him to India. I accepted. What a delight was that journey through the silent valleys, under the shadow of the forests of pine, holly oaks and birches! Far away we encountered small brown bears, sometimes a deer and apes; a grey eagle followed us high in the air, and the mountain flowers of Europe, such as ranunculas, syringas, clematis and anemones, multiplied as we advanced to the fertile hills of High Nepal. We finally took the train at Saran, and wound our way through Behar, Bardwan and Madhupur towards the Ganges until Calcutta. And during those three months what living lessons were taught to me by that mysterious companion, whom I had not hoped to encounter again on this earth."

The sun was already high when Andréas stopped talking. He chose a shadow at the back of a ditch and invited me to sleep like himself for a couple of hours.

Later we descended towards the farm of his friend, which had been visible for quite a long time from the crest on which we had stood. Our host was a tall, old peasant with side-whiskers, who wore golden ear-rings. He showed us his cowsheds and stables, and after breakfast he also showed us his large market garden. He talked alone with Andréas for half an hour, and then we left.

As soon as we were on the road, Andréas said to me: "Did you dream this morning?"

"Yes," I answered, "but it only concerned some memories from the waking state: a farm, work, rain . . ."

"Well!" he said. "And if a material life can influence our dreams, why then can't dreams affect that life?"

"The remark you have made is ingenious, but what science is more obscure than oneiromancy?"

"That is certainly our own error, since we put bandages over our eyes and then complain because we cannot see clearly."

I walked for a few minutes in silence, collecting my powers in order definitely to break through a wall I felt before me.

"Well," I said, "in the name of all my most cherished hopes, from all the force of my most profound desires—make me SEE!"

"Ah! Doctor," he exclaimed softly with a tone of reproach, "for whom do you take me? Realize that I am an ignorant, impotent and incapable person. When I was still young, there were things that I believed I was able to do; but now, during every day, every minute, I come to know that I am worth nothing."

He became silent. His silence was full of things incomprehensible to the mind, but my heart was listening. Even so I analysed my sensations in the full light of consciousness; my legs were briskly walking along the road under the growing shadow of the old apple-trees; my lungs were filling with the fresh, delicious wind of early morning, and a magnetic force was vibrating in my muscles and bones. My head was calm because at that moment I enumerated the logical reasons which could explain Andréas's behaviour to me.

And then, quite within myself, and very far from the ordinary residence of my will, there was another self, not an unknown, but rather a little known one, which raised itself and answered Andréas, with the mouth and voice of the first 'I', that earthly and everyday self.

"Nevertheless, there are men who know, who can. There is a man, perhaps very far away, perhaps very close: he, about whom you have spoken to me," I said, thinking about his travelling companion, whom he had mentioned in his hint during the morning.

I could not restrain myself from associating all this with the memory of the Unknown man, who had presided at the funeral of Desiderius, and also with that passer-by, whom I had met on the morning of my first visit to Andréas.

"I don't know if I should," murmured Andréas, shaking his head. "If I show you the Light which I myself saw, you too will wish to participate in it. But the path leading to that Light as well as everything else has been united in order to remove the wanderer. There are bad pavements, dust, hills, ruts, lack of shade, dark streets where thieves occupy the cross-roads, or where one risks being crushed, nightly traps" (suddenly his voice started to vibrate like the string of a cello), "and when one has bleeding feet, is soaked with sweat or frozen by the north wind, with skinned knees and empty stomach, one still has to advance in spite of everything!" he exclaimed in a very low voice, with an extraordinary concentration of energy in the whole of his powerful figure.

This man could sometimes stir one's heart like a lion shaking its prey before carrying it away. I wondered about all the unknown things of which, to me, he seemed to be a guardian.

And there and then I made the most childish professions of courage, perseverance and everything which came into my head.

CHAPTER XXIV

THE TIGER

To fit in with this narration, I must now mention a story which Andréas told me several months later, about one of his trips to Siam. I am giving it here as exactly as my memory permits me.

One evening he said to me : " You already know that at another period well distant from today, I travelled through the northern basin of the Salween River. My decision to do so had been made by the legends that abound in that region and which were little known at that time. Mountains, endless forests, unmapped watercourses, luxuriant flora, abundant fauna, and tigers for the hunting were all irresistibly attractive.

" Immediately upon becoming free from advice from family and school, I rushed to visit India. Later, with eyes dazzled by thousands of magnificent pictures, I went to Rangoon to rest and make arrangements for a less hasty journey into Laos and Schan. I wanted to penetrate the soul of those people. I received information concerning one of their stratagems, which, at the time, my scepticism made it appear to me as only legitimate. It was, as I noted, the extreme courtesy of Orientals towards Europeans. But it seemed to me to be as if dictated by feelings different from pure friendliness or even fear. I believed it to be inspired by the conviction that they have a certain superiority over us. But what was that superiority? Those people are, at the same time, deeply religious. Even to a casual observer it is clear that India and the neighbouring countries are the proper realm for all kinds of priests. Occasionally, laymen mock at one or another type of priesthood, but, basically, the veneration and fear which are directed to them remain intact. Therefore I considered myself to be very adroit when I pretended to be a Buddhist. I already spoke Hindustani and had studied Pali so as to be able to decipher the words of the Sublime One from the original texts. I had also trained myself to walk barefooted, to control my attitude and gaze, as well as rid myself of the equipment of an explorer. Being on guard because of the speed with which even the smallest incidents fly from mouth to mouth, often for quite a distance, among the population, which is not very interested in working, I boarded an outward bound ship. Then with the help and knowledge of a friend, I quickly changed my attire in his cabin, and returned to the quay transformed into a mendicant monk. Such a radical change in my habits and regimen, also brought about a complete transformation in my mentality. I became anonymous, lonely, possessing only one garment, one wooden bowl and a stick. In a few days I forgot the street stroller which I remained. I felt myself to be renascent in bodily vigour and lucidity of brain, losing myself in the course of the passing days, weeks and months. I was living: that was all!

"I had thought that Siamese bonzes are indolent, and unoccupied. Our orientalists present them as knowing only a few ritual formulas and philosophical passages. However, I was quickly disillusioned, as soon as I spent a few days in a distant monastery, in which I was readily accepted. Every novice is attached to a 'Perfect One' for at least a year. He to whom I was entrusted, was a middle-aged man, calm and sympathetic. But, while most wandering monks whom we encounter have an absorbed attitude, my priest retained a kind face and a constant smile. With rather a strong physique, shaven head and delicate look, and that ecclesiastical countenance, which is to be found in every latitude, he reminded me of those wise and vigorous provincial Franciscans or Benedictines, whom one meets in Italy, and whose silent and always active intelligence is the most effective factor in the perennation of catholicism.

"Such was the man whom I served and called 'Monseigneur', and whose feet I washed thrice daily.

"The first weeks were delightful. I arose before sunrise to sweep the courtyard and put everything in order, while all the others were still in their cells. I revelled in the freshness of the air, which smelt so sweet because of the forest close by, the silence, and the exquisite sky. The whole of each day was as if perfumed by those morning joys, and for me the evening lecture was full of the same quietness.

"In spite of everything, I did not forget the aim of my journey and an opportunity soon presented itself to me to approach closer to it.

"It was the period when France set out to conquer Tonkin, and a fact little known to our diplomats was, that the hostilities aroused all the people in the mountain area where the rivers Clear and Red are born. And I was never able to learn what the reason was for the extraordinary anxiety among those very distant tribes. Anyway my Buddhists in Burma were in contact with the monasteries and hermitages lost in the vicinity of Lolos. There were some buildings to be erected there and such active work was allotted to me because of my physical strength. During the farewell, my teacher addressed a short discourse to me in which he expressed, in very careful terms, mixed with eulogies and advice, the fact that he was not too sure of my religious convictions. And, when being surprised by his penetration, I ardently protested, he smilingly lowered his eyes and said to me : ' But why then do you seek for poison? ' I was stupefied, because he spoke the truth. In secret I had prepared a blowpipe, collected long thorns, and was trying to get the poison of those terrible little grey snakes, whose bite kills in a minute. This was because for my further explorations I needed some weapons for protection against the felines. I hadn't whispered even a word to anyone about these preparations. I believed that I had been spied upon, and cold-bloodedly denied everything. But my venerable teacher retorted : ' My son, lying is suicide: for no tiger is ever able to harm one, who has conquered every vestige of anger in himself. You must still live in illusion before you will see the Permanent. So, go to the mountains where your destiny calls you. There you will learn how one, who has set himself free from the twelve chains, is able to penetrate the thoughts of others.'

"We departed in a party of five or six. All descriptions by travellers are similar, so I will dispense with mine. You can imagine the charm of that long, silent journey, which surpassed my expectations. But the nights were difficult because of mosquitoes and poisonous creatures. Despite this, by an odd chance, not one of us was stung or bitten during the two months of marching through the jungles, forests, rocks and swamps.

"I will omit discussing those long weeks required to build a Vihara. I became impatient, continually preparing new plans only to reject every one of them. We were on the eastern bank of the Black River. Consequently, I had only to follow one of the numerous streams which descended from the mountains, to reach the heart of Tonkin after a few weeks of travel.

" Our abode was set on a grassy plateau, surrounded by forests. The air was aromatic and charged with electricity. And, in accordance with the Scriptures, our superior ordered us a severe abstinence. I alone was entitled to go out to collect the roots and fruit, which were our only food. I felt myself to be quiet, detached, a little drowsy and conquered by the strong influence of luxurious Nature and the collective magnetism of that compact little group.

" One morning, the noise I made when jumping over a fallen tree awakened one of those terrible little grey snakes, for which I was just seeking. It reared itself faster than lightning, and my gaze encountered its fixed and coldly cruel eyes. Then it fled, quick as the lash of a whip. But, instantly the hunter in me was awakened and with a leap I was able to strike and break its neck. Then I extracted its fangs and collected the contents of the poisonous glands into the hollow of a stone. I decided to leave at sunset.

"That night was moonless. I hid my blowpipe in my yellow robe, together with my small poisoned arrows and immediately started on my journey. The whole enterprise was rather a rushed one. I had nothing to be frightened of from the men whom I had abandoned, but there was considerable fear of the country, into which I was adventuring, as it was infested by ferocious beasts. The sharp slopes of those mountains were inextricable tangles of high grass, thorny bushes and rocks where tigers lurked. I began to hear them on the second evening of my march, and from then on, so as to allow myself a little sleep, I had to spend my nights high up on the trees. There was no means of escaping the reptiles. So I simply commended myself to my lucky star.

"I found water only on the sixth day of my journey and I drank for a long while. Then I followed a small stream, assuring myself of its right direction according to the position of the stars. At the end of the week the streamlet became a torrent and later, as its course became stabilized, I decided that I could use its force. So I proceeded to build a kind of raft for myself, fashioned from bamboo and lianas and set out on it without any worries. It was only at the end of the second week that I saw a man. He was a pretty big individual, who was leading some bullocks. I would have liked to stop for a while, but could not, as I had nothing other than a scull to serve as the helm.

"The course of the waters changed twice, and then I found myself navigating a large river. The current was less strong, and several hours after having seen the man, a low, distant rumbling suddenly hit my ears and around the next bend it grew in volume, while my raft started to pirouette in a whirlpool. I realized that a rapid or waterfall was close at hand and my heart sickened, for I hadn't the possibility to manoeuvre like a native craft. I felt that I was lost if the waterfall was high or if there were rocks. But there was nothing to do. The river narrowed sharply between the steep walls, and the noise became deafening. I felt myself being carried like a leaf through the foaming eddies. Then came a sense of falling, a shock, and a dip. Instinct made me surface and I came aground, exhausted and bruised on a strip of sand, where I lost consciousness.

"A sharp pain brought me to, as something tore at my shoulders. An enormous weight was crushing me and a stench of putrefaction suffocated me. I was lying face downwards on the earth and could not move. I realized that a tiger was on top of me.

"It was not in any hurry to carry me off and its sharp tongue licked at the blood that streamed from my shoulders. By now I had completely regained consciousness, and with a lucidity born of despair, I sought for a means to pull out an arrow from under my breast: it was a miracle that I had not pierced myself when I collapsed. But most certainly the animal would kill me in its death throes. No matter! I had to take the chance. With infinite slowness I succeeded in getting an arm free and reaching an arrow. I was just trying to turn my body a little in order to direct my hit, when the animal let out a terrible raucous snarl and pressed me with all its weight, setting its terrible claws deeper into my flesh. I seemed to be dying from the pain. My convulsive movements turned me towards the river bank. Over my head I saw the frightening muzzle of the tiger. But now it was no longer occupied with me, for it saw something else. I followed its gaze and saw a tall man, coming slowly towards us. The excess of suffering brought me back to my presence of mind. I didn't even feel the powerful claws any more as they dug deep bloody grooves in my muscles. I observed the newcomer. He was dressed in a reddish-yellow robe, his naked legs and the right side of his torso showed the perfect musculature and admirable lines of his body. His bulging chest, full, broad shoulders, proud bearing of the head and the nobility of his features all expressed an uncommon power both physical as well as moral. He was certainly a European, or at least one of the pure Brahman caste with a skin colouring as light as that of a man from Provence. In spite of my dizziness I noted the harmonious movements of the man with pleasure. I wondered at his beard, as I wanted to see his face, but by then my exhaustion did not allow me to see more than a purplish blur, as I fixed my eyes on the piercing brilliant focus of his gaze. The tiger was growling. I heard its powerful tail beating the soil with the noise of a scourge on a hard surface. The man was only a few steps away.

"The tiger's claws went deeper, as if it wanted to leap; I felt its paws trembling and heard a sharp mewing. The man arrived and placed his hand on the flattened forehead of the tiger. The terrible muscles relaxed themselves, the crushing weight was removed from me and the ferocious beast went to the feet of my saviour, with flattened ears and bent knees. The unknown man stopped by the furry animal, and I heard him saying to the tiger in French: 'I will not punish you. Go! But never attack a man again.' The beast licked the naked feet of its tamer, then disappeared into the jungle.

"The man lifted me, washed my wounds, made a dressing of leaves and bandaged them with lianas. Finally, he prepared a bed for me on a neighbouring rock and went to seek fruit for our meal. After I had eaten and slept, he consented to speak.

"You will guess who my saviour was," concluded Andréas, after a moment of silence.

Chapter XXV

THE PRAYER

Now I will resume the account of our walk at the point where I left off. Although these remembrances may sometimes take a somewhat romantic turn of mood, I hope that you will understand the intensity of interest which I attached to Andréas's revelations, especially if you place your attention on the fact, that despite the many failures that I suffered in my search for a true master, I still preserved the enthusiasm of my younger years as well as an obstinate certainty of success. Those who have had a similar passion throughout their lives will understand me best.

Andréas, after almost having to acquiesce to my request, again became silent. He offered me tobacco and after lighting his pipe, left me alone and marched off by himself in the middle of the road, and was gone for more than a quarter of an hour. When he rejoined me, I remained silent, not knowing how to renew the conversation. It was he who started to speak.

"Well, Doctor, believe me! The trials about which Iamblicos tells us; the pits of Raguel into which Moses descended; the Olympic dens; the mysteries of Sein's Island; those of Samothrace; the subterranean retreats of Bramatcharia where all the gods of hell come to assemble; the dragons which prevent the yellow races from ascending the tower of the invariable Centre; even the tyrants themselves, soiled by blood, and the coprophages and sodomites, whom some people who have been led astray adore; a sojourn in any of these places, or the presence of any of those beings doesn't require as much energy as an ordinary day's effort, simple and continuous, directed to the Light of lights. In such an ascent there are moments when nobody, nobody, do you understand (and his voice rumbled), would have enough force to raise even an eyelid, if an angel were not sent to help him. Ah! Doctor, that is just the time when you learn to pray!"

These last words perplexed me. I had always considered the ancient Mysteries as the summit of human glory, for the conquest of which omnipotent will-power was required. And now, how my books had deceived me! Things were quite different!

"But," I asked, "about what kind of initiation are you speaking? About which prayer?"

He stopped and eyeing me rapidly from head to foot answered:
" I have forgotten all initiations, I can assure you. Nevertheless, I understand your position. You think: why to pray, if the Primary Cause acts with justice, goodness and perfection? Isn't prayer then a puerility, denoting the blindness of our hearts, or a tenacious egotism? According to your opinion, it would be like a stubborn child whimpering for its toy, like the pride of a being who considers himself important enough that the universe will be troubled because of him, or like a being which cannot conceive that its desire cannot be satisfied!

" O savant! " And his powerful hand rested on my shoulder in a friendly manner. " Did you ever see a foster child at the bosom of its mother, or a wife clinging to her husband's chest? Doesn't the buried stone seek the daylight? Doesn't the plant pierce a wall in order to find light? Even animals stop at least once during a day to look at the sun, and the ocean raises itself regularly to encounter the selenic effluvium, which revives it. People are seeking after happiness, and so do the planets inclining their poles. Isn't your own intelligence so vast simply because it has asked so much? Would you say that every one of those beings makes the right request? No, for the creation as a whole is imperfect, but it has a feeling regarding its impotence, as well as a presentiment of the higher state.

" If perfection and an ideal didn't exist, how could Providence be so cruel as to sow those feelings in our depths? The path of man is similar to that of all other beings: let him follow it in all the simplicity of the spontaneous sense of life throbbing in himself, and it will be impossible for him to err."

I stopped for a long while on the darkened road to repeat these words to myself. They seemed to me to be precious and final. I had never heard anything similar. My emotion prevented my reasoning, and all I could do was to engrave those words on my memory.

Chapter XXVI

THE PHAP

Andreas then continued: " The man about whom you like to hear me speak, Doctor, is the same as the one whom you saw long ago, at the funeral of Desiderius. In Europe they call him Théophane. I met him for the third time in Lhassa, where I was staying after coming back from Siam, following an extensive trip through China, Mongolia and Kiachta.

" I always remember those journeys with pleasure: the trains running through jungle and steppe; the silhouettes of tigers discerned among the tall grass; sometimes the dark head of a hermit with red eyes; the then rare companions of travel, an Englishman or American in khaki; a native gentleman in a turban and white dress; a mob of holy men of all kinds of sects; the hubbub of large towns, caravanserais and ports; the sweet charm of beaches; the majesty of the high, eternal snows that seem to hang as if suspended over your head; the grand melancholy of the sand, or grass and stone desert: that is the way in which I learned to find the beauty which dwells everywhere and in everything. I feel the same poetry in a six-storey block of workers' flats, as in the lofty Himalayas.

" I left the Deccan Brahmans, as I had wearied of the arid study of their occult physics, and hoped to penetrate deeper into the Hindu soul through initiation into their rituals concerning worship.

" So I reached Benares, provided with every letter of introduction, necessary to ensure that the contempt which we inspire in the Orientals, became no more than a slight mistrust. The politeness of these people is a form of savoury irony for those who know their true feelings towards the ' cow-eaters ' as they call us. It is not in just a matter of a few months that our officials or scientists can gain the confidence of an Oriental. But no philologer, or philosopher, at whom they merely mock, will ever gain that confidence, because both races, quite sincerely, consider themselves to be superior to the other.

I first devoted myself to the study of natural science, but didn't draw any satisfactory conclusions from these experiences of mine. I believed that the cause of my non-achievement lay in myself. I thought that my powers of observation and reflection were not sufficiently developed to extract from my work the teaching, which the Brahmans claimed to be in it. It was simply because I didn't have enough documents. Consequently I departed for Java, then went to the plains, only to return to the mountains.

"It was during my second stay in the Himalayas, when I experienced the trials about which I have already spoken to you, and of which Théophane gave me a conclusion, during his fourth visit.

"I was ordained as a lama. And because I knew the Wu-Wang letters and could more or less write in the Tibetan language, I immediately obtained a good position in the hierarchy and was put in the service of the Chief Astrologer of a large monastery called 'Péroun-Mabrou'. This palace or rather town, had a population of about fifteen thousand and protected the residence of the Dalai Lama, although he always remains almost invisible. My duties were to calculate daily the hour for ceremonies in a special small temple, because, in that land, everything is ruled by astrology, and I can assure you that the ritual is quite a complicated one.

"It was on one morning during that time, that I again saw Théophane. His face was the same as it had been twenty years before, but the expression of his features had changed, although all the lines of his body and all his movements remained imbued with the same superhuman power. On my way a caravan escorting an Annamite phap joined us. Théophane saw me and smilingly came closer. As soon as I took the hand he stretched to me, an inexpressible feeling took possession of me. I felt as if merged in a bath of light, of infinite gentleness and force. All the cells of my body from my heart to my toes quivered with the same feeling of deliverance, as if I had risen from the bottom of a dungeon into the pure air that sweeps the mountain peaks at sunrise.

"'How are you, and how is Stella?' He asked me."

At the memory Andréas interrupted his talk and smiled quietly before continuing.

"I wanted to tell Théophane about the work of my mature years, but he said: 'You will soon have some news from me,' and left with that magnificent gaze which, perhaps, you too will see. His escort, which had stopped on one side, moved on again. I remained watching his athletic figure ascending the path, until the curve of it hid him from view. I returned to myself from the kind of ecstasy into which his appearance had thrown me.

"Such was his third visit."

"And even so," I said to Andréas, "you saw a lot of great as well as terrible things, when with those Oriental priests."

I did not hear the answer, for I myself was very absorbed. The deep darkness in which I had erred for so long seemed at last to have been pierced by a ray of light. Nothing remediless could happen to me any more. If I had been caught in a blind alley, I would turn back, if a deception awaited me, it would be less hard to take because I had foreseen it. And if it should be a termination of my efforts? I was merged in my reflections, when a tram-car's horn announced to us the proximity of a gate.

We then separated to return to our respective homes.

Chapter XXVII

AVIATION

One evening some of us were speaking with Andréas about the extraordinary progress then being made by the science of aviation, and how the whole world was expressing its admiration for the boldness, ingenuity and skill of the fliers. But our host didn't seem to partake very much of our enthusiasm, and someone noticed the fact.

"But yes!" he protested. "I find all of it very nice, however, at this time, public opinion is diverted: people care less about indispensable things, which are rather tedious for them."

One of us mentioned about the development of civilization, national defence, the cultivation of energy, and the spirit of enterprise, necessary for a nation to maintain its position.

"Well, yes," replied Andréas, "these views are quite right; but will they work? Do all inventions bring happiness to humanity? You know that for nations as well as for individuals the only thing necessary is to help our neighbour. Undoubtedly, the aviators are bold, but if they don't get any aid at all, their science, selflessness and courage, despite all their perseverance, will not lead to achievement, as they have it at present. Man doesn't even guess just how much assistance he gets in everything he undertakes."

"Well, if Heaven helps aviation, it should be only an excellent discovery from all points of view."

"Heaven?" said Andréas, shaking his head. "Yes and no! Of course nothing happens without Heaven's consent. But it also allows things to be done which, ultimately, are only caprices, curiosity and covetousness. Heaven actually doesn't oppose all the people who like to put too much butter in their soup, but it did not order such a thing, because it commands just the opposite."

"But, then," retorted the young probationer, "if a nation doesn't go ahead, others will overtake it, will oppress it and finally, even conquer."

"Yes!" said Andréas with a smile. "That is true, but I did not say that a nation must drowse in quiet indolence. On the other hand, Nature doesn't allow it. Look at what happened to the Boers."

"Then the English were right?" interrupted an old official.

"Well, no! I didn't say that. The Boers were guilty for not

shaking off the torpor of their patriarchal existence, but Europe was much more guilty because it did nothing for their defence."

"Therefore, what should a nation do?" asked the probationer.

"The same thing as an individual. It should work, be interested in everything, hold its position, and not be frightened to disturb itself and, by opportunity, to spend money to help the retarded nations."

"Didn't France do just that?"

"Yes! And often! It is not without reason," said Andréas, with a degree of gravity, that France is a senior one among the nations, and I am not being a chauvinist when I say so."

"Oh!" said the probationer, who had travelled a little, "we are the lesser chauvinists. One should only hear what Americans, Englishmen or Germans think about their countries, in order to perceive that we really are modest."

Andréas made an evasive gesture, which stopped the young advocate, but remained silent. Then, in turn, I asked: "All right then, what about aviation?"

"What do you wish to know?" asked our master.

"Tell us something!"

It seemed as if Andréas was making an effort to remember, during which his eyes took on an abstruse expression. Then, while remaining seated, he spoke to us as follows:

"Everything comes to a man through clichés, whether their paths lead them down to us, or human desire attracts them; but very few among us are strong enough to be able to make a cliché detour from its route. Clichés constitute the whole world: they are the wholeness of God's designs, the work which He has prepared for us and for all creatures. There are cosmic clichés: the creation is the greatest cliché of all. Then there are planetary clichés, continental, racial, national and individual ones. There are also meteorological, astronomical, religious, scientific and political clichés. A sickness, a marriage, a catastrophe, a book, a disaster, a birth, a death—all are clichés. A battle, assassination, volcanic eruption, big prize, algebra, beauty of discourse, the gathering here this evening, are also clichés. Even objects themselves, like a cannon, a ship, a cathedral, political institutions, a tribunal, a law, a town, a mountain, a piece of apparatus, an automobile, are clichés. The aeroplane is also the materialization of a cliché."

"That is something from Neoplatonist Illuminism," said the doctor of literature."

"You believe, Sir, that Plotinus, Porphyry and others also invented something, that they did not merely reproduce intellectual entities?" and, without waiting for an answer, Andréas continued, waving his hand animatedly.

"No! You see, man is never more than a more or less capable or ingenious copyist, and the brain is only a photographic apparatus, more or less sensitive."

"What then, would you do with will-power?" replied the academician.

"It opens or closes the shutter," retorted Andréas. "But," he added with a sort of bow, "there are exceptions. Very strong and intelligent men can do much with their will-power, while we, the remainder, the common people, are led somewhat like a herd: it is the ordinary case of which I speak. And the same phenomena will occur in the case of a man who is eager to find or win money to make his life more comfortable, or for any other motive. Whether he seeks from his own desire, or God's will, the natural course of events puts him in the path of a cliché. If he refuses that cliché, it goes, but returns. If a man refuses for the second time, the cliché comes back for the third time, and if the man again repulses it, it definitely goes away. Nevertheless, if a man accepts a cliché only on its second approach, he will have more toil in his work than if he accepted it at first. And if he accepts it only after the third time, the action will cost him a lot of effort. What I am here calling 'man' is different to the being with which psychology is occupied. I wish to speak about man's spirit, his *True Self,* which is higher than ordinary consciousness. If the Self is interested in a cliché the latter stops. Then both beings remain together for more or less a long time: they penetrate one another. The human spirit, so to speak, magnetizes the cliché and builds an image vitalized with a greater or lesser amount of power. During that assimilation period of spiritual work, the 'digestion' takes place at the end, and the changed cliché leaves to continue on its way. Then the image rises just beyond the brain, that is the mental which I mean, and when the latter sees that image, an idea is immediately born in the man's head. He doesn't know from where it comes, or he believes that it is the result of his own intelligence, his researches. But that is not important. Nature has no sense of ownership, nor any ambition to be listed as the author. Once the first intuition has been perceived through the consciousness, that which is usually termed 'will-power', can be attached to this flash, or can neglect it. In the latter case the image still floats around the man for some time and if he definitely does not occupy himself with it, the cliché departs. Then it may happen that another brain, more hospitable, open or curious, will accept it.

"If the will accepts the intuition, then a series of anxieties, work and disappointments begin for the inventor, but the final success makes him forget all of them."

"I do not wish anything better than to believe you," said the philosopher after a moment of silence," although all of that is very similar to mythological legends. But how does this mysterious image pass into the consciousness?"

"I will explain it to you," answered Andréas, "when you first show me through words or in writing, how *zero* becomes *one*, how physical feeling produces perception, an idea. We are located, as you may see, in an enclosure, or, better still, between four walls. To study the geometry of 'n' dimensions is a ruse, but not a solution. Instinct, and intuition perceive the non-self through a kind of contact, or confrontation. But this isn't sufficient for intelligence, which wants to render the account to itself. Then it dissects, takes notice and distills the abstractions. If it is sane, it comes to a right conclusion, but often it is not. Then the scientific system does not correspond to reality."

"So, I have a good reason not to study," declared a young man, a powerful one with features indicating energy, who so far had sat quietly.

"No! You are wrong," Andréas told him. "Just the opposite, we have to study and make the mind work. Otherwise, for which purpose has the good God given it to us? But, at the same time, one has to remember that we don't know anything. To reflect, to deduce, to align the calculations, to make the working-plans, the equations, all of these are useful activities, but we have to put them into their proper place. For example, the fundamental idea, for one who desires to construct an aeroplane comes from a cliché, and he tries to realize his desire with the help of his knowledge of the laws of the physical world. To construct a bicycle requires knowledge of arithmetic, geometry and mechanics; but only instinct is needed to ride it. Those who possess a sense of balance will learn faster. They do not make any calculations about the displacement of the centre of gravity and they do very little reasoning about it, since it is experience and the effort of trying which they use. The same is valid for an automobile, swimming, even the simple act of walking. When we were little children, nobody made working-plans for us when they wanted us to learn to stand upright. Let us agree that the work of the intellect is always submitted to an instinctive or intuitional perception."

"But in turn, on what does this perception depend? Upon a cliché? And who directs the cliché itself?" quickly asked the young man.

"The cliché is a living being," answered Andréas. "So the

mowers mean a cliché of death for the ears of grain which are gathered in the harvest. They have their own existence, their personal destiny. In order to remain in the realm of discoveries ourselves, all the apparatus which man has invented in metal or wood have analogies with organs and groups of organs in animal life. The heart is a sucking and forcing pump; the nervous system is a telegraph, and so on. It has even happened, between deluges on this earth, that thirty or sixty centuries later, psychic tensions are becoming an apparatus; and much later, this objective apparatus will, in its turn, become a physiological organ. For example, during the course of the last Platonic year, the Atlanteans were strongly occupied with the transmission of thoughts. Their efforts resulted in the creation in the terrestrial atmosphere of fluidic forces, which account for our wireless; and, perhaps, after one or two deluges in the future, there will be men, who naturally possess a telepathic sense."

"What an imagination!" exclaimed the philosopher softly.

"Isn't it so?" Andréas said to him with his gay smile. "The will-power of a mass of men, used for a long time, attracts everything it likes: it lives and it evokes life. That which transmits thought, as we said before, is not the fluids, as basically they are beings. It so happened, that a little more than a hundred and fifty years ago a planet passed close to our earth, on which were living animals with many paws, protuberant eyes and shells, and looking like gigantic Coleoptera. They formed the cliché of the motor-car. Since about some fifteen years ago, in an unexplored region of our earth, there were a few pairs of winged beings; and it is they who, without wanting to, but merely by their presence, helped to resolve the problem of flying for the 'heavier than air craft'."

"If that is so," said the fitter, with eyes agleam with curiosity, "could we bring these creatures closer to us, increase their numbers, and do something in order to utilize them?"

"Not so!" said Andréas. "It would be possible, but it should not be done. When I say that it could be done, I mean that a very strong and very able man could do it, but I don't know of anybody capable of performing such an endeavour for good ends. You have to realize, if I am right, that the world of clichés is the key to the universal life. The Father does not entrust clichés to anyone other than those who are wise enough not to use them for evil purposes, and one has to suffer terribly in order to gain that wisdom. One must sacrifice, forgive, and work for century after century. All of us will eventually receive those keys, I promise you, but you must start to work immediately. Isn't it your opinion too? " he added addressing all of us. Then, turning to the doctor of literature he said: "You see, Sir, that in the end all of these imaginings aim at simple and common morality."

"Yes!" agreed the old official. "Let us work! Although it seems to me that when, after contacting a human spirit, a cliché leaves, it must be different to what it was when it came."

"Yes, that is exactly the case," replied Andréas. "We have an influence on clichés, an unconscious influence, but quite a real one. Only help your neighbour and you will thereby fulfil your duty under all imaginable circumstances.

Chapter XXVIII

AT COURT

I RETURNED to Ménilmontant the next week and found Andréas at work. An iron ball was attached to his bench for engraving, and with the instrument in his hand he was over-nicely finishing the foliage on a little gong, the whorls on which were framed in hieratic characters. " It is old Chinese writing," he told me with a smile. " The gentlemen who have their works published by Leroux [the famous Parisian publishing house] would be most embarrassed if it was given to them for deciphering."

Stella appeared and introduced a visitor, a big, fat, well-dressed man with exquisite manners. I had once seen him in certain official circles, but had not been introduced to him. Having ascertained as to whether or not Andréas had some time at his disposal, I asked if I could come back again to hear the sequel to a story, which he had promised to relate to me. He acquiesced very graciously, again adopting his paternal attitude. One would never believe that one was in the presence of a man who seemed to read human hearts, cure ailments and restore the weakened courage of a man.

" You will realize," he told me, " that after all you have learned about oriental politics, many reasons forbid me from giving the names of the countries and the persons whom I visited during my last diplomatic journey. It is not because I lack confidence in you," he added, " but all of it is filled with secrets which do not belong to me and therefore, I cannot reveal them."

" I understand your attitude very well," I answered. " And besides you have already bestowed a lot of kindness on me, and I am too much indebted to you to criticize any reserve which you may consider it proper to show towards me."

" Well! " he continued, stopping his engraving and addressing his wife. " The hours successively spent among the splendours of the ancient Orient and the modern Occident were pretty sad for me. I saw you there, very close, my friend, and you did not ignore my proximity; but at no time could I break those chains of state, which nevertheless caused thousands of little wretches, who came from all sides to see a strange ambassador from beyond the mysterious mountains, to envy me. Among the gold-laced diplomats and their staffs, I myself recognized many a face which

I had seen before; but not one among all of them let me see anything on his face except curiosity. I must have changed considerably. Even you, Stella, would you, without that clairvoyance which only love can give, have recognized in that massive person with face wrinkled by snow, wind and sun, and hardened gaze, the man who was once called (and he smiled gently) the handsome Andréas?"

His wife fell on her knees and embraced his thin but muscular hands. He lifted her without any effort and continued his story while holding her close to him. This overflowing of feelings, which no couple of that age could permit without making themselves ridiculous, gave birth only to pure emotion of a superhuman kind, because of its nobility of attitude, the gravity of their faces and finally, because of something that not even I could express.

Presently, Andréas continued in a calm voice: "Then one evening, when I was present at a feast, apparently dispassionate; when my thoughts flew to you, to your dear presence, from which only fifty hours of rail travel separated me; when I sought in vain for a ruse by which to defeat, even for a few hours, the surveillance of my retinue, I saw, beside the monarch, who was my host, the august face of Théophane. My body trembled and I could preserve only enough self-possession in order to salute and return the usual compliments. One of the parents of the king presented to me, under an assumed name, that man in whom I was gradually putting my whole confidence; for in the eyes of all those present he was considered less important than the high Tibetan dignitary that I seemed to be.

"We exchanged a few official sentences in English. He told me that he had travelled throughout the Orient and was very interested in the wisdom of my so-called fellow countrymen. I thanked him in the name of my superiors and we took our places at the royal table. My false position of Grand Lama gave me a place to the left of the sovereign, while facing me, Théophane sat to the right of the queen. My role was a strange one and I could abandon my difficulties only by forgetting about them as much as possible.

"However, I was given a certainty, stronger than at any other time, of the existence of a Divine Principle which leads human steps towards Himself, with a care and tenderness so great, as if our conduct could, in any measure, influence His essential immutability.

"But, Théophane was looking at me, and from his eyes came a power, a fluidic atmosphere, which clarified my confused intuition, co-ordinated my scattered energy and made me discover new and most magnificent horizons, from the peak of the Spirit.

"Don't see any magnetic fascination, Doctor, in this kind of inner ecstasy. My training deprived me of any passivity in that regard, and no gaze, or light could and did not compel me to cast down my eyes. But there is in Théophane something which escapes the senses, reasoning and research: I don't know what it is, I cannot explain it," Andréas added, directing his keen gaze at me. "I believed that I had passed through all the hells and paradises, which the Oriental sages have been able to discover since the last two or three deluges. But the appearance of any other being, the radiation of any other power, could never be likened to the appearance and radiation of him who had previously, as I have already narrated to you, saved me from inevitable death.

"I never saw Théophane use those subterfuges which cosmopolitan, political adventurers exercise with such shrewdness. But his walk, his attitude, the sound of his voice, look and gestures are extremely rich in mobility. At one moment his is the inspired head of a tribune, then a change to a paternal mood as father of a family listening to the complaints of his little children, then an irresistible smile of a god, or an unbearable sharpness of gaze. With friends his words confirm their unambiguousness, as if cast in sonorous bronze; a moment later, being at grips with a quasi savant, they are full of hesitation and polite acquiescence. On the edge of a street he will console with compassion a poor woman, whose husband dallies in a bar; in a palace he will coldly predict to a prince the disasters which are about to descend on him. He is resistant to crushing fatigue, headaches, insomnia and the worry of unsolvable problems. He resuscitates the dead, commands the sea, the earth and the invisible forces, and still repeats that he does not and could not know anything. He says that he has never opened a book, but he knows in which pagoda lies hidden a certain manuscript, the corner of a mountain where a rare plant grows; how to teach a labourer, a soldier, a diplomat, a priest, a sailor, a shopkeeper, an artist, a savant, offering to each one the means by which to see his technical deficiencies, the weakness of his senses, the imperfection of his taste, and the feebleness of his will. He is without any haughtiness, but I have never seen any person become familiar with him; without any courting of favour, yet rendering to everyone the respect required by etiquette, and most of the great personages of this earth feel themselves honoured to approach him. In brief, an enigma which cannot be solved even partially, except by a very rare Oedipus."

While Stella was occupied with the preparation of lunch, I

said to Andréas: "You know what legend tells us about the Rosicrucians. But if I have understood well, the final point of human evolution is the same: whether the perfect man will be called a true Rosicrucian, an adept, a friend of God, a saint, or a reintegrated one. The names are of little importance. Isn't that so?"

"Actually," answered Andréas, "the learned ones (here he was referring to the votaries of occultism) use identical terms to describe very different states and also different ones in order to define the same state. Rosicrucianism is one thing, but saintliness is another; a friend of God reaches a very characteristic development and so does an adept, and so on. But in the end everything is united, so as to become again differentiated in Heaven, according to the Father's will. Only, that which here I am calling the end, is so distant, that Buddha himself has not passed even one hundredth part of the distance, which separates us from it."

"In such a case, what has one to do, what have I to do who want to reach the state in which you are, the state of Théophane?"

"But, Doctor," quickly protested Andréas, "don't believe that I am something greater than others, I cannot do anything!"

"Even so, let me tell you that you are not logical. It is quite evident that you know and can do an infinity of things which I cannot even hope to do."

"I repeat Doctor, that I am nothing more than an average person. I am even less than many others. But your request is, so to speak a little narrow; for, how can you judge in advance what you need to possess so as to reach such a state and not another?"

"That is true," I agreed. "But what have I to ask for?"

At this point Andréas avoided my importunity. "Excuse me, I have to go to the cellar to bring some wine," he answered, in the same tone which he used when speaking about the gravest of mysteries. His natural simplicity, to which I ascribe the kind of charm which his memory still evokes in me, was like that constant mixture of the vulgarities of the material life and the sublimities of the spiritual, which succeed one another, without causing any shocks. I consider this simplicity to be the most indicative sign of true greatness.

When he came back, his arms were full of bottles. He stopped before me declaring almost vehemently: "Doctor, I know only one thing: one should ask to do God's will, to do everything one can and to do more than one can, and not occupy oneself with all the rest."

Chapter XXIX

TOWARDS CHRIST'S INITIATION

ANDREAS went into the kitchen to dispose of his load and then pumped water to permit the wine to be refreshed in wet linen. On returning he asked me to take my place at the table.

Stella was an experienced hostess. She believed that one should eat according to the way of a country, with a climate identical to that in which we live. And, because it was very hot that day, she gave us food with strong spices and a lot of curry. During the meal she allowed me to drink only a little water with some light, perfumed brandy, which she had prepared herself. Both of them rivalled each other in pampering me, as if I was a convalescent, and I let them because the cuisine was so exquisite. However, my host and hostess themselves ate very little.

I paid my compliments to Stella, but she laughingly answered me: "It was Andréas who gave me these recipes. For quite a while he cooked his own meals, and I had to swallow some most extraordinary dishes; but, please believe me when I say that people eat in the best possible way in North India and now you have had a sample of it."

In spite of everything I did not forget the true aim to which my curiosity led me, and at times I interposed a discreet question.

"What is it that you call the 'end'? Is it the Tao of Lao-Tsze? Is it Parabrahm, Ain-Soph, Nirvana?"

"All of them are only words," replied Andréas. "Will you be scandalized if I explain my opinion to you?"

"I will try to understand you," I answered.

"Well, I believe that even the greatest brain on earth is able to reflect the image of only an infinitesimal fraction of the Cosmos. I believe that intelligence possesses life, but it is not life itself. If one cultivates that intelligence alone, one is merely working over a reflection, whereas, in us, there is a Reality, and it is the Heart."

Well, I was thinking, it was something like mysticism, bhakti.

"What I call the 'heart'," he continued, looking penetratingly at me, "is not the contemplative sentimentality of a nun. It is also that, yes, but at the same time it is all the feelings, all the loves, all the hatred, joys, pains, laughs, tears, melancholy, the swelling of the muscles in effort, the emotions of adolescence, the ambitions of maturity and finally, it is the whole life we have to live through. To purify our astral body means to take douches in order to acquire magic powers; it is the act itself which must be purified, sublimated, unified. That is the true imitation of the Logos."

"Ah!" I cried. "I realize why Julian de Campis teaches that the one who practises the first book of the 'Imitation of Christ' is already half-way to being a Rosicrucian. Until now I had not seen anything in it except simple religiosity, without any depth."

"That man was eminently right," said Andréas.

"So, the words of the Gospels must be realized literally and absolutely? If one lives well, that 'rest' which Heaven gives to us 'additionally' means everything: science, power, transcendental abilities!"

"Just that," said Andréas, pushing a jar of tobacco towards me. "Read the Gospels in a very simple way, while using all your guilelessness. Gradually, that which previously seemed to you to be somewhat insipid will become tasty. The Law is simple, do what it tells you to do, my child. To serve is your motto. Who serves men, will some day be served by angels," he concluded, enveloping himself in a cloud of smoke.

Someone may think that perhaps these are only empty sentences, and actually, these words are cold and void set down on paper, but then, when they hit my ears, how they lived, vibrated and awoke the distant, sleeping echoes! How I miss those clear afternoons in that small, picturesque home, the calm of that semi-solitude, interrupted only by the occasional cries of children, or the noise of a rare vehicle on the street, and the appearance of that powerful silhouette, full of its affectionate, good-natured attitude; the view of that rugged, august face, and of Stella, busy, vital and gay, with eyes full of light! The melancholy summer of my life was so well accommodated to their magnificent autumn! And now today, winter has come to me, and only memory of them remains for me, but it gives me power, just as in the past their presence gave me the Light. This memory sometimes brings me that Light again, renewing it in the peace of my nights.

"Thus, my master," I answered, after a short silence, "I can abandon my speculations, can fight against the desire for knowledge, against a love for acting in accordance with the esoteric ideals, for as the books say, a Magus works according to the serene will-power which he has conquered."

"Those books!" exclaimed Andréas, while Stella smiled indulgently. "Ask her advice, she has studied all of the writers belonging to the Western Tradition : Germans, Englishmen, Italians and French alike. For my own part I have examined a lot of others. Let him who wishes to hold to them do so. But for him who wishes to accomplish his true destiny, even to the detriment of his apparently most noble desires, let him hold to the unique book, to the Life which abounds in it, and in whose entanglements, at the appropriate time, he will be permitted to put in a little more order."

"And really, it is much harder to live a completely simple life beyond all the vanities of this world, and beyond all false pleasures, after which the crowd strives, rather than be abstracted through all the days and nights of a whole existence while poring over arid texts.

"You will see for yourself, Doctor, if only you will try," said Andréas, "that the most insignificant deeds can have a great influence on your future as well as on those beings which surround you. Your philosophers make discourses over Cromwell's grain of sand, but they themselves have no doubts that many kinds of immaterial creatures are attached to man. You probably learned something beyond that from 'De Revolutionibus Animarum' by Loriah."

"Oh, yes! I have read that book in Rosenroth."

"Well! Everything has its own importance. For example, marriage which now they try to destroy by every means, exercises very far-reaching reverberations for the future of the couple, and is determined by deep causes. But it should be realized that research concerning that past and future would be in vain for us. Our true realm is just the *present* : to seek on this side or the other for it would be puerile. By this I don't mean to say that people doing such researches are in the wrong : all research is useful. But you, Doctor, you who wish for God's will, and myself who am so ignorant, we should both be satisfied to learn under all circumstances. Understand this well! To forget ourselves always and every where, for the sake of others. Love between husband and wife, is nothing more than an elementary school of love between souls. If that love is flamboyant, the lovers can be separated for the whole extent of the zodiacal epoch, and they will still feel their mutual presence, and the chorus of their prayers will rise in a single flight to the Father, to the Son and to the Holy Ghost."

Andréas stood as he said these last words, so I too rose to take leave of him.

Chapter XXX

THE SPIRITUALIST TOWER OF BABEL

Both Andréas and myself had been looking at a collection of papyri that was being displayed at the Louvre, and we were walking back uphill towards Montmartre. It was raining. The Opera Place and especially the Place of Havre, together with their excavations, puddles and picket-fences, were similar to a bombarded glacis. Trucks, buses, trams and taxis joined the sound of their horns, sirens and bells to produce a most deafening uproar, while the electric lamps were blinding in the morass. The thick crowds hurried through the darkness and the lights to reach the suburban trains. Evidently choleric devils worried these people and threw them out of the shops, offices and workshops only to toss them into another stew. The majority of those pedestrians were silent, but some chatted rapidly in clipped sentences about unnecessary, or crude things just as if the grave was not really quite close to all of them.

"And thus," said Andréas, who seemed to read my mind, "it is good for them that they are here and act so. Yes! It serves as progress for them."

"I was also thinking about another confusion," I answered, one which was much closer to my uneasiness. "They try from all sides in order to reconcile the different sorts of spiritualism; they seek the common points of Yoga, the Kabbalah, Gnosis, Buddhism, Taoism, Pythagoreanism, Catholicism, Hermetism, all the pantheisms and humanisms; they analyse, they reconcile."

"And," interrupted Andréas, with a smile, "they want to build a monument, but instead will only succeed in patching up."

"That is why I have that anxiety, and am seeking an indication, or a direction."

"Well then, tell me about it."

"Thus," I continued, "during these last fifteen years, I have read books by the leaders of different schools of neo-spiritualists, of spiritists, psychicists, neo-catholics, liberal protestants, catholics, who consider themselves to be orthodox, and finally, the seekers who themselves come to believe that they are adepts. Certainly, I believe that all these savants are sincere and convinced, and I am far from the suspicion that they are voluntary tools of an occult diplomacy. But, no matter what they say, I can, in the majority, see them as being antichristian, I would even like to say as being against Christ, if this expression did not have a medieval ring."

"You are by no means wrong!" answered Andréas.

"Listen! Madame Blavatsky uses astronomical concordances, which can be seen in the lives of religious founders, to show that St. John the Baptist was born at the summer solstice, and Christ at the winter one, and that He was resurrected at the spring equinox. Dupuis, Ragon and Vaillant as well as many others said the same before, and even collected analogous dates for Lao-Tsze, Krishna, Buddha, Pythagoras, Plato, and so on.

"Parthenogenesis, temptations, suffering, identification with the Absolute, everything is there . . ."

"But what does it all prove?" Andréas interrupted me. "Don't you see that all of it is only the argument of a materialist, who wants to deduce a spiritual resemblance from a materialistic one?"

"But what about divinatory science?"

"The divinatory sciences go from the physical to the mental, but not to the spiritual realm. From the mere fact that blood, lymph and reflexes in a dog and a man are the same, would you deduce that both creatures have the same intelligence or even soul?"

"I know very well that Christ is unique, that He is different from His predecessors and successors in the history of the universal Messianism; I know that His fluidic body, His astral and mental, if we may say so, were balanced, saintly, wise and powerful like those of the highest adepts, but that His Self, His individuality were a special action and will of the Absolute. In an ordinary man, the self is composed of a focus, it is not any simple principle, but a pretty complicated centre, in the depths of which slumbers the divine light of the soul. In Christ, even the latter was awakened, perfect, resplendent in His Self, His will. He is really the Son of God. The other 'saviours' were only men; but I believe that some of them have been inspired by God, at certain periods, and I still believe that they could and can help their faithful under the simple, but indispensable condition, that they try to practise the fundamental commandment—Charity."

"Yes!" said Andréas. "I see now what those savants about whom you keep talking to me all the time, have written: they cannot behave themselves differently. It is best, or the lesser evil, for them if they will go to the end of the line with their present train of thought."

I did not answer this time, for it was not the first occasion that I had noticed how Andréas did not press people to be converted to his own opinions. Then he continued.

"No! Our Friend did not say: 'My heavenly Father and I (my incarnate *ego*) are one and the same thing.' For, if His visible being was the Father Himself, neither men nor the whole planet could ever endure the dazzling splendour. But what He said was much simpler and more exact: 'I and my Father are One': the same essence but not the same substance. Also, He did not say: 'My Father, I, you and my disciples, who are initiated into My doctrine, are One, consummate in the Unity." But He said: 'Let them be one, as we are One, as you are in Me, and I am in Thee, let them be one in Us. Because these disciples know the intimate and true wisdom, they know that I have come from Thee.'"

Then I said: "Christ stated: 'My Father is greater than Me', and in another place: 'My Father and I are One.'"

"There is no contradiction, which you imagine you see in this text. Sometimes it is God who speaks, and sometimes it is a man: everything could not be told in the Gospels, otherwise people would not understand. Well, if you prefer it this way, everything has been said, but man doesn't understand it. It is impossible to explain to him about a hidden intuition, which he does not possess in himself. Time is necessary for that."

"It is true," I continued, "that there is some economy in Revelation. It is also true that human intelligence is growing, but isn't there only a difference in initiation between modernism and orthodox dogma? The divinity of Christ is incomprehensible, it is beyond and above intelligence; it is a phenomenon, a state which happened apart from the creation, from the relative, where our intellect cannot function except in just these two spheres. There has been a reserve in certain dogmas, an initiation, if you like, in the primary church, but there has never been a word from the priest which could give this light to the neophyte. It is God alone, Who has the quality and power to know whom He judges to be worthy."

"Yes! There is truth in what you say, Doctor. But nobody, you hear, nobody, has ever seen God in the mind. So, how can one discourse about Him doctrinally? It is quite clear that brotherhood, the obligation of virtue, the existence of the Divine, and human immortality are admitted by everyone. But if a school rejects prayer, because there is no God, because it would be unworthy of a man, or because the Absolute would not change itself simply to please us, then such a school would be wrong. There is a God, and man is a sufficiently inferior being not to be ashamed of his pusillanimity. Of course, it would be better if he did not ask for anything material for himself; but where is the person who possesses such Faith? And finally, the Absolute, no matter whether or not it can shock our human logic, does modify His plans and projects if this pleases one of His wise children. A new project does not embarrass Him, nor does any expenditure from His treasury. You must be well aware that He possesses illimitable resources. Prayer is like the antipode of Raja Yoga. There are many kinds of ecstasies, many more than the adepts know about."

"Consequently," I said, "if Paul Samosate formally denied the divinity of Christ; if Arius, in 325 A.D., the Milan Council of Churches in 355, the Council of Smyrna in 357, and the second Council of Ancyra in 358, taught the same thesis; if in 349 the Council of Antioch proclaimed this divinity and in 380, the Council of Saragossa professed that the human nature of the Christ is only an illusion; if the Council of Ephesus admitted both natures—all of this proves simply that the intellectual Light abandons men who do not keep the moral Light in themselves. Here can be repeated, together with a modern Catholic philosopher, the words of St. Augustine, directed to the Manicheans: 'Let them punish you severely, who do not know how difficult it is to find truth and to avoid error.'"

"Yes, it is a beautiful saying," answered Andréas, nodding his head. You are in a great hurry Doctor, but you have enough time ahead of you.

"However, one should not lose one's time."

"Well! But not in this way," he said with an affectionate smile. "To seek whether God is personal or impersonal? We don't even understand how a stone can, or cannot, have free will. If an oriental school were to say that God is not anthropomorphic, we would agree with it; but if it were to say that the Absolute is an abstruse entity, empty and formless, we would then disagree, for in such a case it indicates Nothingness. We don't know what is relative, so how can we comment about the connections of such with the Absolute? What can we say about the Absolute Itself? Let us not rise in our spurs, let us humiliate ourselves, let us recognize that we are really quite small things. And then will come the light of that unknowable, pure Spirit."

Then I asked: "Isn't the Christian Trinity also Krishna's Trimurti, the Sat-Chit-Ananda of the Upanishads? And their Atman, isn't that the platonic Logos?"

"No, but it is not too important. When you were still a small boy, was your mother occupied with your far-fetched ideas more than with your obedience?"

And then passing on to another idea, which apparently had no connection with the former conversation, Andréas continued as he used to do.

"The parthenogenesis of such extraordinary men, especially that of Christ, is not at all a symbol. It is a reality; it is even a physiological necessity which motivates the excessive tension of the work to be done. The Gnostics were wrong when ascribing feminine qualities to the Holy Spirit; for the Holy Spirit is just the member of the Trinity which will remain the most deeply unknown. No! God does not incarnate Himself in all religions. The ancient Brahmans knew very well about this; one only needs to read their theory of the Avatars. I am telling you about all of these things only because perhaps some of them will be useful to you, but this is the subject, which needs centuries of study in order to make the first approach to it with any success.

"Many modern hierophants, although rich in precious flashes of intuition, lack the practical sense in them. The resurrection of vanished cults, a revivification of petrified dogmas, skill in the Hebrew language, in Greek, in Sanskrit, or in Chinese, in the theories of self-deification, are all the respectable illusions of pious juniors, the touching guilelessness of the learned ones, lost in their dream worlds. But it should openly be said, that they are also forming the underground courses of a future religion, cemented with tears, sweat and blood. Those pioneers, who do not accept either positive science, or religious faith, grow old over their metaphysical hieroglyphs, phantoms and neuroses; they are lucky if, after twenty or forty years of study, they perceive that the symbols, arcana and rites exhumed by them, are the veils of the axioms of common sense, of a sane mind. But simple people feel the same through their instinct, because the human heart is the tabernacle in which shines that eternal Light, of which the great arcana of occultism are often only deformed shadows.

"Modern man is poorly balanced and Nature rarely gives birth to masterpieces. Consuming flames are burning in us, and the gods of money, glory, science and arts pull away their poor devotees and lead them astray. That is why, for example, a doctor finds so many psychopaths among the spiritists, mystics, and in the crowd of believers and pseudo-leaders of that crowd.

"The experimenter of the hyperphysical realm will be able to remain cold; but the sentimental one, who darts to the Mystery with all his heart, anxious and pained, desiring to touch the impalpable and to speak to the dwellers of hell and paradise, in brief, he who has all occult phenomena as his objective, finds a thousand and one opportunities to sink into any mystery, a mania, a partial mental alienation, or into pride as naive as it is exaggerated.

"However, all such sick people are pioneers; we should neither despise nor mock them. Even so, my dear Doctor, don't exaggerate your apprehensions. If you tell a certain Mr. So-and-So, a grand founder of societies, that he is simply a proud man, what good will you do, even if it is true, except to wound him? Will you change his heart? Look into yourself, and you will see that it is not so.

"Well, leave alone those initiates, esoterics, amateurs of ecstasies and abstracters of the quintessence. Don't provoke them. Listen to them if they like to expound their theories to you, and don't stop them if seemingly they end in wrong. Try to get some practical improvement from them, in their deeds and thoughts. That will already be very good."

And so, under this penetrating rain, my ideological enthusiasm received another shower.

Chapter XXXI

THEOPHANE

On my next visit to Andréas I found him painting pottery in the Norwegian style, as was fashionable at that time. While he was still working on his leaves, I asked him for an explanation of prayer, the act to which he seemed to attach great importance.

"One can see that you have never had any heavy blows on your head," he answered with a smile. "Your Kabbalah puts an axiom in the forefront of its teachings, which you have probably read without paying it much attention : 'Everything is a living being', as Siméon-ben-Jochai said somewhere."

I nodded in agreement.

"Then happiness, or trouble are, in a certain world, beings which possess form, intelligence and freedom. If your physical self is limited, your astral, moral, and so on, selves are equally limited. If an orangoutang is seven times stronger than a man, why then shouldn't there be invisible beings stronger than the interior forces which are put together under the term of willpower? When one of those colossi takes you by the nape of your neck and shakes you, as if you were a rabbit, what remains for you to do except to cry for help? That is prayer. If you are attacked in a forest your servants, providing that you love them, will defend you. Therefore, one should attract the love of God's servants, that is, to fulfil the will of the Father. That is the way in which our prayer is granted."

"Thus," I said, "the moral force of man is illimitable."

"Yes! If it is granted to him. But if he is deprived of it? Doctor, do you perhaps believe that even the smallest of atoms of your individuality are yours, or really belong to you? Stop deceiving yourself, the whole of your 'I' is a loan granted to your soul. And, believe me," he added, as Stella came in and sat down beside us, "there is only one thing through which man can conquer this world."

"Don't tell him," exclaimed Stella. "I will find a letter for him, which you know." And she ran upstairs to her room, then returning gave me a piece of Chinese paper, carefully protected in a leather portfolio. "Read," she said gravely.

There were a few lines in French, written in strong, hastily formed characters, similar to those of Napoleon I, but even more energetic. Emotion overtook me, without any reason, as I slowly deciphered the hieroplyphs. Here is the text:

" My child, you should not be disheartened being as you are; you have in you the eternal power by which subsist the cosmic armies. It is Love. It is he, the father of what we call time, good, evil, pleasure, suffering. His omnipotent virtue transfigures souls. It is the supreme Master from whom we learn all the lessons; it is the password, which removes the guardians of all the temples; it is the sword whose sight alone puts enemies to flight. He ignores the obstacles of evil, he sees only the weakness; he forgets the past; the future does not make him anxious; he knows only the present; without counting, he pours all his treasure into every minute of that present; he is the phoenix which immolates itself without end, and which, after each sacrifice, receives the rich treasures of Hope and Light.

" Continue your path, Stella, and have no fear whatever. If you have made the same sacrifice fifty times, be ready to make it for the fifty-first time, and again if you are asked to do so."

The signature was like an illegible paraph, but I felt certain that this letter came from Théophane.

After a long silence, Stella said to me : " I received this letter through the Chinese Embassy. It came with another packet addressed to the Ambassador, instructing him to deliver this paper, sealed with the imperial seal of the five-clawed dragon, to me.

" Fortunately, one of the attachés at the Embassy, who was my neighbour in Neuilly, where I was living at the time, so long ago," she added, as if apologizing for herself, " knew me, and brought me the envelope which most certainly the Son of Heaven had held in his hands. I have never been able to discover, for which reasons Théophane was allowed access to that monarch, guarded as he was by a most infrangible ceremonial."

We looked in silence at the five-clawed dragon. " Don't you find," continued Stella, " that, even after so many years, the words of that . . . man bring with them a virtue which I don't know, but which, like a breath full of sylvan perfume, restores hope and presentiment of an unknown Eden? "

" Who is Théophane, who is he, what is he? "

" But, dear Doctor, do you believe that I would tell you, even if I knew? Do you believe that if he so wishes, he would not tell you himself? Did you ever think seriously about the true discipline of real secrets? "

" In short, Christ spoke well when He said : ' I am here with you all the time until the end.' "

" Yes ! He said that to His disciples."

" Everything is possible for God ! Certain sects have announced the return of the Christ. I know that their Christ is false; but the idea is right."*

"Well, yes, dear Doctor! The idea is exact. About two thousand years ago there was a man in a certain house; he went about his business like men of today do, and in the evenings, he spoke to other men in the market place, just as we do in a café. If he were alive now, he would wear a jacket instead of a robe, and so on. You should become accustomed to these ideas, so that you clearly realize the possibility of the Friend's presence."

"But, to know that in such a street, under such a number, dwells a person who would be . . . No, I don't dare to finish."

"You see! You see quite well, that sometimes one must remain silent. To pronounce it would be terrible. However, do continue to discourse about human nature and the divine nature, about the inborn knowledge, experimental knowledge, and so on; dissect Thomas Aquinas, read again the Jesuit theologians of the Blessed Heart, and you always will arrive at the same result: nothing is impossible for God."

"Yes! I realize that one must remain silent. Anyway it seems to me that the simple intimate relations of a soul with God are so grave, so sacred, that, if this favour were to happen to me, I would never dare to speak about it."

"Finally, remember again that we were warned: 'If someone tells you that Christ is here or there, do not go there.' That is," he continued after some moments of silence, "all that we can teach you, as I believe in the matter of Théophane. The rest depends upon you yourself. You will meet him, when you will give proof of your good will, and will not be afraid to take the path to his country. Perhaps you will see him on a street, or in your home, or among important persons, or in a hovel, or in any other sphere; but certainly, he will come to you, once you have shown humility and charity which are the hallmarks of the children of Light. You don't know him, but he knows you; you don't know who he is, but he knows from whence you come and where you are going. Anyway, remember that a doctor is for those who are sick and not for healthy persons."

"And you have seen him only five times during your life?" I asked, a little disappointed. For surely, if a man of Andréas's knowledge, energy and goodness had received only such rare recompense, what hope could I have, with my vacillating will and lack of courage?

* This undoubtedly refers to the unsuccessful attempts made, at that time, by certain Theosophists to create a new Messiah from a Hindu youth.—M.S.

"On another occasion both of us saw him," answered Andréas, "and he will probably pay us a final visit, before we leave this earth."

"Thus, you are evidently thinking that you will die?" I said with considerable astonishment. My reading had taught me that a man, who had reached the degree of knowledge and power which I felt belonged to my interlocutor, should be able to extend his earthly existence for as long as he wished.

"The legends concerning the elixir of a long life have some truth in them," Andréas told me. "There were such men, and still are a few of them who have been on this earth for centuries. Even you know them, but I will not tell you their names in order that you will not be tempted to judge them."

"Then, they are doing wrong?"

"Yes, it is not warranted," he answered. "When a man is born here, his destiny is fixed. If he violates his norm, no matter how pure his intentions may be, he transgresses his rights. And he cannot do that without illegally kidnapping certain forces, without violence to certain beings, and without causing trouble and suffering all round him."

"Then, the best thing to do is to submit oneself in everything and to everything?"

"Yes, Doctor! One must learn to obey before having the desire to command."

The hour was late, so with regret I took leave of my host and hostess. But my store of new ideas was now large enough, and I had many opportunities on which to draw upon them during the following months.

Chapter XXXII

THE COMETS

At that time, there was a comet, whose appearance had been announced in advance. Everyone wanted to see it and I used this pretext to entice Andréas on one of those nocturnal walks which he seemed to enjoy as much as I did. So, one night an electric train from the Invalides Station took us to Val Fleury. From there forest paths led us to the plain of Villacoublay, from where almost the whole of the firmament was visible. This enabled us to study the long-tailed star at our leisure.

The beauty of the night was tempting and we descended into the dark and rustling forest, while talking about various matters.

How peaceful it was, to leave the feverish city; what freshness was in that perfumed air! The beauty of Nature remained serene even in its variety, whether we skirted little innocent pools, or removed the branches of the thickets where the noises of small nocturnal animals intruded into the silence, or when the moon, shining clear on the plain, showed us the high roofs and small towers of a farm, at least five hundred years old.

In the homes in the forest dogs barked from time to time and on the edge of a road we stopped for a moment to watch the palavers of the rabbits. And then, in a quiet voice, Andréas made one of his remarks about the habits of animals and plants. He showed me tufts of the noble mugwort, which feeds on small pieces of stone and refuse, the humble colt's foot which marks the hygrometric changes, and the proud good-fellow John, preparing its fragrant flower spike for the next moon, as well as dozens of others: that placid population of the forest, that variegated, but harmonious multitude, amiable and familiar like the delicate clarity of the skies of Ile-de-France, so well rendered by Corot. Andréas also drew my attention to the noises of field, rivulet and wood, to the anxious barking of a fox, which would probably be very afraid of having its hunting activities disturbed, to a rustling of insects, and a flutter of wings.

After leaving the Chêne-Sanglant and the cordon of Enhaut on our left, we emerged on to a sandy stretch, where badgers' holes criss-crossed among the heather, aspens and young bushes. At our feet a landscape of magic serenity was displayed. The hill, on which we stood, sloped steeply to the pool of Sarcelles, which sent its freshness to us. The low ground of Velizy, sprinkled with small houses, stretched away to the railway lines, and then, in the distance, rose to meet the coppices of Viroflay and Ville-d'Avray and the forests of Fausses-Reposes. The great moonlit silence bathed the profiles of the nearby hills, and myriads of stars animated the motionless sky.

We sat and smoked like two sachems, no doubt to the great despair of the badgers and beech-martens, for we were certainly disturbing their return. Andréas talked in a voice that did not resound, which he preferred to use when he did not want anyone to hear it. Once, when asked about the reason for such a precaution he replied :

" The fields have eyes and the woods ears."

" Why are there all those stars, and how? " I asked him.

" The 'why'," answered Andréas, " is a secret that belongs to the Father, and it is probable that He will tell us about it when we shall be ready to return to His house. But the 'how'? All parts of creation are alike and reproduce in themselves. It is just that while contemplating it, we don't perceive the continuous Whole : we see only the unco-ordinated fragments. This breaking up is not without reason and corresponds to another breaking up in our faculty of cognition. So, on this earth, we perceive human beings under the aspect of individuals, but minerals under the appearance of a mass. If we lift the eyes of our spirit to the inner sky, we will also see men as a compact Whole, and if we lift our physical eyes to the firmament, an immense army of stars, enlarged beyond measure, will be shown to us : the same sight as a microscope unveils in a molecule. The rhythmical battle of electrons, ions, magnetons, and so on, is nothing other than an infinitely small astronomy."

" In that way," I said, " you want me to realize a new point of view in the old Greek Hermetic axiom : *everything is contained in everything*. If I have understood well, the real ontology would list the following ways of existence : arithmological, mechanical, fluidic, energetic, astronomical, collective being and freedom? And every living form, every creature, morphous or amorphous, definite or indefinite, conscious or unconscious, would contain all these ways together, but they would all be so organized as not to perceive between themselves more than one mode of existence in the environment in which they live? "

" Yes! What you say is a kind of reduction of biology to the table of Pythagoras. This proceeding certainly gives some light, but it it still only a proceeding, and it will unveil to you only one aspect of Truth, although vast and just enough. Even so, human wisdom, as far as I could see when delving back into the secret doctrines, has not found anything better. But a man, on becoming pure, throws away these intellectual instruments and turns directly —without any intermediaries—to the beings, about whom he needs to realize."

" Is there an end to that star-dust? "

"Yes, that is a field," he answered, " to which the Father has set limits, and the Polar star is one of them."

"Really!" I replied. "If it is a limit, that star must be the farthest one, and astronomers say that among the stars closest to the earth this Polar star has the smallest parallax. This signifies that it is very distant from us; but there are some which are much farther.

"Then the earth is in the centre of the Universe?" said Andréas. "And the Cosmos itself has the form of a sphere? And the sun is not motionless?"

"No one says such things."

"One cannot judge about distance, size and brightness except in relation to us. Moreover, one can ask whether, by travelling through inter-stellar space, rays of light are not subject to refractions and metamorphoses, and could they be calculated, if such influences do exist?"

"I don't know about that," I replied.

"So, you see, that as exact as it appears to be, the science of astronomy is not at all certain. Therefore, its usefulness should be defined as purely a moral one, because it gives us an idea of our smallness, of the greatness of the Father's work, and through the successive errors of its theories and uncertainty of its discoveries, astronomy humiliates our vanity."

"That is about as little as all the sciences produce. But then, what is it, this whole Universe?"

"This Universe? For us, its inhabitants, it means everything that exists; beyond it there is only Nothingness. And in any case, if we could see things from the point of view of God's kingdom, we would perceive that Nothingness lives just the same. Also, what will always prevent the metaphysicians from agreeing between themselves and with one another is just the co-existence of two points of view in the human soul: that this soul is at once dual, both—created and uncreated, and the perceptions of the natural and supernatural selves are always mixing together in us."

"Then it is useless to try to know anything."

"I beg your pardon, Doctor! One must try, with all one's forces, not in order to gain any personal satisfaction, but, if I may say so, because of charity, so as to let live the rational and intellectual powers which the Father has entrusted to us through obedience and love for Him."

"But," I objected, "to take away from a man the bait of personal profit, isn't that equal to cutting off his hands and legs?"

"Yes! If the man doesn't believe in God; but, if he does, where is there greater bliss than to obey the One whom he loves? Which motive can give more energy, constancy and enthusiasm? If you are a man, a bearer of the torch of the Infinite, don't behave like the little fox which, walking here and there behind this tuft and that tuft of grass, believes that the only reason for its existence is to swallow as many eggs and crunch on as many chickens as is possible, and to teach its young to do the same. But we have a different purpose. Now, if you wish, we can sleep for a while on this sand, where we will not feel the dew, while we await the breakfast hour in Bruyeres."

After sleeping for some time, we resumed our walk through the delightful morning air, when the whole of the forest shone in a clear light, like a virgin coming from a spring, shaking out her damp hair. At that hour tomtits, wrens, warblers, blackbirds, and yellow-hammers were singing in full voice. The air was filled with fresh perfumes, and the leaves were a clearer green, the sky a more delicate blue and the clouds more vaporous. The grey past seemed to be very distant, the future promising, and the peaceful kindness made us livelier.

I attempted to renew our conversation. "The Puranas also say," I began, "that the egg of the world floats on the unfathomable ocean. But what about that ocean, where is its foundation and its shores? Aren't such conceptions, besides being undemonstrable, rather rudimentary ones?"

"That would be so," answered Andréas, "if the world's substance were everywhere identical to the earthly substance. But it is nothing like that. Also, very close to us, there is an invisible planet in a space, which is different from ours, and whose density is almost twice that of this earth. Further, an imponderable, fluidic projection of will-power can act on a heavy mass, and I could quote many analogous facts. Our consciousness functions only under certain conditions which limit sensible things for us. We cannot imagine different conditions. Nevertheless they do exist. The strongest reason is that we cannot imagine Nothingness, just as we cannot imagine how we come to see the stars and everything else."

"Then, this means that one should ask oneself whether or not things do exist, and whether there is something other than mere appearances?"

"But yes! Things exist. Man has life in him. He cannot

create any absolute illusion; the whole of his weakness lies in seeing the changeable forms instead of the pure essence. In every world and in every plane of every world the appearance is the proportional average between the essence of the object, its actual form, the pure essence of the perceiver and his more or less sane abilities of perception.

"This is the basis of the science of signatures. The trunk of that birch would not appear to us as a terrestrial expression of a universal power. The silvery leaves so much in movement like the red, green and yellow stars, which we can see at any time, are also signs."

"Then, people have some reason to see in comets the abettors of calamities?"

"Yes and no!" answered Andréas. "When rain is imminent, snails appear; but the rain doesn't fall because they come out. When a comet becomes visible, it does not provoke a war or an epidemic, but it is an astronomical consequence of a demiurge's act, of a cliché, the earthly social result of which is a war."

I had a number of questions to pose in the matter of comets, but this morning, as so often happened in similar circumstances, our conversation deviated according to Andréas's wishes. Despite this, he never spoke first and only answered my questions.

I had forgotten the queries I had prepared, or perhaps an indefinable timidity prevented me from putting them. However, I consoled myself by thinking that my master knew better than I did, as to what were my needs and what knowledge would be profitable or useless for me.

But as far as I can remember, I asked that morning, for some information on the role and usefulness of comets.

"When a man is sick," answered Andréas, "and when medicines are not helpful, we seek a different method of ingestion for the therapeutic factors, rather than via the stomach, skin, lungs, and blood circulatory system. A serum, for example, when injected, follows a different path than usual. A comet is such a regenerator of the solar system, that it too is a tonic. It brings something unknown into our zodiacal system and consequently—coming from another zodiac—is of an enormous dynamism: it restores a given troubled function.

"As far as the comet itself is concerned, its journeys are like studies. It gives many things to the worlds through which it passes, and it also receives something. After its completed world tours, its speed diminishes, and subjected to the reactions of other celestial bodies, its path is gradually changed, it slows down, and in turn becomes the centre of a system. You have a similar process in embryology during the first hours following the fecundation of the ovum."

" It seems to me that there are some similar things in the Hindu Jataka."

" No doubt about it; these are very simple things. But a comet has still a third function, not of any kinetic order, but of an individual one."

" How is that? Is a comet a person, like you or me? "

" No! It is the covering of a person just as our body is the covering of our individuality. All celestial bodies are garments and the beings which wear them each fulfil their functions, although we don't know them, nor can we perceive them, except to approach them by very hard work. The comets are their prophets, for good and for evil, they are their artists, and distribute to them joy, hope, enthusiasm and news."

" If you were to say such things in public, you would be judged to be an anthropomorphist."

" Therefore I am silent. Anyway, it is man who has been built and who acts after the image of Nature, and not Nature after the image of man. But we are so strongly convinced of our importance that we believe ourselves to be indispensable for the world's course. How many things would we know, if only we were humble! "

Our walk led us to Fonceaux. We stopped in order to do justice to a rustic lunch and the course of our conversation was changed.

Chapter XXXIII

THE INUNDATION

It was the time of the great rising of water which did so much damage in the basin of the Seine. It was completely impossible for me to see Andréas for more than fifteen days. I had to abandon my laboratory work in the hospital so as to assist with emergency cases. All beds were occupied, with stretchers in every corner, even on stair landings. The staff were overworked and supervision disorganized. Our old brick building had not seen so much activity since the year of the influenza epidemic. I ended up by putting a bed of sacking in the room of an intern, who admitted the sick at any time. But on my first free morning, although I was weary from lack of sleep, I hurriedly slipped away to the little home at Ménilmontant.

Andréas seemed anxious that morning. Usually so active, this time he was stretched out in a cane chair, slowly smoking a long earthenware pipe, that was brown and polished like those bamboo ones used for opium, when they are about fifty years old.

"A beautiful pipe," I said.

"It was quite white yesterday evening," he answered absently.

"Then, you have been smoking all night?"

"Yes, and I have run out of tobacco."

I offered him mine. A few minutes later Stella appeared bringing coffee and milk. She started to talk about the disaster, which, for the past two weeks, had laid waste Paris and its suburbs.

"Where is all the water coming from," she asked her husband. "Certainly, it is not only rain or melting snow!"

"Nor deforestation either," I added.

"I don't know," answered Andréas, "whether it is really necessary to search for the cause of this inundation; what is the use of it?"

"To prevent a repetition."

"Ah! And if there are subterranean sheets of water, which have changed their levels? Would engineers drill shafts two, three or more kilometres deep?"

"But are there waters so deeply buried? All Parisians know of a small lake which was under the Opera House, and another which is located under the hill of Moulins, the remnants of the ancient stream of Grange Batelière. It is true," I added, "that Savoyards tell of a subterranean lake into which the River Rhône disappears, and the Vaudois say that a similar one exists at the end of the Lake of Joux."

"There are many more of them, Doctor. In France alone, I myself know of about four large bodies of water situated at different depths, varying from two to four thousand metres, and several extend under one or two departments."

"In such a way," I said, "if deep upheavals occur, and these waters have some connection with certain holes, like that of the Côte-d'Or, where the peasants throw the carcasses of their cattle, rivers can swell without any limit."

"Yes, Doctor, but this doesn't happen except in the case of a break in the balance of the mineral mass. These modifications come only from the precession of the equinoxes, or a subterranean eruption, or from the birth of a new magnetic fulcrum, which can follow because of the proximity of a comet. And such phenomena do not happen by mere chance; they are desired by the cosmic intelligences or invoked as a reaction to social diseases, or ethnic ones, if you so prefer. Thus, it is wise, a priori, to let them be fulfilled."

"And if there was an extraordinary action by an evil power?"

"There are no beings absolutely evil. That which we judge to be such is only temporary, relative evil, and in any case, it never acts without the tacit or express permission of the Father. However, if there would be a place for the modification of the march of phenomena of this sort, the operator must talk face to face with the prince, lord and spirit of the earth. He must possess an exact knowledge of the conditions of the whole solar system, as well as be conscious of the plan of the cosmic clichés."

"And is there such a man on this earth?"

"You have a certain idea about it, dear Doctor," Andréas told me smiling with that marvellous benignity, which often transformed his immobile and rugged face.

"And what about us, can we do anything against such cataclysms?"

"It is a bit too late; what would be needed is some courageous men, fifty or a hundred years ago. At least, unless an innocent being hidden somewhere devotes himself to this, nothing remains except to endure."

"What do you call 'an innocent being'?"

"Well, someone whose spirit does not yet know any evil."

"How could he prevent the catastrophes?"

"The gods would make a pact with his spirit. We would not know anything about it, and probably the intelligence of that man would not be conscious of the fact. We will see only his misfortunes, the enmities, treachery, ruin and moral suffering."

"There is still one thing," I continued. "How does it happen that astrologers and seers have announced practically nothing about this disaster to the public?"

"Heaven doesn't like soothsayers. Long ago, through its friends, it has told us everything that could be of use to a man in order to amend himself. Everything else is nothing more than curiosity, intermingling, confusion, fortuitous flashes of intellect and fallacious lighting by the powers of darkness. For my own part, even if I knew the future, I would have no right to unveil it. We always imagine that our fate is of interest to the universe; but you know very well that we are only poor little creatures."

I made a gesture of discouragement and remained silent, thinking about those thousands of poor people, the anaemic women and badly fed children, without a home, fire and bread. Stella left us. Andréas kept silent, lost in a deep reverie. Outside the rain his the window-panes. Then drowsiness overtook me for a considerable length of time. It appeared to me that a man entered the room: he was tall, but I could not discern his face or clothes. However, I saw that he was radiating light. Then, everything became dark. I opened my eyes to find Andréas standing before me, looking into my eyes, with his head held high and his chest thrust forward, as if he was about to shoot away from the earth. Something like a fluidic aura radiated from him, fresh and powerful; something mysterious seemed to join us and I felt that we were both united ' in the name of Someone '.

Then in a flat voice he said to me: " You will go and find such and such persons," and he named a carpenter, and a grand lady known to the whole of Paris because of her elegance and the pomp of her home.

" In my name you will ask them to do three things: not to slander, not to defend themselves no matter who may attack them and to pray for whatever they would consider useful, until their prayers are heard, even if they have to spend whole nights in prayer: and you will engage yourself with each of them. And, if you hold firmly in this way until the day of St. John, some misfortunes will be spared your fatherland. It is Heaven which promises it."

Chapter XXXIV

THE CHINAMAN

The inundation was not stopped at all, but Andréas no longer talked about it. He had been expecting a visitor for some days, an elderly Chinese, and I was very surprised to hear his celebrated name.

I did not know how it came to be that this very high dignitary, famous, rich and powerful came to be a guest of Andréas. He arrived one evening after dinner, in a pretty democratic way, in a cab accompanied by a taciturn little mandarin, and a marine, who was on convalescent leave was also present. I had been invited to attend these interesting meetings, at which a yellow gentleman—a master next to his Emperor, of four hundred million people,—strong enough to upset the whole of European diplomacy, spoke in all simplicity to a soldier, an obscure doctor and an antiquary.

In order to do honour to her guest, Andréas's wife had arranged a room in the Chinese fashion. There was a large ebony bed, mats, embroidered panels, a set of shelves full of jades and bronzes, and a magnificent perfume burner standing on the floor, all of which completely transformed the small room.

"But you have had a lot of expense!" I said to Andréas.

"Well, dear Doctor, that is so. But Oriental people like formality, and we should never offend anybody. Anyway, when I visited this prince, all his retinue was mobilized. Aren't you acquainted with their forms of politeness? Then, just watch me and do as I do. We have to respect the habits of old people. Moreover, speaking in social terms, this man is very much above us, so let us keep in our proper places. It is for him to indicate to us, the manner of speaking he desires from us. And you, Marius," he said to the soldier, "imagine yourself to be an orderly to a Commander-in-Chief."

When we heard the cab, we all three went to meet the prince. He entered, after a mutual exchange of compliments, bending his tall figure and shaking his wide sleeves which, according to the Confucian rules, signifies pleasure. He spoke very good French, and his voice was loud and gruff. In spite of the good-naturedness of old age and his desire to remain courteous, his face, which was fat, motionless and seamed with numerous wrinkles, still showed the immense pride of a man who was conscious of his forty-five hundred years of unbroken genealogy. And, despite all the flowery eloquence of his compliments, too many things separated us, and I was often made uncomfortable by the clear, piercing gaze of his sloe-coloured pupils, framed by the narrow slits of his puffy eyelids.

He took his place on the low bed, and in courtesy, first smoked a pipe which Andréas presented to him. Then Marius prepared opium, and after having smoked some ten of such pipes in silence, Tsoun-Hing started to inquire about all kinds of things. He also answered my own questions. He had an astonishing memory, and, according to the custom of educated men, unceasingly quoted the poets of his country, indicating by a special recitative, different secret meanings, hidden under the outer literary form. Andréas, in turn, quoted from the classics, romantics and contemporary sources, and he too was able, equally well as his illustrious interlocutor, to suggest—at least for myself—unexpected symbolism by means of the melody of his utterances. That evening Tsoun-Hing spoke about the inundation.

"What, my brother," he asked Andréas, "say the mandarins of your country when your dragons become furious?"

"O venerable one, our learned people do not even know what a dragon is: for them it is as good as non-existent, always sleeping on the bottom of the ocean."

"Is that possible?" said the astonished prince, although not even a wrinkle moved on his face. "Then, if you permit me this silly question, what do your mandarins do when the deluge comes and later goes, although it is hardly conceivable, that they are unable even to foresee that happening?"

"They do just what the Manchu officials in your innumerable villages do. They issue orders to build dams and look for money to rebuild the houses. The neighbouring nations send help, and by this fact, as far as my small intelligence can judge, this inundation is beneficial, because it has permitted different nations of the white race to perform a gesture of fraternity."

"They really need it," said the old man. "But who can fathom the will of Him, Who has no will at all?"

"My left side," answered Andréas, where there is my heart, is the right side of my brother, and his left is on my right, and we both have only one heart."

"Great is your wisdom," answered Tsoun-Hing, smiling with pleasure, and his narrow eyes flashed although he remained silent.

"Deign to remember," continued Andréas, "that I am not a mandarin. But he," and he pointed towards me, "is versèd in the art of curing. But, in this country, men possessing wisdom without words almost never become high dignitaries, as it should be. So the law of Tao is realized. Merit lives with us in shadow and apart from honour and offices."

"I know that, seeing how you yourself live," interrupted the prince with a gesture of deference.

"Those who suspect the existence of the dragons do not wear any insignia, nor do they wield any power, and command nothing except their own homes. Among them, some have only to feel the wind of the dragons' wings to open themselves, while others, very rare ones, think that these divine animals live only above the clouds. But, alas! Among all the coloured people, I do not know the man, who could follow the six movements of the Dragon with Five Claws."

"Don't you know such a man, O veracious one?" murmured Tsoun-Hing, rising to stand on his feet in a single movement.

"Yin and Yang never separate one from another," answered my master, also rising. Then he added: "I know the man."

The old prince bent his tall figure and Andréas approached closer. They remained facing one another in silence, lowering their eyes, while their fingers performed quick movements, and in that way exchanging the signs of recognition of the most secret Asiatic fraternities. Later each resumed his place again. The pipes were lighted once more and rare liquors were drunk, while Andréas started to talk by addressing me.

"A hundred cycles ago, if we will count as the astronomers of the Heavenly Empire do, we European people knew about the existence of gods, goddesses, geniuses and fluids. Men resemble each other everywhere; our ancestors dedicated their cults to those spirits and thus violated the Law of the Supreme Regulator, just as the population still does in the empire of our very venerable friend. And so the world goes, to the extreme left, then to the extreme right. It calls this rewards and penalties and, if someone conceives after the example of Kong-Tse, the invariability of the middle, they seek that middle in the chaos of the five elements, instead of finding it in the spiritual equilibrium of the Path."

"Your people," said Tsoun-Hing, "lose themselves in the five elements and twenty-four asterisms."

"Yes, you see correctly, O old man with sharp intelligence," answered Andréas, staring at his interlocutor, who seemed to be asleep. "But remember those days, when I received, without being worthy of it, your virtuous hospitality. During those years I entered into the gateless temples . . . and I went out of them."

"I do remember, my older brother."

"Don't the lamas of the Roof of the World say that Tzong-Kapa came from the West?"

"Yes!" said the prince, observing me, for he seemed to notice how much my interest was aroused. "You speak like a very old man, and I will try to answer you with the same wisdom, while not achieving it. But milk suits a foster-child, elaborate cuisines are for an old man, and healthy rice and fish are for a mature one. Perhaps our younger brother would tell us what he thinks about those dragons, which make the river overflow and the clouds to burst?"

"I can only read printed books, and in them I have seen that all the nations believe in similar things. The subjects of the Heavenly Empire also know about the unicorns, lions, strange birds and fish of dreams. Our Aryan brothers have their vulture Garuda, their swan Hamsa, and their many-headed serpents and Gandharvas, as well as many kinds of beings which visit the contemplations of the naked ascetics in their forests, while those of Tibet, on the icy plateaux and those of the Crescent in their torrid deserts, see all sorts of creatures passing in the night. What can I say, about which both your wisdoms do not already know, O venerable fathers? I have only read some very old books. All people in their natural state know about the existence of the dragons, as well as animals and beings which our narrow sight cannot perceive. They are everywhere: in the ocean, in a gulf, in a strait, in a lagoon, lake and pool; in a mountain chain, in a peak, precipice; in a desert, in a city, a forest; in a stone, plant and tree; in cloud, air, and under the earth; in thunder, wind and rain; in a continent, nation and people; in the Sun, Moon and stars; in the eclipse and in a comet, a meteor; in the night, day and dawn; finally, in the month, a cycle and a year. I ask you! Is it true, O knights of the dragon?"

"Lao-Tsze said that they are wandering forms."

"In the meantime," said Andréas, "old Lao-Tsze wrote that every being has a name, which is not a Name, although contained in the Name."

And Tsoun-Hing, approving the comment, recited in his growling voice the verse which Andréas had mentioned in his remark.

"Could that old sage say that indefinite things have a name? Thus everything is an individual? What do you think, O very prudent one?"

"You entered into the temple without doors," answered the Chinese.

"Look at this rock, for example, look at it with all your powers," continued Andréas addressing me. "I mean that not one of your powers is to be occupied elsewhere. For that purpose set your immobilized bódy free from any shuddering action it may perform, even from the very remembrance of such an act; remove every former polarization from your fluids; remove every feeling from your heart, and every thought which is not about this rock from your intelligence. Look, with your eyes lowered; listen with closed ears; feel with immobilized hands. At first you will not see the spirit of that rock, but only different kinds of beings which are like envelopes, guardians, travellers. Only after you have removed them will you see the genius, and, if your virtue is equal to your force, you may be able to talk with it, because your spirit knows every idiom."

"A somnambulistic subject? Magic?" I asked.

"You know very well that magic is forbidden," answered Andréas. "You will never find any medium able to penetrate so far."

"What then?" I said. But Andréas continued, seemingly giving me no answer.

"Yes, everything exists: the fauns, satyrs, nymphs, dryads, hamadryads, and demi-gods; Hercules and the others, the goddesses, Aphrodite and her sisters, the Muses, the Fates and Furies, Zeus and all his pairs; and jinn, and houris, and kobolds, trolls, gnomes, nixies, fairies, elves, sprites, brownies, korrigans, all of them are not at all merely the hallucinations of superstitious peasants. Teutad, Thor and Walhalla; the Hindu deities having four and ten arms, and their saktis; the Egyptian gods in animal form; catoblepas, basilic and roc, and the whole menagerie of the Middle Ages, all of them and many more all exist, and at some time, all of them have lived on this solid earth, on the plains, in the forests and cities, or they will live there."

"Do you really wish to say, that all of them are real creatures, individuals, like a dog or a horse? That they are not merely symbols of meteorology, astronomy, philosophy, or of natural forces? Would they be animals or half-human half-animal? Then what about the demonologists like Peter of Abano, Agrippa, and Rosicrucian legends, Sinistrari, de Guaita?"

"Nature makes the beings: it is man who makes the symbols," answered Andréas, smiling. "Do you believe that the bull of Assur, with a human head and the Sphinx of Thebes were only cleverly combined images? When a Rishi sings: 'The soul of a yogi mounts the divine bird Hamsa, which takes him on a flight as fast as a light ray to the dwelling of the supreme Brahma', do you believe that he quite foolishly does not say what he saw? Do you believe that he is amusing himself by playing at being a rhetorician? Then you are neither a professor of philosophy, member of some mysterious brotherhood like the so-called Rosicrucians, nor a Buddhist, nor a Templar!

"But," he added, stopping to smile and bending himself towards the old prince, "if my very respected guest permits, we could learn a lot of things from his eloquent mouth, which his people know and which they keep secret from those with coloured faces."

"I am ignorant," said Tsoun-Hing, in a modest and grave tone. If I speak it is only to obey my older brother, and because sometimes it is necessary that such a thing should be said, even by an unworthy voice. I have forgotten many characters which I once admired and copied with my respectful, but unskilled pen. Ah! How virtuous were the sages of ancient times! And it was just then that they were praised when, during my long career, thanks to their invisible presence and steady assistance, it was granted to me to do something useful for the people in accordance with the Supreme Will! But please forgive a feeble old man, who in trembling approaches naked before his beloved ancestors.

"And what will I say," he continued after a short silence, "which our younger brother has not read in our old books? Ten thousand beings, animals of the air, earth, waves and forests, and of fire, all appear on the rice-field, grow, then diminish and disappear. And so the cruelty of men evokes demons in the reverse world, and such demons suborn their victims; later, when many crimes have been committed, these demons take the shed blood and dead flesh, and their princes build bodies from them. Thus appears the tiger, which kills the same men, whose malice has opened for it the door of the earth. And when the 'man-eater' has already killed all those men who bear its mark, its power diminishes, its body becomes smaller, and in the course of many cycles the tiger becomes a cat, an elegant, egoistic and timid creature.

"Similarly, long ago, there were gigantic lizards and crustaceans the size of a bull, and many other creatures which have vanished in the reverse of this visible world."

"The hidden knowledge flows from your lips, O very venerable one," said Andréas. "Tell us more!"

"Thus are the ten thousand beings," continued the prince. "A hundred families appear on the earth, but they have already appeared on thousands of other earths. They first dwell in the dreams of the wise men, then these creatures are born with scales, feathers, or fur, with or without bones; then they diminish and disappear from the view of the wise men. Later the gods take them to other earths. Thus this world is a sea with innumerable waves. Therefore, look on it, younger brother, with a pious and firm heart. No being should be feared or disdained, and know that you yourself are nothing, and you will become everything. But, if you wish to become everything, you will have to be reduced to nothingness, like a clod crushed in a mortar."

"Speak further my very wise father," I requested the old mandarin, because a kind of emotion animated his discourse and I felt that a grateful sympathy was growing for him in me.

"I will remain silent," he answered, shaking his pipe, while the marine rounded a ball of the required opium over the fire. "Yes! I will keep silent," he repeated, addressing Andréas, "because only you, who have fought the dragon, can act, while I can only speak. You are the father of this junior brother; open one of the white doors for him, cut off his ear here, so that he can hear on the other side; close his eyelids to this darkness, so that he may see the torches held by the lions with short manes; Wen-Wang comes with us."

Then, turning his face towards the wall, he remained in silence.

"Did you hear that?" said Andréas. "Do you wish to try?"

"Try what?" I asked. And then realizing what was meant I added. "Yes, provided that you will be with me and it will not last too long."

"One or two minutes? Leave your pipe aside and be seated comfortably."

But hardly had he spoken the last syllable, when the room disappeared from my sight and I saw myself standing with Andréas, who held me by the arm, while Tsoun-Hing sat looking at us. A gate from the Far East appeared and disappeared; then came a large river, covered with malodorous junks, followed by ricefields, a mountain, trees and a cave. Everything passed very quickly, like a movie film in a cinema, but with extreme clarity. Suddenly I found myself in the nave of the cathedral of Notre-Dame in Paris, then in the first crypt, which is known to everybody; next in the second one, which was, according to my considered certainty, the floor of a temple of Jupiter. Finally, in the third crypt I saw large stones, Gallic lances, a rusty sickle, and the white phantom of a druid. I heard a dull blow, as if made by a strong blade striking on stone; then the sound of an enormous breathing, heavy and rattling with death, and a few steps ahead of me I saw a monstrous body extending into the sticky shadows. It seemed to be about fifteen metres long, with flat paws, twisted legs, that were slender and naked and covered with unhealthy looking skin, and which could not possibly lift that body. It was grey, glossy, viscous; the back was covered with scales and surmounted by a fish-bone type ridge, jagged with pointed spines. Its ferocious head, furrowed with deep wrinkles, ended in the enormous beak of an octopus, filled with several rows of teeth. Filamentous, trembling antennae protruded from the half-open beak, and tried to extend themselves far enough to touch Andréas and myself. But my master merely raised his hand, as if to calm a snarling dog. The monster shone with chatoyant colours, livid and poisonous, while its membraneous wings hung shuddering on the earth. Its big, protruding, naked eyes, with their greenish, sickly eyelids and unbearable gaze, threw human glances at us.

The beast was evidently furious, and its rage was further augmented by fright, for Andréas obviously fascinated it.

"You see," he said to me suddenly, "one word would suffice to induce this animal to terrible anger. It would then demolish everything, and in three days, high above our heads, the River Seine would disappear and Paris would collapse. Will you remember this? Will you try to understand?"

I nodded in the affirmative, and everything disappeared. I again found myself in the Chinese room, with its three occupants in the same positions.

"Well, dear Doctor," Andréas said to me, speaking slowly with expressionless face and thereby answering my hidden question. The fire of his gaze became unbearable, but he retained his fraternal kindness. "Work! Work! And keep awake!"

"Ah!" said the loud, gruff voice of Tsoun-Hing, sounding without echo in the heavy air of the room. "We sons of Heaven remain motionless, and, by its secret essence, the Path comes to us. But you, men of coloured faces, your hearts burn. Which of us has taken the shortest way?"

"Omnipotent brother, so very old and wise," Andréas replied, "what is the Way? It is Movement. What is Movement? It is Life. What is the result of the Way? A crowd of innumerable living beings, that is—the Truth!"

Tsoun-Hing raised his hand to order another pipe, but midnight was striking. The young secretary entered, and as I took leave of him, the old prince quietly turned his face towards the wall, while Andréas continued to smoke in the opaque atmosphere of the room.

Chapter XXXV

THE PYRAMID

I HAVE always believed that in every epoch, no matter how many divergent doctrines are manifested in it, there will always be among those inimical sisters a common link, a secret architecture, a profound armature, in which such doctrines, in the ultimate meaning, are only discordant resonances of the same word, inaudible for the masses, but perceptible to the few.

On that evening I was seeking from Andréas, an indication which would allow me to catch an example of this secret unity, which organizes the metaphysical world. A completely impartial mind must find the resemblance between, say, Alfred Fouillée, Secrétan and Bergson, also, for example, between Taine, Péguy and M. Seillière, and between l'Action Française, la Démocratie and Clarté. And also go beyond all the points of contact placed in that region of the penumbra where loom the classical disciplines of the intellect, romantic spirits of the passions and regimes of the will, but where gradually the Spiritual Sun appears.

Consequently I tried to arrange and put into order the arguments of different thinkers. Andréas listened to me patiently, here and there putting in a few appropriate words.

"Every rule," he said, among other things, "is bitter from the outside and sweet inside; contrarily, every caprice produces inverse sensations. Every passion is exhausting, every action regenerates according to the quality of its motives, and everything alternatively rushes from one extreme to the other. Also, truth doesn't belong exclusively to the intellectual realm: a brute can catch it at the moment when it escapes from a most liberal thinker. Truth does not at all reside either here or there; it is not one thing plus another; and it is not this combined with that. Neither analysis nor synchronizing, nor synthesis nor analogy are able to embrace it infallibly.

"The full view of a tree cannot be obtained either from above or below, or by turning round it, or if one would put oneself into its vital focus, which is impossible. The prehension of the true, admits of a series of treatments of phenomena and concepts, very similar to chemical manipulations. Equally well there is a psychological as well as a philosophical catalysis; an affinity exists between sentiments and ideas; a passionate crisis is similar to a battle of ions in an atom, and inspiration is like a flash that combines heterogeneous bodies."

"In which place in the Gospels can there be found opinions about this matter?"

"A little everywhere," replied Andréas. "In the parable about the Virgins, then in the one about the wedding and also perhaps, in a story which happened during the stay of the Holy Family in Egypt. I will relate it to you.

"You know that because of hostility from some people, the family changed its place of residence several times, and finished up by settling not very distant from a small fishermen's village, close to the Great Pyramid. Nomads camped beside it, but they were of a completely different type to the local natives, speaking a foreign language among themselves and refraining from mixing in with the life of the villagers, although these nomads treated their sick. They were said to be natives of the Numidian West, where the Bedouins live, although they were rather similar in looks to the ancient Ninevite invaders. They constantly observed the stars, and the peasants noticed that those people left and returned in such a way, that no trace of their camels could be found in the sand. They were believed to have discovered ancient underground passages, and they were also feared.

"Their servants, who went to the village every day to get water or to buy grain and fruit, soon knew about the arrival of a poor Jewish family. St. Joseph went to work and the Holy Virgin, who encountered some of the nomads, talked to them and explained her story in a few words.

"One evening our exiles visited the Pyramids. The sun was sinking low and in the shadow of those enormous triangles of stone, the fires of the Bedouins' tents grew red. There lay the beginning of the desert, the world of petrified immensity, where only thunder and winds speak, and the solitude surrounds the traveller and sets him face to face with himself alone. Black kites flew in the glowing sky, while its declining splendour painted their poor patched cloaks with royal pomp. One after another the tall, bearded Bedouins raised themselves to greet old Joseph and his young, silent wife, and let the little blonde child play.

"The little one had already astonished them. One day, in the distance, they had seen a lioness licking the boy's feet, and on another occasion, a ferret, usually too timid to leave its hole during midday, was seen running with him. They also noticed that snakes left their lairs among the thorny bushes, and also some other things. Finally, one of the hermits asked Joseph the birth date of the charming child.

"While his father and mother talked, the little Je*s*us, in the shelter of a rock, seemed to be amusing himself by tracing some lines in the sand with a reed. Then he ran to the oldest of the Bedouins and led him to his work, just as all children do when they have built some fragile wonder. But, as soon as the old man with an impassive face looked at the drawing, he became pale and leaned quickly over the confused geometry. In its large isosceles triangle he discovered the plan of the inside construction of the Pyramid: the crypt, the rooms of the King and the Queen, the passageways, the pits, in brief—everything. But those nomads were the only ones who knew the secrets of those structures. Inheritors of the antediluvian traditions, they knew that the Pyramid, together with the Sphinx was one of the stony books in which the patriarchs deposited all the keys of their knowledge. The geodesic position of the Pyramid, its orientation, exterior and interior measurements, the angularities of its edges and passageways, the position of its rooms, all give the elements of general and earthly astronomy, geography, sociology, laws and political, philosophical and religious history, as well as those of physiology and psychology."

"But," I interrupted, "the works of Brück, Piazzi-Smith and Lagrange tell us the same."

"Yes!" continued Andréas. "But those scientists didn't tell everything. Apart from that, in the Ptolemaic epoch nobody had any idea about it. So, when our nomad had looked well, measured and studied the drawing of the little child, and when he recognized its exactness, his surprise became enormous and a feeling of profound fear arose in his soul."

"Indeed!" I exclaimed. "I can imagine how such a man would feel, who, after having battled with all his ideas, vanquished all his passions, faced all the gods, and finally, having achieved certainty, saw his treasure in the hands of a child, and is confronted by a miracle: him for whom every miracle was only an application of a certain secret formula! What a collapse of his whole self!"

"Yes!" answered Andréas. "The earthquake shows its maximum power just on the most solid mountains. Now, in order to finish my story: when the small child considered that its work had been admired long enough, it again took a reed and finished the drawing, tracing some new lines inside its original triangle, which resulted in the figure of the cross, exactly similar to that which the Jewish executioners were to raise on the Mount of Calvary. It said nothing to the Bedouin except indicating the points of the landmark. After having measured and calculated the lines, the brown face of the adept became ashen and his tall figure prostrated itself at the feet of the mysterious little being. But it merely behaved as an ordinary child: sat beside the frightened man and started to play with the fringe of his cloak."

"Your story is curious," I said. "Doesn't it refer to the ancestors of the Rosicrucians of the XVIIth Century, to that school which pretends to have had its beginning from Enoch, a son of Cain, the powerful centralizer, who takes the name of Elias, is attracted to the High and who develops himself through hardship and hope?"

"That is yet another legend," replied Andréas, raising his hand. "What I would like you to see is the way in which that solitary Libyan, possessor of all the elements of the combination, from which Truth is born, could perceive and catch that truth. Think a little about it."

"Well, on one hand there is Nature, the sunset, centuries old monuments, and a few men who study them, and on the other three foreign persons, who neither study nor say anything. Two of them are basically concerned only with the preservation of the third, who is the smallest and least noticed of all. And yet, he shows them the Truth while playing. What more?" I asked.

"But your analysis is complete," answered Andréas. "That is the way in which one finds the Truth. You don't understand me, because you don't stop your reasoning. At certain moments one must not reason any more, but simply—see. That is why woman accepts better than man, the intuitional truths which form the primordial rays of the Truth. May God be agreeable that woman doesn't lose this beautiful privilage, and begin to reason just as a man does.

"Of course, we have to reason, that is certain, but only to a degree and not all the time. Clearly, one should not become blind. We must stop the mental machine when it starts to revolve in emptiness and then start to look, feel and inhale Life, to live and to love. Here, dear Doctor, is a method which actually is not a method; but only those who have previously tried all other methods are able to realize its use."

Chapter XXXVI

THE AVE MARIA

Andreas and Stella had recently returned from travelling in Poland. There they had been the guests of a great landlord, who had showed them all the corners of his immense estates. Andréas had brought back some rare plants and a peculiar kind of mistletoe from which he wanted to extract some unknown medicine. He spoke to me for a long time about these preparations, then the conversation turned to the Polish people, whom he praised.

"Have you ever noticed, dear Doctor, how those people love the holy Mother of God, their ' swienta Matka Boza'? "

"They truly are," said Stella, " very much devoted to the Virgin, and in all classes of their society, except the intellectuals who used to go to Germany for their studies. It is a curious thing that such a popular cult, which flashes spontaneously from the hearts of the crowd, is almost always created on the plains, among the forests where there are many oaks."

" Yes ! " I replied. " They have their famous pilgrimages to Czenstochowa, likewise to the vanished forest of Beauceronne where there is the ancient black Virgin of Chartres. Also in Britanny, where people love the Virgin very much, there are plenty of oaks; even in Meudon the seminarists of Fleury erected a statue of the Virgin carved from oak."

" But," objected Stella, " Lourdes, Salette, Puy-en-Velay are in the mountains."

" Yes," answered Andréas, " but those centres were created from Above, they don't stem from human beings."

" Why," I asked, " are all the miraculous Virgins on the plains black, and why do people often admire them in crypts? What is the reason for this? "

" But, dear Doctor, the oak, mistletoe and crypts all go together. You know that the most wonderful medicines can be extracted from the most harmful substances. The mistletoe is a parasite, and the oak is a tormented tree, just like the olive, which suffers a lot in order to grow, and which yields the olive oil from which the symbol of peace has been made."

" How does it happen that the olive tree suffers? "

" Most certainly it does. Did you ever look at an olive tree? Electric light can be produced from coal, and when the ancient people wanted to attract some fires from the firmament, they operated in crypts. You should know all of this as well as myself, because you have studied the mysteries. You should therefore tell us your ideas about the Virgin, for you certainly know a lot of theories on the matter."

"Actually, I am acquainted with many of them," I answered, "but not one of them satisfies me."

"Tell us one of them," said Stella, to encourage me, "and he will give you an explanation later."

"Well, all right," I said, seeing Andréas's sign of approbation. "There are two kinds of theories: those in which the Virgin is conceived of as a symbol and those which consider her to be a living force, personal as well as impersonal. The first ones belong to the philosophical systems, more or less derived from Platonism, and I am not interested in them. To me ideas are not merely abstractions; they have form, substance and energy. So I will keep to the second group of theories."

"Have you ever noticed," Stella said to me, "that the popular beliefs in the Virgin, as well as in natural forces, ascribe a personality to all the forms of the *Invisible*. So on every earth there exists a religious legend about a Virgin giving birth to a Saviour."

"Yes! The people quite honestly believed in it, but the savants declared that it was only a symbol. However, every kind of initiate wanted to make that symbol exclusively his own."

"Well, Doctor," interrupted Andréas, "initiates don't possess the whole Truth, although among them are impartial and tolerant savants. We should render justice to everyone. But please, do continue," he added, seeing that I was a little amazed.

"I saw," I said, "in the books of the alchemists, that they consider the stone and an image of the Word to be in the mineral, and that, according to them, their real, primary matter is the Virgin. Robert Fludd explains it. A Brahmin from the Deccan taught me that the Father, the Son, the Spirit and the Virgin exist in man: the Father, according to him, is the root of the will; the Son is the point of the projected will, the Virgin is an imaginative form nourishing this exteriorized point, and the Spirit is the vibration of the whole system."

"I know that theory," Andréas told me. "It is almost the same as that which Sri Srimat Sankaracharya expressed in his Ananda Lahari, about the relationship between Shiva and his wife."

"For orthodox Brahmins there is Maya, the universal illusion. "Maria," I added a little pedantically, "is Maya plus the letter 'R', which is the sign of the proper existence."

"That is one of the many opinions," said Andréas, "and I think it belongs to Fabre d'Olivet. But how does it explain that while Brahmins desire to escape from Maya, Christians, on the contrary, throw themselves into Maria's arms?"

"I haven't read anything about it," I replied.

"I believe, Doctor, that an oriental man wants to escape evil while escaping life, change, and becoming: he takes his refuge, or at least tries to take it, in the zero, the nought. The Christian, on the other hand, tries to escape evil by raising himself to another way of existence."

"That is it!" I exclaimed. "I understand! If Maria signifies heavenly space, the place of the absolute life, she is the mother of the Word (the Logos), although also its creature, because, if we can say so, she provides the substance for the development of that Word. In Fabre d'Olivet's grammar the Name is the Father; the Word, the Son; the relation is the Spirit, and the sign is the Virgin."

"Oh, well," Stella said to me, "it is not worth studying Sanskrit, Hebrew and calculus in order to find it. What you say is written in French in all prayer-books!"

But smilingly Andréas stopped her. "How exacting you are! Didn't you seek for a long time for the thing that was in front of you? And likewise didn't I travel thousands of miles instead of merely stretching out my hand? Therefore let him alone for nothing is useless." And turning to me he said: "Here is what I would do in your place. I could tell you long stories about all the Mahadevas, Kuan-Yins, Saktis, Hirams and Miriams, which you can only imagine.

"If I don't do so, it is not in order to play the role of an initiator and thus hold the bonbon high before you, as you are well aware. I am doing so only so as to let you have time.

"Thus, look around you, seek what Nature and the crowd, which is obedient to the vital instinct, have devised. In no country apart from Europe would you find a cult of the Virgin. What forms the basis of such a cult? It is the *Ave Maria*, extracted from the Gospels, the litanies and some other special small fragments of different liturgical feasts."

"It is true," I conceded, "the *Ave Maria* contains the Angel's salutation and that of Elizabeth, which can readily be found in the liturgy of St. James the Minor, and in the antiphony of St. Gregory the Great. Baronius tells us that the third part came from the Council of Ephesus in 431 A.D., except for the words ' *now and at the hour of our death* ', which are attributed to the Franciscan monks. The prayer itself, I believe, has been imported from

Alexandria: it was introduced into France by Louis the Fat. Therefore, the *Ave Maria* certainly originated from Apostolic Christianity."

"How erudite you are!" smiled Stella.

"It is the erudition of a candidate! But," I said to Andréas. "What is the real reason for the suppression of the Virgin's cult in protestantism? Why did Cromwell forbid the recitation of the *Ave Maria*? I believe that its importance is vital, because even the king of Protestant mystics, Boehme, re-invented it under the name of the *Sophia*. And it is true that the pastors did persecute it."

"Protestantism," answered Andréas, according to his habit of never criticizing, "Protestantism is excellent because of the spirit of liberty animating it. It is going ahead; but—and there is a big 'but'—its founders, when cultivating free thinking, also cultivated rationalism. And rationalism is gradually sapping the belief in the divinity of Christ. In the XVIth Century, all the reformed still had this conviction, but today great numbers of them, versed in exegesis, deny it, seeing in Jesus a more advanced man, a social reformer, an adept, a disciple of the Egyptians or Hindus, and even as only a myth. This blindness has been prepared for three centuries, in a hidden way, by certain beings, by means of lack of appreciation of the real dignity of the Virgin. This is a commentary on your question; but the 'why', dear Doctor, is too difficult to conceive."

I was astonished to my depths, that a man, who was such a savant and so wise as Andréas, professed to the popular and common beliefs about Christ and the Virgin. But, when Stella served tea to us, he answered my thought.

"Don't believe, Doctor, that I would allow myself to confirm simple opinions in such a way. I tell you these things only because I know them."

"I would like you to say: 'How do you know them? Where is your criterion?' but," he added, "everything is alive, nothing dies, and Truth comes to the one who searches for it with all his heart."

We drank our tea in silence. Then, offering me tobacco, he asked whether I could explain to him the orthodox doctrine of the Roman Church concerning the Virgin Mary.

"Here is what it teaches," I replied. "The Virgin is the first among creatures, queen of angels and men, conceived without a sin by the grace of the Almighty, because of the merits of our Lord Jesus Christ, and she always remains a virgin. Mother of God because the Son is God, and although she does not participate in His divinity, she has been assigned a crown by her Son, at the same time, both in the soul and in the body. The cult of hyperdulia is due to her. She is the channel for all the graces which descend on to us and consequently also for all ascending prayers; her Son never refuses her anything. The Greek Orthodox Church professes the same doctrine."

"I remember," said Stella, "having read some books on the matter. It was at the time when I knew Eliphas Lévi about 1872. That doesn't make me any younger. That poor Eliphas already had his dropsy; he liked to go out with me. At the time he lived at the end of the street of Sèvres, which was almost a village, and the whole suburb of Plaisance was covered with market gardens. On the street of Meudon there were some small hotels, and people went there to lunch and drink some white wine. I had ordered the Clavicules from him: he did them in coloured pictures and symbols. When I succeeded in selling such a manuscript for him, for a good price, he was eager to invite me to be the first to take from the pile of gold coins, just as the Bohemian students do, for at least he always remained one, despite the fact that his beard was already quite white. They were good hours of relaxation for me!" And Stella smiled with her husband over the old memories. Then she continued: "Look how old I am. I'm already starting to talk nonsense. But I wanted to tell you that Eliphas Lévi was a deacon, the 'enfant terrible' of the whole Seminary. Under the name of *Abbé Constant*, he published the book—'*God's Mother*'. He was then thirty-three years' old and he had lent the book to me."

"But," I said, "I beg your pardon for this interruption, have you had the manuscripts of Eliphas Lévi? Perhaps you still have some of them?"

"I saw him draw about a dozen of his Clavicules,* but I don't know what happened to all of them. You know," she added, casting a look full of love and confidence at Andréas, "it is long since all such things lost their attraction for me. Anyway, in that book Eliphas, the deacon, summarized the theological doctrine about God's Mother. He quoted Bonaventure and Galatinus, and in a very oratorical style he explained all that you have just said to us, describing the Virgin in her historical person, in her theological essence, and commenting on the VIIIth Chapter of Proverbs. He also showed her in her mysterious intercession and, together with Marie d'Agreda, conceived her to be Jerusalem of the

---

* The Clavicules, as Eliphas Lévi liked to call them, are the arcana cards of the Tarot (see the Encyclopaedic Course "*The Tarot*" by the translator, published by G. Allen & Unwin Ltd.).

Book of Revelations, as the spouse of the Canticle [by King Solomon] and as the *symbol of the Church.*

"It is St. Epiphane in the IVth Century, who first assumed the Virgin to be the Spouse of the *Canticle* and St. Bernard develops the same idea. Marie d'Agreda has slightly copied St. Bonaventure, who wrote the *Commentary of the Salve Regina,* a *Little Psalter, The Praises,* and *The Mirror,* all about the Virgin. The latter treatise is a commentary on the *Ave Maria. The Praises* are explanations of the figures of the Old Testament: the Fountain of Paradise, the Tree of Life, Paradise, the Ark, the Rainbow, the Dove, Jacob's Ladder, the Burning Bush, the Vase of Manna, the Tau of the Copper Serpent, the Rod of Aaron, the Star of Balaam, the Temple, Judith, Esther, and so on."

"All of these are actually figures of the Heavenly Virgin," said Andréas. "If you are curious, Doctor, you can study in order to possess knowledge of them, from the point of view of the symbol as well as according to the hieroglyph of the letter. However, remember that knowledge acquired through understanding alone will vanish."

"I have read," interrupted Stella, "*The Mystical City* by Marie d'Agreda, but in Spanish, although it is very beautiful when the French translations flow drop after drop like fountains of marshmallow. That Dominican nun made a dithyrambic eulogy of the Virgin."

"Which you only half-heartedly like," said Andréas. "You have some Huguenot blood in your veins. What Marie d'Agreda said is true enough, only one should be able to give her vision its exact place. But please continue your reminiscences, I shall tell you my ideas later."

"However," said Stella, "*The Mystical City* is useful. It shows the idealistic life of a young girl, wife and mother, adding a feasible touch about the possibility of interesting Heaven in even the most common-place actions."

"Do you know anything more?" asked Andréas.

"No!" I answered. "Everyone repeats themselves: St. Ambrose and St. Epiphane were the first to teach the Immaculate Conception from the dual point of view of the primordial and actual sin, while St. Bernard, Jacques Sanazar and M. Olier have copied one another to a certain extent."

"And what about the non-Catholic mystics?"

"I know only Boehme and his school, Law, Gichtel, Pordage and Frankenberg. They say little about the Virgin. According to them, she provided the matter for Christ's body and His human nature; she was, as regards her soul, an emanation of the Virgin

Sophia, of the Nature-essence, but only after the conception of her Son: by herself she is only a saintly woman, who does not participate in the prerogatives of Divinity. And now," I added after a period of silence, " can I ask you to tell me something further? "

" Listen Doctor! Don't let me judge the theories which you have expounded to me. I will tell you my own opinion quite simply. You may compare, weigh and decide about it for yourself. It is your duty to do so, for it is a grave subject. Here is what I understand from that mystery. When the Logos assumed an earthly body, He had to remember the weakness of physical matter. It is said that the blade wears out the sheath. If this is true for men, the stronger the reason, in the case of a body destined to become an instrument of the Almighty, for it to obtain a very pure temper. Therefore, it was necessary that the physical mother of Christ, the instrument of that miracle, should be exempt from the defects of ordinary physical matter. Because of that, she is the queen of saints, just as she is the queen of angels, so as to remain pure after having passed through the mire."

" It seems to me that I am catching hold of a new idea," I said in answer to Andréas' mute question.

" It doesn't matter," he continued, " whether Mary, as the Church teaches, had been created pure before her first contact with the earth, fifteen years prior to the birth of the Logos [Word], or, as some adherents of reincarnation say, she had descended several times on earth leading, without any lapses, a constantly saintly life and so preparing herself for the highest glory of her last incarnation."

" Now I can explain to myself," I said, " why Boehme calls her: the ' Salvation of this valley of pain ' and otherwise ' the purified affliction '."

" That is why," continued Andréas, seemingly not hearing my words, " she is the way to go to the Christ, for no matter what theories are concocted, the fact remains that the Virgin has satisfied the whole Law."

" All the Fathers of the Church give her the title of the Gate of Heaven," said Stella, " and also Vintras," she added.

" And I think," I said, " that the titles which are bestowed upon her in litanies and liturgic hymns are somewhat different from the poetical praises."

" That is certainly so," replied Andréas rising. " Everything is true, I tell you, but in its plane. The reasons for those titles is implicitly contained in the Angelic Salutation. I shall try to show it to you now." Then he went into his workshop to write down a forgotten note. Stella, so to speak, continued his teaching.

"You see," she said, "there are three parts to the prayer: one said by the angel, another by a privileged creature, the mother of the Precursor and one invented by pious men. And each of these three parts is divided into two sentences, while the *Amen* terminates the septenary. Likewise, the number '7' is found here, in order to play a great role in her life."

"How is that?" I asked.

"Andréas told me that at seven years of age she had intuition of her message; that at fourteen years she was married, and at sixty-three she received her crown."

"I see! There is a complete planetary cycle: *I am greeting you, Mary, full of grace,* it is a prostration; *The Lord is with you,* is the divine radiation; *Blessed art thou,* is the multiplicative energy; *Blessed is the fruit of thy womb, Jesus,* is the solar heart of the system; *Saint Mary, pray for us,* invokes the heavenly gentleness; *at the hour of our death,* revives the guides of the dead: Anubis, Hermes the psychopompos [leader of souls], and Yama. *Amen,* is the form of the number of seven, which, according to Boehme, embodies every desire and . . ."

The sudden reappearance of Andréas cut short my Hermetic development. He sat down and resumed the conversation at the point to which his wife had led it.

"The number 'seven' seems to be the one which is encountered most often on this earth; it should therefore have a close relation to the law of human life; but we don't consider it for a moment. Rather note this: it is the Angel who salutes the Virgin; it is the righteous woman who issues just praise to her; it is the fishermen who elect her; or, if you so prefer, the Angel shows us what she is in the sight of God, Elizabeth shows us her place among the human species, while the third part is the irresistible conclusion of the two former ones."

"Thus," I said, "you recommend the cult of the Virgin, the cult of hyperdulia?" I asked.

"My dear Doctor, I don't recommend anything; those who feel themselves inclined to present their prayers through the Virgin are not in the wrong. That is all that I can say."

"Would you like to continue the explanation for us?" Stella asked him.

"The *Ave Maria* in Latin and in French, as well as in any other language has a different sense and interpretation; but, note well, Doctor, that happens only in the realm of human language. In the realm of the divine word there is only one meaning. The language of that realm is the Spirit, which teaches us about it.

And we should prepare ourselves for receiving its lessons through work, through action. Here is the whole mystery in its simplicity. The Virgin was not a feminist; she never presided over a masonic lodge, nor supplied any copy to a large daily paper. She was an obedient child; a young girl, married without even being consulted, a woman exposed to the suspicion of her husband, to gossip, to housework; a mother doomed to the worst anxieties, crowned by the most enormous pain; an active and charitable widow, still occupied with the household of the Apostles. She led an obscure life, a common life, an anti-intellectual one.

"Those who will best understand her will be the people of the same class, the poor workers, whose paltry existence is consumed between fatigue and anxiety about their daily food. Those people would not perform any gematria or mantrams. When they ask, it is with a cry from their poor exhausted hearts. And they are very close to the Kingdom of the Logos. Heaven listens to them much better than to the initiates."

"Then Catherine Emmerich is right when she says that the Virgin is a model for a woman?" asked Stella.

"She is a model for humanity. But it is hard to speak about someone without judging him. She will forgive me if I say something inexact, or which shocks you, my Doctor."

"I think," I said, "that I am wise enough not to reject what I am unable to understand. But, I beg you to tell me, why the Archangel Gabriel describes her as being 'full of Grace'?"

"What about her name, Doctor, permit me not to say anything when we are not in a position to bear the knowledge of names, and anyway, I don't know that name. The title '*full of Grace*' means that in Mary everything had been renewed by Heaven. You know that she did not experience bodily death. Thus, from the central light of her soul, from the marvellous organs of her spirit to the smallest molecule of her physical body, everything in her was cleansed of the stain of egoism."

"But, how could that be?" I asked.

"Well, when a man succumbs to anger and hits his opponent, the muscles of his arm, which do the work, develop themselves, and they function well according to their purpose. But the intention which put them into movement, the desire, as said St. Martin, was perverted, and hence their work produced the fatal results, which extended over all the ulterior movements of the same muscles. In order to purify them, Heaven has to '*convert*' all those muscular fibres, apart from the moral conversion which must follow. Therefore, if the Virgin spoke little; if the affability, simplicity and dignity of her appearance reached a state of beauty, it happened because every evil which reveals a tedious word, every unpleasant attitude, was removed and replaced by Grace, by the gratuitous Light descending from Heaven."

"Now I realize, my master, why the litanies call her the Mirror of the Trinity, the Throne of Wisdom, Mother of Grace, and why St. Bernard said that she is Heaven and the Ark of God."

"There are still some other reasons for these titles, dear Doctor; but believe me, you should not embarrass yourself with these too distant speculations. Of what use would it be for you to know that she is a star above the universal ocean, on which invisible ceremonies confer such titles as the *Gate of Crystal*, the *Room of the Feast*, the *Mystical Rose*; and in which cosmic drama she plays the role of *David's Tower*, of the *Ivory Tower*, of the *Golden Castle*? We should not be too curious: it is one of the lessons I had to learn at my own expense."

"Then," I said, "one should not study at all?"

"Don't throw yourself into extremes, but perform what work is possible. Limit your studies to those which concern your present life; that field alone is a sufficiently vast one. For example, returning to the subject which is occupying us just now; realize that, if the Angel said: '*the Lord is with you*', that was because he saw that she was one of the most humble of creatures."

"At one time I read a Jansenist manuscript, which said the same," interrupted Stella.

"That is also because she is in essence, indissolubly bound by love to her Son; that is why, not only during her earthly life that is known to us, but always and everywhere, she is in constant communication with Him, not by any magnetic or mental effort, but through the effect of her love. It is that presence of God which enabled her to bear such suffering, to overcome such trials, material and moral alike. I believe dear Doctor, that you have not yet read the Gospels in a proper way."

"My God!" I said, "the Gospels, like all sacred books, contain many meanings, which can be discovered by means of literal and numerical calculations of the words, numbers of the letters, chapters and verses. Just as every language has its hieroglyphic aspect, so ordinary translations are susceptible to such manipulations, but Latin, Greek and Aramean versions are still the best."

"You are going too fast," Andréas interrupted me. "In order that such a study will show a true result, it would be indispensable for you to know at least the science of numbers and letters. But, nobody, do you hear, nobody, even the most reputable ones, knows anything beyond the first letter of the alphabet of those sciences.

Even so, what sort of certainty would those theosophical operations, transpositions, magic squares, and so on have?"

As I did not reply, Andréas continued:

"The Gospels then do not have many meanings, as you, an occultist, understand this expression. The different meanings of the sacred books are just like new sentences which appear in a cryptographical text when read with different grids. The Gospels are always one, always central. In them the reader perceives the centre of the plan in which his spiritual life develops. Therefore, the signification of the word of the Logos appears to us as more or less high, profound or universal, depending upon how far we ourselves are distant from the true *Centre*. Do you realize now, my dear Doctor, that every word in that book is an absolute one?"

"It is true," said Stella. "When I am a little tired, I say that I am terribly fatigued. But it is not strictly the case. We always apply exaggerated terms, extravagant even in the smallest things. But the Gospels give an exact expression to every idea, feeling and fact. That is what literary men call its 'simplicity'."

As I nodded my head, being completely astonished at never having thought about such evident things, Andréas continued:

"The angel saluted her. It was politeness. Do you know what politeness is, or rather, what it should be?"

"It is," I answered laughingly, "to ask, with feigned sympathy for news about the health of a bore."

"Or," said Andréas seriously, "if someone bores you and you do not like him, then your politeness is a lie: it comes from darkness and produces darkness. It is not an enormous business, of course, but how can we undertake great things, if we cannot do the small ones? The salutation of Gabriel is thus animated with sincere feeling. What are the qualities of angels? Obedience and innocence! Without these they would not be angels at all. If Gabriel saluted her, it was because he recognized in that woman, purity and obedience greater than he himself possessed. And, truly, the spirit of Mary, when it came into the world, was pure and she kept herself pure during the whole of her lifetime."

"Then you do recognize the immaculate conception?"

"Look Doctor! If a sick woman has a child, will it be healthy? If the character, temperament, mentality and, briefly, the whole human nature of Christ were perfect, could the one, who was the laboratory of that diamond, be perverted, even in the slightest degree?"

"And what meaning do the words '*full of Grace*,' have? They surely don't concern physical beauty alone?"

"Why not dear Doctor? The holy Virgin was very beautiful,

but not in the way in which people, except for a few rare artists, understand that word. The intensity of her inner life modelled her face; it was extremely mobile and because, in every action, she did everything wholeheartedly, her face expressed the ideal type of whatever faculty she was using. I am not sure whether or not I have spoken in an understandable way."

"Oh yes! For it seems to me that when, for example, she prayed, for an artist, she must have been the living incarnation of Prayer; when she gave alms, it was Charity itself, and so on."

"That is just what I wanted to say, dear Doctor. But there is another thing. What the Church calls ' *Grace* ' is the power which Heaven sends to us gratuitously, even when we believe we merit it by our good deeds. To you, Doctor, grace is an operation by which Heaven replaces a sick cell in us whether physical, mental, or astral, no matter which kind it may be, with a pure cell, which comes from its *Treasure*. But, in the case of the Virgin, all visible and invisible organisms had already been renewed; all that remained, if it is possible to say so, was the web of Nature's work."

"It seems to me," I said, "that there was something like this said by Henricus Madathanus."

"That is possible Doctor, for the first Rosicrucians loved the Virgin, even though they were Protestants."

"And also," I said, "wouldn't there be something in common between the grace she received and the nine choirs of Angels?"

"Actually, from the Catholic point of view there is. St. Bonaventure spoke about it. But, I am repeating it to you again. It is only a detail, but it is still too difficult for us."

"But you didn't tell me anything about the name of Mary?"

"Oh, Doctor, you know as well as I do about all those mystico-Hebrew glosses, to which that name has given birth. I don't want you to lose your time. Believe me, we will review it some centuries later."

"If only Providence will grant me the favour of finding you again," I replied.

"Ah yes!" he exclaimed with a charming laugh. "That would be a nice favour! Let us speak about it! You shouldn't have such ideas, Doctor!"

"Oh!" cried Stella gently with a tone of reproach in her voice, "why do you say such a thing? You will make him suffer!"

But he, rising, embraced her with one of his arms.

"Well, Doctor," he said to me gravely, "because you want so strongly to accompany me, I promise you, that I will ask Heaven to give to you, no, rather to both of us, the force to fulfil Its will forever. That is the surest means of which I know, in order to remain together, and forever."

I too rose, and it seemed that a lighter air filled the room; a perfume of spring invaded my being. I was not thinking any more and I relaxed as if in a bath of rejuvenating light. It was not the first time that similar feelings, which were always sudden, had rushed into me. Their purity, their force by far surpassed everything I had ever imagined after reading accounts of ecstasies. And I was not merely tasting these inexpressible effects of their charm. Always, after having experienced one of these very brief moments of paradise, I noticed that, without the slightest effort on my part, I acquired a kind of prestige, I exercised an indefinable attraction for other people. When my sick patients left me, they said that they experienced a noticeable improvement, a relief which was moral as well as physical, the cause of which neither they nor myself could ever explain. After a few moments, Andréas started to smoke again and continued his discourse,

"The blessing, which Gabriel gave to Mary, was specially chosen for her. She was the first creature in which was accomplished the mystery the Church calls Christ's birth inside us. She is the perfect type of an obedient being, humble and loving. Actually, woman, or better still, the whole of the female side of the Universe, lives more conformably under the Law than the male counterpart. And the life of the Virgin was fully conformable, in every way to that Law. So, properly speaking, it is not to the imitation of Jesus Christ to which we should devote ourselves, for the model is an almost too perfect one, but, to His Mother."

I opened my mouth to ask about the reasons for such an exceptional elevation, but Andréas anticipated me.

"After all," he said, "don't conceal from yourself that everything I have said to you is only an approximation. The Christ and the Virgin are mysteries. Their figures surpass our intelligence. Their secret is like creation itself; we cannot know it without knowing the cause of Life. Perhaps some day the Logos will unveil Itself; but we will never be worthy of such a favour, and if we receive it, it will always be a gratuitous Grace for us."

"Thus, the blessing of Jesus, which Elizabeth celebrated, is just the recognition and love from those whom He saves."

"It is all very simple, Doctor! And yet only a few think about even such a simple thing. Pious people, or those so-called, know very well how to ask when they have need of something, but they almost always forget to thank. We should not do so because Heaven takes offence at our impoliteness, because our gratitude, no matter how insignificant, is pleasant in its eyes, and sets a good example for the beings which it is our mission to educate."

"What about the third part of the *Ave Maria*," I said. "It seems quite clear to me. The holiness of the Virgin is deduced from the titles given to her by the Angel Gabriel. However, is the role of interceder, as ascribed to her, a real one?"

"Yes, dear Doctor! You know that everything that happens on this earth leaves a trace. The Virgin lived here, the elements of her body came from physical matter, and the luminous trail produced by her departure can be more easily found by us than, for example, the wake of her Son, whose physical body was foreign to our planet."

"A Druidic triad says something analogous about the body of the Logos."

"It is a distant intuition," replied Andréas, "but let us talk about it another time."

"Yes," I answered, "it really is pretty late. But one last question before I leave. Why is the Third Order added to '*Pray for us poor sinners*', which is '*Now and at the hour of our death*'?"

"You don't know your true self, dear Doctor. The actual field of our consciousness is a very narrow one, it doesn't embrace more than a little corner of our being. Thus, when we pray, our body participates in our action; the spirit of its material cells—if I may say so—emerges and seeks the light, like a dog, asking for work, like a somnambulist seeking a lost object. Our spirit will more quickly find a trace of light, which has been emanated at some previous time from a physical body, similar to our own. Thus the prayer of the Virgin is more easily heard."

"But, *at the hour of our death*?" queried Stella.

"Well, you know that after death there is an individual judgment. At this tribunal justice is represented by the geniuses which had the mission of watching over, helping and guiding us. If we took advantage of their good offices, they say so. But Heaven always interferes so as to mitigate our errors, and to excuse our negligences. Thus, the Heavenly form, the ray of the Absolute closest to our earth is the Virgin. That is why religion presents her to us as helpful for those who are suffering."

I thanked my host and hostess and took leave, for the noise of the milk carts, descending from Montfermeil to Paris announced the approaching dawn. And so I returned home, walking slowly, under the ash-coloured dawn, through the streets gleaming with rain, in which moved the vague silhouettes of the sweepers.

Chapter XXXVII

THE VIRGIN

The peculiar sweetness of that December day seduced us. We walked in Andréas's little garden, under the watchful eye of his dog, and among the familiar quarrelsome sparrows. We talked about Olive Schreiner, who had died in the Transvaal. Then the femininsts entered our conversation, followed by the 'modern-minded' young girls and the grandmothers with their 'ancient minds'. We agreed that the fighting amazons of today, in spite of their declamations, diplomas, congresses, journals and leagues, greatly risked exercising nothing more than a very superficial influence from the outside, and a very incoherent one at that. On the other hand, women whose recognized sphere does not transcend the kitchen or granary, exercise a much more effective, deeper and saner regency. Once again, the shadow seems to be taken for the substance.

"Even so," I objected, " there is a lot of excess, much abuse of authority, and legal abuses on the part of fathers, guardians and husbands. Also what about the destiny of unmarried mothers and their children?"

"Oh, I know," replied Andréas nodding his head. "A lot of tears have flowed and many existences have been poisoned by prejudice, covetousness, and haughty people. But, nevertheless, all these heart-rending things are useful, all of them, without any exception. Ah, if only men could see what women are, and women, what men are! If they would just look at one another without taking sides for love or hatred, how much pain they would escape!"

"But how should they act?" I asked.

"Eh!" said Andréas. "They only have to look at the Virgin Mary!" And Andréas took a few steps, merged in his thoughts. Then he continued:

"You cannot imagine what a marvellous creature the Virgin was. Truly, no artist ever saw her, and so far, no artist has had a soul vast enough to see her. Her person united all the beauties of the Jewish race, in which, contrary to the opinion of ethnographers, the vast historical Orient has melted its many-sided loveliness. The fine Egyptian features, the vigour of the desert nomads, the Chaldean power, the clear gracefulness of exiled

Celtic girls, the Syrian languidness, all of these things reposed in her, and reappeared in turn, according to the palpitations of the inner life, so very rich and vibrant. There is no doubt that Cimabue depicted her mystery for us: Giotto her nobleness; Angelico her entreating fervour; Lippi and Botticelli her joyful grace; Leonardo da Vinci the subtlety of her intelligence; Bellini her sadness; Michael Angelo her power; Van Eyck her suffering; the French artists of the Medieval epoch her heroic, hidden virtues, and Raphael, the painter most alive to feeling, her virginity. But all of their portraits are only accidental. You cannot imagine the incredible richness of her vitality. In the violet shadow of a small house she was resplendent like an ardent topaz, and all the torches of enthusiasm and intelligence shone in her eyes during those rare moments when she did not cover her radiant, rose-windows with her long eyelashes. She leaned over the ashes on the hearth, over bread dough, or a jar of olive oil, like a large, living flower. She magnified everything, beautified everything.

"You have probably noticed that there are people who wear extremely ugly clothes and can produce factories full of ready-made garments, and yet, who even appear to look like aristocrats; people, whose hands, deformed by the hardest of labours, still remain expressive, whose features marred by misery and long exposure to the weather still remain noble and rich in their numerous facial expressions. So it was with the Virgin; a half-raised hand, an inclination of the head, a sinuosity of the lips, hope and despair, poetry and dejection, fatigue and ecstasy, all stood before the gaze of an observer and displayed their infinite dramas. But her eyes, Doctor, her large eyes that were so pure, her eyes in which all the glances were thronged together, like vessels in a port! And her voice, that remained clear until her death, transparent, limpid, winged, except in those rare moments, when, half-opening the gates of her soul, she allowed others to guess in the intonation of a single word the gorgeous harmonies of a sensibility as exquisite as profound! No, my friend, one cannot even conceive what a marvel that woman was, and for my part, I know that no outsider was able to understand her, only her Son. It has been permitted me to measure the width, length and depth of the abyss of her humility; it has been granted to me to conceive of the motives which caused her never to complain, or defend herself, and why she steadily buried in silence, all the treasures of grace, understanding, and tenderness with which the Father had so magnificently endowed her. She always kept silent. Imagine dear Doctor, that silence in suffering, against admiration, compassion and veneration! No one ever saw even one of the Virgin's tears, and what virginity! The Mother, and of what a Son! And of what adopted, thankless children!

"When after all of this, I hear women lamenting and men, who never suffer as much as women, whining even more, then I have to consider deeply the unfailing mercy of our spiritual Mother, so that quick compassion will arise in me for the suffering of all beings. Ah! Never, never will anybody understand that woman!

"Thus," I ventured, "we suffer, we weep, we even kill ourselves so as to escape the torture of existence."

"Yes, there is no doubt about it, I tell myself. I know very well that the same pain can render one man insensible and make a martyr of another; but I also know that if we suffer, it is because we do not want to suffer, hence, so as not to suffer we should put our dear pride under our feet. Ah! When God imposes on one of His servants a formidable burden of discernment of the conscience, He might as well remove the man from this world, which is the antechamber of hell! And yet, everything God does is good."

I did not know how to answer. I caught a glimpse as of a precipice beyond which float the clouds, of the terrible conflicts which should arise between the two natures—the human, and the divine, of the master of Andréas, of the master of us all. Long minutes passed, and reconciliation between those incompatibilities did not come. Then Andréas rose, took a few steps and said:

"Anyway, it must be quite forcibly and absolutely realized, that some day or another we will live as Mary lived. When unhappy creatures come crying before you do not repulse them, but do not hurry. A superficial compassion is worthless and touching sentences are also worthless. Listen to the complaints in silence, and don't speak until, in the depths of your heart, you feel the same ploughshare tearing at you as is tearing at those sufferers. Then, and only then, the three words which you will pronounce will act effectively. All suffering is, at the same time, both illusory and real. Therefore, touch it only with pure hands and a respectful heart."

"Truly," I said gently, "all of our anxieties come from our hatred; we immediately want to possess this or something else, and we never admit that our desires can be erroneous. A mother cannot understand that her son can love a young girl, whom she doesn't like, and the son understands his mother even less: the mother in her love has not lost her critical sense, led by considerations of luck or social fitness. A wife doesn't imagine that her husband desires to be loved in a way different from what she imagines. Everyone believes that he possesses the perfect intelligence."

"Yes! Doctor," interrupted Andréas. "One should sit all one's life on the back bench in the school of Life. We don't know even the alphabet of that language, let alone to speak about it. Ah! To keep silent! Not to speak except to keep alive the courage and joy around us. Here is a good rule: never to govern, nor to claim!" he added with a smile.

"Isn't it so?" I said, laughing in turn. "Not even to bore others with peevish sermons about the uselessness of making sermons?"

Chapter XXXVIII

THE LOUVRE

On that particular morning Andréas led me to the Louvre, to see the Camondo collection, before the opening. There was a Buddhist statue, remarkable because of its very rare detail of gesture. In seeking it, we passed before an open window. A Siamese bust stood there on a socle, it was made of old blue-green bronze and behind it the spring sky of Paris flaunted its changing silks between the classic perspective of the Carrousel and the elegant trees of the Tuileries. And there, much lower, on the top of a stout base, mauve and grey, the Arc de Triomphe detached its jade-coloured silhouette from the mother-of-pearl roses of the west. A delightful landscape, the smile of Paris, French grace, orderly with charming unexpectedness, full of nuances and airs, with that cleanliness of outline which stops a dream and compels it to become a thought.

"Look," Andréas said to me, "look on the soul of France."

"Yes! I am looking with all my sight."

"And still you are not looking enough. Ah, my Doctor, I have known a lot of countries, but France! One doesn't know everything that Heaven has given to France."

"But," I said, "there is a question. How can it be, that France seems to lead Europe into all sorts of disorders—violence, scandals?"

"Firstly, it is by God's grace. When France does evil, it does it more openly than any other nation. It is a great privilege to be in the position to act in such a way. Also you remember your alchemy very well. Forces must be pushed to the extreme left, in order that they can return to the extreme right. And France, in that athanor of the white race, is the lion's blood."

"Wouldn't it then be the reason, because of which, in our day, and especially in our country, all the political, philosophical, religious and social tendencies are becoming angry and stiffening? Would it be an example of the angry world about which Boehme speaks, which foams and boils with rage, simply to crack at the lighting of a fire?"

"Use these images, if they suit you, they are true enough. Look around you in your own realm, that of medicine. Don't you feel that the boldest efforts lead to the violation of Nature's laws?"

" You wouldn't say that the works of Carrel are anti-vital, for they are among the boldest efforts? Isn't that so? I can see the dreams of the alchemists almost being surpassed in them. I can foresee a future of almost frightening splendour in them, it is . . ."

" Dear Doctor," Andréas interrupted me with a smile, I can see you are in one of your esoteric crises. Truth according to Nature and Truth according to God are two truths, not one. You know very well that alchemy, seen from the point of view of Nature, reaches results which are scientifically true; but seen according to the Super-Nature, they are false."

" Yes! But Carrel is not an alchemist."

" But yes, dear Doctor! Alchemists enforce a mineral to live like a vegetable, and today they compel an animal tissue to live like a vegetable. This is a spiritual rape. And what about all those future complications with the displaced cells? What suffering for sick men and animals! What a cry, from the ' other side ' when they die! "

" Ah! " I exclaimed in a low voice, " it is something like : ' Do not put a new patch into an old garment ', isn't that so, my master ? "

" Yes, of course, and yet everything is so simple. If only men had good will, Heaven would steadily send them miracles. If only you knew how good the *Father* is! "

And old Andréas bowed his head and bent his broad shoulders. And the subtle breath of the Spirit, the pacifier, came upon us there, in those halls on the walls of which were resplendent the greatest efforts of an extreme human culture. What a difference between those two atmospheres!

Chapter XXXIX

IN COMPIEGNE

There came a year in which European politics became terribly entangled. One of my friends, who was attached to a certain office in the Foreign Ministry, confided to me, that these complications were provoked by the wife of a very important banker for the profit of her lover, a cosmopolitan adventurer, who was greatly in need of money. In order to satisfy him, the woman arranged an intrigue with the mistress of a monarch, and after some repeated press campaigning, the latter was able to arouse a nervous tension in public opinion to such a degree, that the parliaments of three countries simultaneously voted credit for national defence. The big bank was thus enabled to realize hundreds of millions in profit, and so the adventurer got his money. Even so, war became imminent. Andréas confirmed the exactness of this report.

"Great historical catastrophes, as you should see, have not had less futile causes. Thus one should grant attention to them, if one is in a position to interfere usefully. More than anyone else we Frenchmen have the right and duty to love our country in every way. If, dear Doctor, you have some light in the matter of the Realm Invisible, you will realize how much light and generous beauty has come to Europe because of our France, despite all the foolishness of her sons and all the freakish behaviour of her rulers. Apart from ours, no other nation has insufflated so much of her spring into minor peoples. But also, with no other nation has Heaven been so directly mingled as with France. Therefore, it is proper for us to love France because we are her children and because we are also the children of Heaven."

"Yes, Master!" I answered. "But what sort of connection would there be between that bedroom story of today and that of which you speak now?"

"Well, Doctor, let us speak about medicine. If a witch-doctor of Annam can establish his diagnoses from the relations of the red corpuscles with the vital light, mental light and will-power, when for the same purpose a probationer searches for those relations with salt, mercury and sulphuric oil, if Van Helmont analyses the tension of the arcs, if today they seek microbial ferments, if a magnetizer dissects fluids and if a spiritist seeks invisible beings, all of this doesn't prove that one or another of them are completely in error, or in full truth. That is because everyone judges after his own point of view. And this proves that a physical phenomenon is only the last link in a very long chain. It proves that such a phenomenon is born through the conjunction of a whole row of non-material causes, and finally, this proves that every phenomenon develops of itself from an imperceptible seed." At this point Andréas emptied his pipe with great care. "And you will be able to see that almost always, a human being is the soil in which grow all of those seeds."

"But then," I questioned, "what about the present case?"

"Eh, it is quite simple. You know that ingratitude is not the privilege of men alone. Individualities, which the grandiloquent Eliphas Lévi called Egregors also have this fault. The Egregors of other nations don't feel any recognition of our country: on the contrary, they would very much like to enslave and kill it so as to enrich themselves from the spoils. And the Enemy, who watches for every chance of a quarrel, assists them as much as he can. In the three persons about whom we just spoke, he found a wonderfully cultivated soil. All three have no fatherland, or religion. Their God is just themselves, and, for their own profit, the invisible forces will try to manipulate the egoistic passions of these three persons, who are pulling the most powerful levers of social life, so as to defeat our country in full."

"I begin to understand. But," I said, "if I am not committing an indiscretion, do you in anyway intend to interfere with that coalition?"

"Most certainly, dear Doctor. Isn't it my duty if Providence has furnished me with the means to do so?"

I had become accustomed to Andréas's habits; but the fantastic character of the views just expressed so quietly by a man, who this evening had been like the figure of a brave, retired contractor, perplexed me a little.

"Would you be able to spare me some three or four days?" Andréas asked me.

"When will we depart?"

"Tomorrow evening at five o'clock from the North Station."

"In that case, I will arrange things so that half of my visits will be for tomorrow, and the rest next week."

Next day I found Andréas at the station.

"I should," he said, "beg your pardon. I took third class in the train, and it is not too comfortable, but we are only going to Compiègne and I hope to gain some information on the train."

I answered what politeness indicated and we went to the platform. According to his habit, Andréas walked the whole length of the train, examined the locomotive, spoke to the mechanics and finally chose an empty compartment. Presently a peasant woman entered with her little son, and then a fat man with his young daughter and suitcases. It was raining as we left. Andréas and the man exchanged some words of courtesy. We spoke about the bad weather, the endangered crops, the diseases of wheat, wrongly distributed taxation, and so on. The man was a wine merchant from Epinettes. He was taking his little girl to stay with a cousin, a farmer and it became clear that he had his family in Compiègne.

"We are going," said Andréas, "to make a trip for a few days in the forest. It seems that there are some old churches there, which are Roman antiquities."

"Quite right!" said the man. "In Compiègne there is still an old tower on the property of a cousin of mine, almost on the shore of the River Oise. We could go there, if you like."

"Very well," said Andréas, "and we will dine together. It is the tower in which Jeanne d'Arc suffered the first stage of her Calvary," he added speaking to me.

"I cannot," said the wine merchant, "because of the little one. It is two miles distant from my father, and we would arrive too late."

But Andréas persuaded him to accept. We passed Chantilly with its white barriers, its plain meadows and comfortable houses, Coye with its factories, large fields cut from the groves, the amiable horizon of Ile-de-France, and the grey and peaceful River Oise. Then we arrived.

We dined in the Bell Hotel. The cuisine was appetizing, the service hospitable and the wine tasty. Our guest was delighted and talked a lot, and renewed acquaintance with his old comrades. Andréas was cordial to everyone, he offered cigars and joked, but did not lose an opportunity to give advice or a prescription.

"You see," he said to me privately, "that was good fortune. If we had travelled second class on the train, we would not have met that man who, for twenty years was a porter at the bank of the Jew, about whom we were speaking yesterday evening. Undoubtedly he is giving me information."

"I don't at all know what an old tower can have in common with the political situation in Europe," I said. "But you have made me accustomed to incomprehensible things. Perhaps there is a hidden string, linking the banker, the tenor, both women, politics and the heroine of Vaucouleurs, and the places to which we are going to on excursion?"

"It is almost exactly four hundred and eighty-one years ago to the day, when Jeanne d'Arc was incarcerated in the place to which we will now go," answered Andréas.

I did not understand anything further, but did not ask him any more. After dinner Andréas found a pretext to bid farewell to the wine merchant, promising to see him again soon.

"Do you realize," he said to me, "that it was necessary for me to see whether or not Jeanne d'Arc had actually been imprisoned in that tower. I needed to have some one from this area beside me, and that man is just from these parts, and for even much longer than he suspects. Now, we have to be alone in that tower."

We returned to the town. It was about eleven o'clock at night and we directed our steps to the house which our travelling companion had shown to us when we passed by. As soon as Andréas opened the gate a dog barked; but he whistled to it very softly and when we entered, the guardian seduced, as I supposed, started endlessly caressing us.

"Keep this dog with you," Andréas told me. "Hide behind these casks; do not fall asleep and do not move under any circumstances, no matter what you may see or hear. Don't smoke. Otherwise, there is no danger at all."

He went up into the tower, and then everything became silent. Only the sound of a clock, the horse-team of a carrier and the whistle of a fast train interrupted the nocturnal quietness. From time to time a torpor fell on my eyes like a stunning blow. Then I shook myself because I had promised not to fall asleep. Thus half an hour passed. The dog lay between my legs, and suddenly I felt it tremble. Seeking around me for the cause of its fear, I could no longer see the house, hencoop, or sheds. Old stone walls rose up from the earth, while torches in brackets were fixed around a portal; people came and went, clad in the dress of the XVth Century. There were men in gowns, knights and servants. They spoke a language hard to understand. I recognized both Burgundian intonations and English words. Then I realized what had happened: Andréas had renewed, under the most difficult conditions, the famous supper of the dead by Cagliostro. This man had reversed the wheel of time. We had gone back four hundred and eighty-one years. And all that without any ritual, preparation, or assistance, with only a formidable gesture of will-power he had succeeded in evoking Jeanne d'Arc.

Actually, a few moments later, the vision changed and I saw Andréas standing in a vaulted room speaking to a young woman dressed in a costume attributed to the heroine by all painters. However, it was not just a vision, because under my hand I felt the coldness of the walls. I heard the voices of the questioners and even took part in the conversation myself. An hour later everything had disappeared. The little house, the courtyard, the dog, everything was there again. But Andréas's first words compelled me to promise secrecy concerning all that I had heard, and about everything that I could still see or hear tomorrow and afterwards.

We could not dream of finding hotel accommodation in this little town at two o'clock in the morning. So we returned to the forest using the small paths and took rest in an abandoned quarry, which Andréas was able to discover. In the morning, we soon found an inn in which we had breakfast.

Andréas struck up a conversation with some of the rare customers: a gamekeeper, a teacher and a peasant, and I then realized that he was seeking information about the location of the ruins of a castle, which was not mentioned in any guide-book. After providing ourselves with a quantity of matches, we left the inn, and before starting our further explorations, wandered along some of the country paths, so as to baffle the curious. We went to the Cistercian priory of St. John of the Woods, to the Benedictine monastery at Renardière: all without success. Next day we visited Pierrefonds; but Andréas declared that he found too many people there. Only two days later at the exit of the Chemin des Plaideurs did he give me some hope of imminent achievement. There was a large circular plain about a kilometre wide, covered with old, straight, high and silent ash trees, which offered before us the start of a short and steep path. The damp, dead leaves which covered the ground deadened the noise of our feet, while the short call of a loriot, hidden far away in the forest, the angry cry of a jay fluttering among the branches and the call of a magpie perched amid the foliage heightened the silence around us. The musty smell of morels blended with the exhilarating perfume of the forest trees swollen with sap. Between the columns of large, smooth tree trunks gleamed the blue of the sky, while the low rays of the setting sun flashed like golden javelins in the hands of warrior-angels.

"There they are," said Andréas, "the assembly of the elders among the forest people. Being wiser than men, they speak little; for too long they have seen the dwarfs appear and perish at their feet. They are hospitable to weak creatures just like a Sannyasin, during his struggle for deliverance, sitting in a humming jungle, with birds dwelling in his entangled hair, they give those little ones food and shelter. Immersed in the great hospitable soul of the paternal soil, their spirits contemplate and look at how the wheels of generations turn. Day after day, snow after summer, south winds after zephyrs, people after people, all of this circulates around them. They know the law; they know that everything obeys a great god, which is time. Time which causes them to be born from a miserable seed, time which makes them grow, and which, at the hour inscribed in its invisible book, will send the killer—the wood-cutter to them."

It was midday. The whole forest was enjoying its siesta. Suddenly, Andréas stopped me; he had discerned an unusual movement in a coppice some three hundred metres distant. Soon I saw something moving.

"It is a stag and two hinds," he whispered softly. "They have come to drink because it is the stag which is behind, or perhaps something frightened them. Therefore, let us walk over to where they came from; we will find water or something else."

And sure enough a few minutes later, we reached a small stream, which enlarged itself into a pool, but later resumed its capricious course.

"Do you see some irises?" my master asked me.

"Yes, over there, to the left."

"There you are, now I have my antidote."

And two minutes later he gave me some handfuls of serpentaria plants, which he had pulled up by their roots, so as to put them into my bag.

"Now," he said, "we have to find the ruins. Since nothing is visible in this forest undergrowth, we will have to locate a vantage point. Let us take a by-path."

And he went to the left slowly inspecting the trees with full attention, hitting the soil with his cane, and from time to time taking up some pieces of earth.

"You see, we are seeking for brushwood and snakes, and therefore dry terrain sandy, or rocky, with heather, sharp grass and perhaps juniper, oak and birch. Ah! Look! No doubt behind this clearing of ferns, there it is! Anyway, it seems to me that I see the barrel of a rifle in front of us . . ." and he accelerated his pace.

Sure enough, a little further on, a guard appeared on a path which crossed ours. Andréas answered his greeting and said to him:

"Did you see a stag, just now, close to the stream?"

"No!" answered the man.

"But it was walking towards the small pool over to the left, and had two hinds with it."

"Ah! Yes!" said the guard, "he must have come from far off, you know; some poacher has probably dislodged him this morning."

Andréas turned away, still talking. He took a few steps backwards and tripped over a bundle of twigs lying on the edge of the path. Regaining his balance, he cried:

"Look, a snake!" And showed the guard the faggots.

"Ah!" said the latter, they usually don't come this far. There is a whole nest of them on a slope, a few kilometres from here. One cannot see it because of the high growth of the forset; but there is a large stony circle with a lot of brush around it, where some time ago there used to be quarries. But I never go there."

"Oh well, neither will we."

And Andréas sat down and offered tobacco to the guard, and having lighted his own pipe in turn, asked about the way to Compiègne. We continued talking for a few minutes, and then the guard saluted us and left.

"Now, we will both set to work," said Andréas rubbing his hands together. "Let us go to that part of the forest."

Arriving there, he took the bundle of herbs he had collected by the edge of the stream, gave me half and tucking the ends of his trousers into the top of his boots, he placed a band of the herbs around his ankles, pressing them well together.

"In this way," he said, "no snake will bite us. Even so, let us walk with care, which means we cannot go very fast."

And really, we soon found ourselves in such a tangle of nettles, hawthorns, acacias, brambles and thistles that it seemed impossible to take one step after another. Serpents of all sizes slithered away on every side. The strong sun and heat which arose from the soil oppressed me and the large silent trees looked like battalions with immobilized lances, watching us with their innumerable eyes.

The massive body of Andréas moved here and there in the undergrowth, making its way without any noise. I was following him, already completely soaked in perspiration, when suddenly, he gave a low cry. The terrain descended steeply, and on the other side of a ravine we saw the ruins, completely covered with overgrowth.

"Let us follow around," he said to me, "instead of descending, because there must be the remains of a postern."

It took us almost three-quarters of an hour in order to complete the circle, and after almost returning to our starting point, we discovered the remains of a drawbridge. We had to descend over the loose stones and then work our way up again, frightening an enormous number of lizards. I sat, while Andréas cut dry branches and made several bundles of them.

"These will serve us as torches," he explained.

"So, you want to go down there, into the cellars?" I asked with some apprehension.

"Of course! Moreover, if I am to believe the smell around us, we are going to discover some very rare things. But hold yourself well, dear Doctor, and let us seek the stairs. Follow me!"

There remained parts of enormous walls, but so well buried in humus, so well covered with creeping plants, and so defended by the old trees, that one had to touch them in order to see them. Very rare fauna and unexpected flora were there. Enormous Coleoptera, big nests of wasps, wild bees, enormous fox-gloves, clumps of ferns man-high, euphorbias, and some oaks adorned with mistletoe.

"This is rather rare in France," Andréas said to me. "There is mistletoe on oaks only in Menez, in Brittany, and the peasants preserve them with great care."

I had to place too much attention on where I was going to put my foot next to be able to continue any conversation; but Andréas went here and there without any apparent fatigue, just as if he was walking in the Tuileries.

"Here is the courtyard and there are the pits, where we will not go; and the dungeon cannot be in the middle, but in the front, on the periphery. And that is the way in which they had to descend into the oubliettes, so let us look."

Half-way down the stairs Andréas entered a narrow passage let into the thickness of the wall and soon we found ourselves in a subterranean chapel, where we sat down. And once again, there appeared a scene similar to that of yesterday, but a much more dramatic one. I cannot say anything further about it. The only thing which is permitted me to add is that some years later Europe entered into a most terrible storm, the worst its people had ever experienced.

Chapter XL

CHRISTMAS

It so happened that I rendered to a young married couple of the cosmopolitan world, one of those trivial services, the annoying consequence of which is that one is compelled to accept, with a delighted attitude, kindness as payment for such service. Thus they asked me to attend a Christmas eve function in a luxurious Paris environment, in the best style. However, the elaborate delicacy of the food, and the elegance of the diners did not shorten the whole ceremony for me. Finally, the hour of departure arrived, and then, at the very moment of farewell, I saw in a group of departing people, the powerful figure of Andréas. He was in evening dress and his companions, among whom I noticed some celebrated faces, seemed to pay him the attention usually accorded to important persons.

He saw me and came over after taking leave of his friends, and suggested that I spend the two or three hours still remaining before daylight with him. Later in the morning he had to visit some interesting sick people, so we could go together to his home and then I could accompany him. I accepted and we started our walk. Andréas had become thin. His handsomeness, usually as if shadowed by the halo of bodily vigour, appeared more visible in this exhaustion occasioned by too long fatigue. His hair, which was now long, heightened the superhuman character of that face whose features and lines more and more radiated the power of his kindness. The wrinkles were accentuated on his admirable forehead, around the vigilant eyes, and about the mouth with its moving smile. But his gaze remained luminous, limpid and magnificent. According to his custom, he questioned me in short sentences, of which the connecting links were not always immediately apparent.

" What do you say, dear Doctor, about all the morass in which the whole world is floundering at present? What do those around you say? "

" Nothing that you most surely don't already know," I answered, " if I can judge by the diversity of conditions prevailing among the people we encounter. Everyone complains or gets angry, but it is only due to discouragement, so disheartening among men of good will which seems to me to be significant and it makes me anxious."

"However, there is nothing to be discouraged about," answered Andréas, lighting his pipe. "At least if the men whom you call 'of good will' are not servants of Heaven. You might perhaps think: who is a true servant of Heaven? Yes, you have the right to ask: who serves Heaven? And I too ask: am I a servant? There are so many things to be done, so many of them."

"In that way," I remarked, "you are the one who pronounces the most discouraging words! If you believe that the work surpasses your forces, what then have we, the others to say? What have I to say?"

"You will say," replied Andréas with a smile, "that I am an old dotard. You see, I know well that things appear to go wrongly, and I am in distress. But I also know that things go as they should and it is well that they are going so; and then I preserve my confidence. You! You are a young and simple being; you see everything in either white or black, while I am an old complicated grumbler."

"Say what you like," I said, "all that I think about you is that you are helpful and good. Actually, I believe that I am forming a too simplistic conception of beings and life; therefore I am not a simple, but a simplistic one, whereas you are really simple, and that is not the same thing."

"In reality, life develops itself into innumerable nuances. That is why no system has so far been invented, which can possibly embrace everything. That is why the destiny of any creature is not a definitive one. No one, not even the tools of the Adversary is merged in the Darkness to the same degree. No servant of Heaven possesses exactly the same quality of the Light. Even the majority, that is, the large part of both armies are only an incoherent floating mass, undecided in their dim flashes of tepid twilight. That is why, if you wish to join in the talk with men about God, you have first to gain caution, then prudence, and finally caution again."

"With such prudence, would I not quite simply finish in being completely still in myself?"

"No, never!" declared Andréas energetically. You would be wrong. One has to emerge. Do you thus believe," he continued after a while, "that when I occupy myself with someone else, I am not shown his future and what he will do with the Light I am giving to him? Do you thus believe, that for a hundred individuals who come asking me for work, that I see only one, perhaps two, who possibly will perform that work to the end? Knowing that, could I refuse the other ninety-eight their little bit of Light? Have I any right to refuse them?"

"No doubt!" I said. "The treasons, or, if you prefer the conscious defections, neither surprise nor move me; but what about the involuntary cowardice, the unconscious resignation of those hearts which one loves dearly, and to whom one would like to give everything, but who cannot receive, who are going left believing they are going right, who imagine themselves to be working, when in reality they are living only from the work of others?"

"What is it that could satisfy you, my good Doctor?" answered Andréas. "They ask, you give; they offer themselves, you accept; they reject your gifts, you pick them up carefully; they go away and you pray to the good God for the venturesome travellers. If you wish to do something for your brethren, let no fantasy from their side surprise you; you cannot restrain anyone against his will: the most essential thing is that when they hear you, you really pronounce a word of life. And those of your friends who want to work, let them work twice: for themselves and for the novices whom you believe to be your friends, but who do not work at all. The courage of the few and the indolence of the others will balance out later; nothing is ever lost. If they don't abandon you, they remain with you. Isn't that so? Therefore, don't be anxious about anything except to give them today what they ask for today. Tomorrow there will be another day for you, for them and for me."

"I accept your good words with all my heart," I replied. "But, finally, forgive me for this indiscreet question: don't you ever commit a mistake yourself, in your choice? Do you know with whom you are dealing?"

"You also know from your first glance with whom you are dealing, but you don't think about it to yourself, because Heaven has given to you some humility, but all the same you know. I do likewise, I know, or, rather, I don't know: for it is the Light in us which gives us the information. For example, didn't Jesus know from the first meeting in His childhood, that Judas would betray Him? And Peter too? Isn't that true?"

In the meantime we had reached the old cemetery of Belleville. A few gleams from the Aurora were piercing the blue obscurity of the night that was ending. The cold was sharp. Some isolated songs reached our ears, and, to us, they seemed improper towards Him, Whom they pretended to commemorate. The enormous city, with all its lights still burning, floated in the undecided darkness like a large vessel, full of dull rumours in the mist of the Northern Ocean. It was a mysterious scene, which corresponded to my own irresolution. The deep voice of Andréas finally interrupted my enchantment.

"Yes," it said, "we are ignorance itself and the blind leads the blind. Sometimes the omniscience transfixes us. Its brief, unexpected flash should suffice for us; for it always coincides with certain important possibilities. Let us not expect any regular crop from our present work. Even so, no matter how rare the ripening ears of our wheat might be, their value will always surpass our toil. When we consider the immense solicitude of the Father as against the small number of hearts who agree to accept it, it may seem that He too is disappointed without end. However, He is never mistaken. So, dear Doctor, let your soul be strengthened, consolidate it, make a firm rock of it. The defections, the treasons are nothing other than retreats for future progress. Are we each not someone, who, in reality, no mishaps disconcert? The others who scatter themselves will most certainly return a little later, and the solid and flexible link which attaches them to us is just our first welcome, which you wrongly blame as being a lack of clairvoyance, or firmness. Go ahead: I certify before the Truth that you are walking on a right path; but always remember that it is a rough one. And," he added, regaining his usual attitude of affectionate kindness, "let us go home and ask my wife about a good cup of coffee."

Chapter XLI

ANTIBES

That morning a mistral was sweeping away the rainy clouds, which, for some days, had been dropping their beneficial moisture on to the fields, so dry for months past. On the northern horizon the Italian peaks extended their snows which the rising sun painted with precious, rosy colours. The hills awakened in the amethyst-coloured fog, which rose from their valleys, and in contrast, the sea deepened its metallic blue from days of full sun. In the little port the fishing-boats slowly set sail, displaying their patched canvas, brownish white and red, under the eyes of the old, motionless fishermen.

Behind a barque from Leghorn, a man was talking to the sailors. His silhouette seemed well known to me. On approaching nearer, I was surprised to see Andréas. He gazed at me as I passed by and with a wink let me know that he would join me presently. I waited for him, while strolling through the shipyard.

Then, the barque slipped its moorings and a few minutes later Andréas joined me, with the same quiet pace, the same fatherly smile, and with the same gaze full of power and kindness.

But his face, now grown older, bore traces of oppressing fatigue, and I immediately expressed my anxiety about it to him.

"It is nothing," he answered, "absolutely nothing. Don't be disturbed. You know very well that if I would ask Him, the Father would grant me victory in three days from now; but we have enough time for victory, do you understand? We are not pressed to finish it. We should only be pressed when spreading the Light. The longer the battle will be, the higher the beings will rise."

"Ah!" I replied, "I again find you as you were, irremovable and as if standing on the threshold of Eternity."

"Look, dear Doctor, let us not make any literature: I am a man quite similar to the others. Don't raise your head. Life is complicated enough as it is. Everyone of us has his little work to perform, so let us do it simply, but thoroughly. But, what is with you?"

"You know the rest," I said, "I am not too satisfied."

"What could it be? Look at that barque, she has a good wind, and she will reach the Port of Maurizio in due time. You see, things always arrange themselves when we have confidence. Yesterday evening nothing moved; but by tomorrow everything will go smoothly, if God wants it so. You, dear Doctor, are always the same: you are too anxious. Patience, more patience! Let every day suffice for its toil. When you become a saint, only then will true difficulties arise: for the moment the work is simple."

"The work is simple," I interrupted, a little surprised. "No doubt about it; but still one has to do it. I find it very difficult in order that the twenty-four hours in every day become perfect, definite, and that there will be nothing to return."

"You are perfectly right," Andréas continued in a grave tone, "nothing is more difficult. The wrong lies in the fact that one lives today thinking about after tomorrow. I don't forbid any foresight, but this foresight, even of today, belongs to the work of today, no matter even if it aims at the next month."

"Yes! It is to be whole in the real work! It is possible for you, but what about us?"

"It is so for everyone, dear Doctor, because, if I have a *Friend*, you will also have this *Friend*, because you are my friend; and your friends can have Him equally. To all your comrades, who passed through the war without any accident it happened so only because they were able to be simple beings. and I confirm for you, that if they continue to remain simple, they will be able to pass through the peace, or through that which they call 'peace'; but they must not use phraseology in their hearts when talking with the good God. You see, everything is simple! Christ is simple; His commandments are clear; it is we, who make the complications."

"However," I ventured, "to find money for the poor, to find force for the afflicted, cures for the sick, it doesn't seem to me to be too simple at all. And to earn one's bread honestly among all this covetousness isn't too easy either."

"But yes, it is simple! Only that you are all seeking simplicity through complication; better for you to go towards simplicity through simplicity, which means making quite little ones of yourselves, very little ones. Look at those great men of letters, great painters, there are some of them even in this place, at this moment, and some day we will go and talk to them. In their beginnings, all of them created very complicated books or pictures, with a lot of research, procedures, understanding, rare words and learned techniques. And then they saw that they practised the trade, but not the art. So they discarded or restrained their vocabularies and their pallets; they made visible their sensibility, augmented their comprehension, and ennobled their souls. Now, they are almost simple. They could have become so thirty years earlier, if they had read the Gospels. The same applies to you. Become simple in your heart and then you will find simple processes for curing and helping."

At this point Andréas seemed to merge into one of those long silences according to his habit. And, as if I was anxious of losing him from my sight again, perhaps for months, I asked him for further advice on how to reach this state of inner firmness, favouring the most intense activity and at the same time allowing the freest soaring of our noble desires and enthusiasm. Here, on broad lines, is how he answered me.

" You see! Those who believe that, because they have devoted themselves to Christ their lives must be peaceful and monotonous, are in the wrong! Likewise, those who believe that because they have devoted themselves to Christ, their lives must be one long martyrdom, are also mistaken. Both types of people have only one thing in common: *to be devoted to Christ*. But since they gave themselves to this Christ, of Whose omnipotence and all-goodness they are certain, why are they still anxious? Because they are in the hands of the Father, let them perform their duties thoroughly, let them ask for everything, and this will suffice. If He hears them, it is good; if He refuses them, it is equally good. If He sends them a trial, it is well; if He sends them some happiness, it is also well. Now, just look at that old gentleman, who is leaving his car and coming over to us: without any doubt you recognize him.

" Really, he was a very great person, whose name at one time was known to all the world."

The man stopped, waiting for Andréas's gesture, exactly as I had done recently in the port.

" You see, your comrades, during those five years, risked their lives ten thousand times, but they live. Three years ago, he was hunted by thousands of men, persecuted, without money and refuge. They believed him to be imprisoned in a fortress, or buried under snow somewhere in the East. But here he is. He knew how to remain simple. Let us go and shake hands, for you know him. We will lunch together."

Chapter XLII

THE BATTLE

A TELEGRAM had called me to Nyon, and I was late at the station. As I ran to the counter, someone appeared before me and greeted me saying: "Don't be in so much of a hurry dear Doctor, we still have ten minutes to wait, for I presume you are taking the train to Pontarlier? Their locomotive doesn't work, so it has to be changed." It was Andréas. He did not let me express my surprise.

"I am going to send a telegram," he continued. "Wait a few seconds for me. Do you wish us to make the journey together to Dijon? I am going to Creusot."

The train finally departed after the announced delay. We found an empty compartment and Andréas offered me a journal and asked for my permission to let him work. He did so for less than an hour and then we started talking. I knew what he wanted to say. I understood about the accident to our locomotive, and why, in this crowded train, we had a chance to be alone.

I took my place at the other end of the seat and turning towards the curtain did not take any notice of my companion. When, as very seldom happened, Andréas did not 'work' alone, he liked to be completely ignored. I had the leisure to enjoy our happy encounter. One evening on leaving me, he had dived into the crowd and it had closed over him, just as the sea does over a sinking boat. How many times, during the bloody cataclysm which was devastating Europe, my heart had turned sorrowfully to this man. What was he doing during that immense nightmare? Forgetting the rule imposed by Christ on His soldiers, I was astonished not to hear the secret chronicle talking about Andréas. I would liked to have seen him consulting with the great chiefs. And now he was here, equally calm and affectionate, with his paternal smile. Certainly he did not slow down his mysterious activities, and I felt it very well. As usual, the air around him vibrated with all kinds of *presences*: I breathed the power and immutability. He was the same man, definitely the same.

A little after Fontainebleau he interrupted the silence.

"Well, my Doctor, what do you say about it all?"

"Ah! I have too many questions, too many requests. You see very well everything that I lack, everything lacking in all of us. What can I do?"

"But France possesses all the necessary elements for victory. Heaven will give it to her at the moment It wishes to do so. What does concern you is that you are in the storm; remain in your place; endure to the end; you should . . ."

"But enduring is not enough. I am doing nothing: I am a useless one."

"Nobody is useless, dear Doctor, just be patient. You know very well that I don't like to give advice, for it augments difficulties, especially for those of us who are held under observation by the invisible tools of the Enemy. For it is the realm of the Invisible, where the true battle takes place. This war is quite remarkable at the same time from the military, political, ethnographic and spiritual standpoint. The physical armies represent the exact extension of the two mystical armies: of Light and Darkness. We are lucky to live in such an epoch!

"Yes! For those who have fought; but what about the others?"

"Let them fight now; there is a civil war. All your writers have indicated about this. However, one can do more."

"What more, tell me?"

"Nothing other, than to do more thoroughly those things which are already being done: social aid, moral attitude, propaganda by the press, through conversation and still other attempts, for there are also other kinds of battle," added Andréas, directing a searching look at me.

I collected myself and then said:

"Listen! It is probable that you wouldn't like to give me any orders. But do explain to me what you believe I am able to undertake, and then I will think about it."

"Yes!" continued Andréas, as if he had not heard me at all: "The trenches, grenades, shells, poison gas, hand-to-hand fighting, all those frightening horrors are only a shadow of that which passes beyond the *Veil*, And if, in order to face them, one must be heroic simply by being a model citizen, who then will be able to face the spiritual war? What man could ask for such a thing? What man could dominate it?"

"But Christ is seeking for such men. He wants me, I know that quite well, and I know that it is not without a purpose that I have found you again."

After a short pause, Andréas answered: "Splendid actions are precious; but activities which God alone sees surpass them. The first are flowers, the latter are the seeds, and Christ is the gardener. Only those can fulfil them who know how to keep silent. Do you know people who know how to be silent?"

"I know some people who are discreet."

"Yes! Everyone is discreet; but under the condition that their neighbour perceives that they have sensational information." And Andréas laughed a little.

"Then there should be an inner discretion, a mental taciturnity? Then one should not only keep silent, but also not allow oneself to see the possibility of talking? One should 'forget' effectively, and remember when desired? This means that the most discerning eye would not be able to read from my face that I am hiding something and so, that even the subtle demons would have no doubt about it?"

"There, my Doctor, are the first orders. You know that orders on the battlefield are sactioned by death; imagine now what the soldier of Heaven risks? And that is justice, because the act alone doesn't bear in itself the whole value; it depends greatly on him who performs it. It is useless to seek after an example, isn't that so? That is why such a small thing as *not to slander* is so important for us. Hundreds of beings set their patterns by our attitude, and hundreds of others are watching us in order to make us fall."

"Yes, I remember! You told me about it some time ago. But one never ascribes enough importance to simple work. Also, in the future . . ."

Andréas stopped me. "Well, it is enough. You know your duty, fulfil it to the end, with stubbornness. If you are going to die of fatigue, would it be important?"

"Agreed," I said, "and beyond it there is still prayer."

"Which? An opportune prayer, an economic prayer in ready-made slices, a pusillanimous prayer, an egoistic one? Oh, no, Doctor? But a perpetual prayer, which embraces even the smallest details as well as the vastest objects; a prayer of overflowing tenderness and even impassiveness; a naked prayer, right, sure of Christ, but one made in profound abasement: that is what it should be. From an incandescent heart falls the refreshing rain of the good God on to the soil parched by hell. Nothing is puerile or irremediable before our King. Thus, let everything appear before you as a seed of eternity. For the one who at that moment assumes the office of prayer there will be no waking, no sleep, no rest, no lecturing, no relaxation, but only toil and prayer. He should enforce his ego until it is broken: let his body submit or fall. And, if the body falls, the spirit will continue the work on the *other side*."

Substantially, such were the words Andréas spoke to me in his familiar tone as if in ordinary conversation. But a whole avalanche of forces rolled from under that tranquil voice. Supreme certainty, wisdom and the vastest conceptions could be discovered in those words, while the instinctive enthusiasm which stirs up fanaticism did not come from them; but my will-power rose in a new fashion. Certainly the lights were rising in me, and I felt myself becoming a different being.

I was still listening to the inner echos of his last sentences, when Andréas continued: " Apart from that, there are reactions, it is the hardest work in prayer. Among our enemies there are intelligent men, men of strong magnetism. It is evident, because they serve the Prince of this world, he who governs magnetism, among other things. The spirits of those men attack our spirits, by force and by cunning. For example, a soldier of Christ asks that an embezzler may be stopped: immediately, the geniuses of all the administrative machinery attending that embezzlement, the spirits of the enemy's accomplices from all his related formations, his knowledge, his factories, intellectual centres, all the false angels of his religion, all the servants of the Beast, briefly, all these react and try to attack the servant of Heaven. An Army of Matter against the Army of Spirit. If the soldier of Christ on provisionally seeing that all his efforts are in vain, becomes discouraged, his calm changes to irritation, or criticism and then everything has to start again. A general in the midst of his staff, disposes of his plans in relative peace. But the soldier of Christ is at once the strategist and the combatant. He must suffer and yet remain lucid. Apart from that, he should take on a material occupation."

" I see then, that no one can say: ' I will be a soldier'."

" No, Doctor, at least—no and yes."

" Well, I have realized."

" In that case, go! " concluded Andréas, and try to have others follow you. Heaven assists the weak. Have no fear, dear Doctor," he added smiling, and fixed his gaze directly on my eyes, a clear, strong gaze, whereat a peculiar feeling of quiet joy began to spread through me, alleviating my body and illuminating my faculties.

After some minutes of reflection I said: " There must be, among the moral purifications, something specially appropriate to make our prayers be heard."

" Yes, firstly there is Charity: the act of Charity is the best for everything. Apart from that, if one doesn't fear pain, let him abstain from slandering, not only persons, but also animals, even objects, even time. But yes! " added Andréas, seeing my surprise. " An animal has intelligence; an object, rain, all of them are beings which live. It seems to me that you forget that a disciple of Christ finds himself in spirit in Christ's home, where there everything is life, intelligence and love."

"Yes, I really have forgotten it," I murmured.

"You will not forget forever, go!" he said with a kind of consolation. "You know very well that we are the servants of Christ, of the Logos . . . of the Logos, do you understand? But the true Logos-Word is action. That is why, during the war, it was the soldier who had the foremost role. The civil one, even a saint, even a man of genius, was only on the second plane. And of those who remained in their place, woe to them for they have prolonged their earthly lease by six thousand years, perhaps still more. But, as you see, I advise others to keep silent and I myself am talking. Good-bye, dear Doctor, good-bye. Don't disturb yourself, remain seated!" And as the train rolled into the station of Dijon, Andréas prepared to leave.

How quickly those hours had passed! And again how many questions, how many things to tell him, how many wishes to formulate. But, inexorable despite his kindly smile, Andréas went out. While walking to the exit, he still waved me farewell with his hand. And, in a measure, as he walked away, I realized further that everything he has said to me, even in this small amount, in sum total, has encompassed the whole *Necessary Unique Thing*.

CHAPTER XLIII

RESURRECTION

THE last episodes which I have related, produced a definite impression on me which, because of the awkwardness of my narration, the reader doubtless will not share. I threw myself with ardour on to the 'narrow path', which I believed I had now perceived. But I did not have to wait long to collect the fruit of my lack of experience. I wanted to check the truth of Andréas's doctrine with facts. I started attending to the sick free of charge, I gave away my money and time, sacrificed my nights, endured the caprices of my friends, limited my pleasure in art and literature and sold my books. Then people started to mock at me, and later accused me of weakness of character. Fruitful consultations became less frequent; my corrospondents considered me timorous because I would no longer flatter their manias for magic, divination and phenomena; my reputation in the circles of 'illuminism' diminished; desperate cases, which I was unable to cure revived old doubts in me, which gradually grew into dreary despair.

Little by little my courage abandoned me. Everything became insipid and tedious: I started to take drugs so as to be able to sleep and not to think any more. Going out was odious, but to remain at home was torture; reading annoyed me and to take food was a compulsory toil.

At the end of three months of such melancholy, when I was already resigned to await the end without making any further movement, when it seemed to me very clear that the universe and myself no longer had any aim or sense, a visitor came to me one evening.

A young woman in the neighbourhood had been dying of consumption for more than a year. Now she was at the very end. No doctor would take care of her and her husband, in despair, explained to me that he did not expect her to be cured, but that she was choking herself, and some alleviation must be given to her for at least an hour, during the time of the agony. I was too indifferent to everything in order to think of refusing him. So I went with him. It was about 2 a.m.

Then a man appeared on the street in front of us, coming towards us. He was tall, but had such good proportions to his body that I did not perceive this fact until we were close to him. There was nothing remarkable in his dress, but he had the style of a grand lord. Passing him, I raised my eyes towards him as if mechanically, and received his look like the flame from a kind of light. He passed us. I turned back to him and he did likewise at the same moment. Then, without any deliberation, I went to him. He took off his hat and said to me: "Doctor, I believe that I know you, forgive me my indiscretion, but aren't you a friend of Andréas?"

I also removed my hat, being nonplussed.

"Yes!" I answered him. And while I was seeking further words, he said:

"I guess that you are going to see a sick person, perhaps I could be of use to you, if you will allow me to accompany you."

And suddenly, I realized. It was Théophane, it was he! My heart started to beat in leaps, the despairs, rancour, grudges, bitterness, disgust—I felt all of them being dissipated in heavy, creeping mists, during the time I was explaining to my client: "He is a doctor of my friends, a specialist: we will take him to see your wife."

But the man, lost in his suffering, did not answer and we soon arrived at his home. It was a poor and moving dwelling of a minor official with its banal decoration and false air of being well off. The mother of the sick woman was there, without any more tears in her eyes, and her features stiffened in dullness. In an absent voice she said to her son-in-law: "It is too late, she is dead."

I leaned over the sick-bed. No sound in the heart, no breath: the delicate nose had already thinned; the face had recovered that unmistakable motionless calm; a little warmth still remained in the hollowness of the stomach; but the poor body, so terribly emaciated, with large swollen joints, seemed to beg to be left in peace in the quiet darkness of the coffin.

"Do you believe she is dead?" suddenly asked Théophane, and his voice seemed to sing in the silence. I made a gesture of confirmation.

"Do you love her? Is it so? You have children?" he asked the husband time and time again. And then, without awaiting his answer, Théophane continued: "If she will come back to life, if she will immediately be awakened from death, would you show your thankfulness to Heaven, would you remain with her, not leaving her either in your heart or body?"

The poor man, confused, not daring to realize, looked at us and said nothing.

"Be calm," Théophane told him in a very kind way, "don't grieve, but answer me conscientiously."

"Is it possible?" stammered the husband. "But it is impossible that you would mock me. If you say so, she can come to life again. Yes! I promise you." And he fell down all his body shaken by sobbing, while the old mother collapsed and desperately embraced the already cold body of her daughter.

Théophane approached the corpse and took both its hands in his left, raising the inert head with his right, and said into the ear of the body, very tenderly and in a low voice, but loud enough for us all to hear it:

"My child, my daughter, come, return: it will be counted to you, they need you!"

And no chill even touched us for it was quite natural, the dead one must be resuscitated. The woman opened her eyes, drew herself up and looked around the room.

"I have been dreaming," she sighed. Her mother and husband kissed her hands; but she, leaning against Théophane's breast, started to silently weep.

"Light another lamp," ordered Théophane.

The mother staggered, raised herself and came back with the lamp, which was placed so that the sick woman was well in sight.

"You see," Théophane told us, "she is recovering."

And really, in about a quarter of an hour, a little flesh came back around the bones; the face became fuller and more coloured. Exalted with joy, the husband threw himself at Théophane's feet, but the latter lifted him up just as I would a child.

"No, no!" he told the husband. "It is Heaven which must be thanked." And taking a step back, he added: "Remember what you have promised. There is a book in which are written stories of the dead returned to life; do what that book teaches. Well! Good-bye!"

And with the whole of him radiating affectionate kindness, he embraced the woman, mother and husband, and went out with me. I thought that I was dreaming. However, I recognized the street on which we were walking; here a picket fence, further on a vacant allotment; then a bake-house, and to the left a bar in which some night customers of the lower classes were shouting. Yes, I was still on this earth, in Paris; I was walking beside an unknown man, and it was he, Théophane, the enlightener, the so long expected guide, whose presence alone dissipated my darkness, expelled my doubts, and comforted my fatigue.

He explained to me, that he must take the express train for

Brindisi at about four o'clock in the morning, and that he could not defer his journey as that train left only once per week, while, on the other hand, he had many things to tell me. So, if I was free, he asked me to be kind enough to accompany him to Modane [the station on the Italian frontier]. We would be qiute comfortable in his reserved compartment. I was delighted. Quietly we arrived at the station from which the trains leave for Lyons. And during the next ten great hours he continued to teach me, smoking all the time, for it seemed that he lived in an ordinary human way.

He spoke without any haste, in short, simple sentences, without looking for effect. He seemed to be a witness of everything he spoke about to me. He explained myself to myself, showing me the most hidden machinery in my consciousness; his gaze penetrated the opaque obscurity of the past centuries. I cannot tell here everything that he taught me that night, for all reason opposes this; but imagine only the greatest mental concentration, functioning in harmony with perfect limpidity of the intellect; imagine an immediate and always true understanding of the relationship between cause and effect, a memory clear to the smallest detail; an exquisite sensibility, extending itself equally to the beings of the present as to those far distant in time and space. A very intimate joy, very calm, very limpid, such was the state of my soul during that night, so that my fatigue, fever, weariness and somnolence were forgotten. But, in any case, words cannot render the exquisite, ideal freshness, vigorous vitality and serene confidence in whose waves my weakened spirit bathed. This bliss, and that which followed it, I think I will never be able to repay, even if I have to suffer without interruption through my whole existence and in the whole of my being. My only anxiety of today is, that so many men are passing so close to Heaven without knowing anything about it. And not because it is hidden, but because, not wishing to go out of themselves, they do not want, nor can they perceive it, for—*they do not look.*

THE END